Study Guide for the Telecourse

MARKETING

Sixth Edition

Study Guide for the Telecourse

MARKETING

Sixth Edition

David P. Stone
Valerie Lynch Lee
Judith D. McDuff
for
Coast Community College District

Costa Mesa, California

The Dryden Press
Harcourt Brace College Publishers

Fort Worth   Philadelphia   San Diego   New York   Orlando   Austin   San Antonio
Toronto   Montreal   London   Sydney   Tokyo

William M. Vega, *Chancellor,* Coast Community College District
Leslie N. Purdy, *President,* Coastline Community College
Peter Vander Haeghen, *Administrative Dean,* Instructional Systems Development
Michael Werthman, *Publications Editor*

Marketing **Telecourse Design and Production Team**
David P. Stone, *Senior Instructional Designer*
Valerie Lynch Lee, *Instructional Designer, Fifth Edition*
Sandee Harden, *Executive Producer,* KOCE-TV
Carol Dunn Trussell, *Series Producer*
Peter Vander Haeghen, *Academic Advisor*
Jack Wichert, *Academic Advisor*
Joseph V. Anderson, *Contributing Consultant*

Marketing, a telecourse, is produced by Coast Community College District and KOCE-TV, in cooperation with The Dryden Press.

The telecourse is distributed by   **Coast Telecourses**
Coastline Community College
11460 Warner Avenue
Fountain Valley, California 92708
Phone: 714-241-6109   Fax: 714-241-6286

Some material in this book has been adapted from *Study Guide for Contemporary Marketing,* by Stevens, Kaiser, and Loudenback, CBS College Publishing, 1983, and from *Study Guide for Contemporary Marketing*[WIRED] by O'Connor, The Dryden Press, 1998, which is part of the ancillary package that accompanies *Contemporary Marketing*[WIRED], Ninth Edition, by Boone & Kurtz. Used by permission.

Address for Editorial Correspondence
The Dryden Press, 301 Commerce Street, Suite 3700, Fort Worth, TX 76102

Address for Orders
The Dryden Press, 6277 Sea Harbor Drive, Orlando, FL 32887
1-800-782-4479

ISBN: 0-03-019029-0

Printed in the United States of America

7 8 9 0 1 2 3 4 5 6   202   9 8 7 6 5 4 3 2 1

The Dryden Press
Harcourt Brace College Publishers

Preface

To the Student

Welcome to the telecourse *Marketing*. Whether you are taking this course as a part of an academic course of study, for self-improvement in your job, or simply because you are interested in the subject, we hope that you will find it an informative, stimulating, and educationally enriching endeavor.

This course is designed to introduce you to the fundamentals of contemporary marketing by providing you with both the theoretical and the practical aspects of modern marketing management. As with most classroom courses, this television course has a textbook, *Contemporary Marketing Wired*, ninth edition, by Louis E. Boone and David L. Kurtz (Fort Worth: The Dryden Press, 1998); a study guide (this book); assignments; and, of course, tests. Unlike most classroom courses, this course includes 26 video programs that focus on examples of companies that have successfully applied marketing concepts and principles. These case studies vividly illustrate many of the marketing concepts discussed in the textbook.

Marketing has been continually reviewed and refined. This is the sixth edition of the study guide, and the new ninth edition of the textbook has been extensively revised. Since the telecourse was originally produced, eight of the video programs have been updated with new information, and one completely new program was added .

This study guide is your road map through *Marketing*. It is a starting point for each lesson because it contains step-by-step assignments for reading, viewing, and doing related activities, overviews of the content of the textbook and video programs, and a complete array of learning activities to help you master the learning objectives for each lesson. Each lesson in this study guide has the following components:

Assignments. A guide to reading assignments and other activities to be completed before and after viewing each video program.

Lesson Notes. An overview of the main points emphasized in the textbook that helps you focus your attention on the most important concepts in the lesson.

Video Program Notes. A capsule description of the video program for each lesson plus questions for you to consider while watching the programs. The Video Program Notes are *not* a substitute for actually watching the video program.

Learning Objectives. A list that identifies what you should learn from the Lesson Notes, the textbook reading assignment, and the video program.

Review Activities. These activities include both Key Concepts and Completion exercises. The Key Concepts exercise serves as a check to see if you understand important marketing terms. The Completion exercise reinforces what you have read in the textbook and seen in the video program. These activities will help you to retain important concepts and information.

Self-Test. A short multiple-choice quiz to help you evaluate your knowledge of material presented in the textbook and study guide.

Applying Marketing Concepts. This analysis exercise gives you an opportunity to apply what you have learned to a specific marketing situation. Some of the exercises involve straight-forward applications of concepts; others require more creativity and involvement. Each application is tied to marketing concepts presented in the lesson. A number of questions are provided to test your understanding of those concepts.

Additional Activities. Included in this section are Experiential Exercises and Questions for Exploration. These activities have been developed to enhance your understanding of the material presented in the lesson. (Your instructor may assign some of these activities as part of the basic course work or for extra credit.) The Experiential Exercises provide a variety of unique marketing learning experiences based on the principle of "learning by doing." For example, one of the exercises asks you to create a new package for a product, giving you firsthand experience in branding, labeling, using color, and deciding what information to provide and where to place it on a package. In these exercises, you will encounter tasks similar to those assigned to marketers. The Questions for Exploration contain two parts. The first addresses a conceptual issue; the second addresses a practical issue related to the video program. The goal of the Questions for Exploration is to stimulate your thinking and to help you integrate course material into your own frame of reference. Your answers to these questions should be supported by facts and based on strong logic and reasoning.

Answer Key. The final section of each lesson provides answers for the Key Concepts and Completion items and for the Self-Test and Applying Marketing Concepts questions. Check your answers after you have completed each activity. If you have any incorrect answers, review the material.

Course Goals

The instructional designer, academic advisors, and producers of this telecourse have specified five major goals for students taking *Marketing*. After completing all the assignments in this telecourse, you should be able to:

1. Understand the marketing process and the functions it accomplishes.
2. Describe the major elements of the marketing process, including the influence of external factors on marketing, marketing planning and research, buyer behavior and market segmentation, product strategy, distribution strategy, promotional strategy, and pricing strategy.
3. Understand the relationship among the major elements of the marketing process.
4. Recognize how the major elements of the marketing process apply to actual marketing situations.
5. Explain how marketing principles relate to international marketing and nonprofit marketing.

To accomplish these goals, the telecourse emphasizes the concepts and principles of contemporary marketing and the correct use of marketing terms, and the textbook and video programs provide numerous real-world examples and case studies to illustrate the practical application of marketing concepts and principles.

In *Marketing*, you will learn that marketing is vital to every organization, large or small, for-profit or nonprofit, local or international. You will also learn that marketing is much more than just selling and advertising. This course will show you that marketing encompasses a myriad of activities, techniques, concepts, and systems, all of which are essential to the exchange of goods and services between producers and consumers.

Not only is marketing a vital part of every organization, it is also a vital influence on each of us in our daily lives. No matter what role you play as an individual, whether you are self-employed, part of a corporation, or a consumer who wants to buy a particular item, you are affected by marketing. Understanding marketing and its relationship to contemporary society is increasingly important to everyone.

How to Take a Telecourse

Telecourses are designed for busy people—people with full-time jobs or family obligations—who want to take a course at home, fitting the study into their own personal schedules. To complete a telecourse successfully, you will need to plan in advance how to schedule your viewing, reading, and study. Buy the textbook, the study guide, and any other materials required by your instructor before the course begins and look them over; familiarize yourself with any materials supplied by your college and estimate how much time it will take you to complete special tests and assignments for each lesson. Write the dates of midterms, finals, review sessions, and special projects on your calendar so that you can plan to have extra time to prepare for them. You may find it enjoyable and instructive to watch the video program with other people, but save the talking and discussion until after the program so that you won't miss important information. After the program, take a few minutes to write a brief summary of what you have seen and to answer the questions listed at the end of the Video Program Notes for each lesson.

If you are new to college courses in general, and to telecourses in particular, you may benefit from the following suggestions about how to study and how to complete *Marketing* successfully. These suggestions have been compiled from students who have successfully completed telecourses.

- *Do* buy both the textbook and the study guide for *Marketing* or arrange to share copies with a friend. Do *not* try to get through the telecourse without these books.

- *Do* watch each of the video programs. In order to pass the examinations, you will need to read and study the textbook and to view the video programs. If the programs are broadcast over a public-television station or cable channel and you have a videocassette recorder, tape the programs for later review.

- *Do* keep up with your work for this course every week. Even if you do not have any class sessions on campus or any assignments to turn in, you should read the textbook and do the assignments in the study guide, as well as watch the video programs. Set aside viewing, reading, and study time each week and stick to your schedule.

- *Do* get in touch with the faculty member who is in charge of *Marketing* at your college or university. The instructor can answer any questions you have about the material covered in the course. Your faculty member can also help you catch up if you are behind, advise you about additional assignments, discuss the type of test questions you can expect, and tell you where you might be able to watch programs you have missed or wish to review.

- *Do* complete all the review activities and self-tests provided in this guide. These will help you master the learning objectives and prepare for formal examinations.

- If you miss a program or fall behind in your study schedule, don't give up. Many television stations repeat broadcasts of the programs later in the week or on weekends. Your college might have videocassette copies of programs available in the campus library or media center. And *do* call on your course faculty member or manager to help if you have problems of any kind. This person is assigned specifically to help you succeed in *Marketing*.

Contents

Anything that won't sell, I don't want to invent. Its sale is proof of utility, and utility is success.
—Thomas A. Edison

1

The Marketing Process

Assignments

For the most effective study of this lesson, we suggest that you complete the assignments in the following sequence:

1. Read the study guide Overview (Lesson Notes and Video Program Notes) and the Learning Objectives for this lesson.

2. Read *Contemporary Marketing Wired*, 9th edition, Chapter 1, "Developing Relationships through Customer Focus, Quality, Technology, and Ethical Behavior," pages 2-16 and 23-40 and Chapter 2, "Creating Value Through Customer Satisfaction and Quality," paying particular attention to "Chapter Overview" and "The Importance of Satisfying Customers," pages 47-51, "The Quality Movement, " "TQM in Action," and "Delivering Customer Value," pages 54-71. Also read Chapter 10, "Relationship Marketing," pages 357-358.

3. View "The Mouse That Roared: A Marketing Overview" video program.

4. Review the textbook assignment for this lesson.

5. Complete the Review Activities (Key Concepts and Completion), Self-Test, and Applying Marketing Concepts for this lesson.

6. Check your answers against the Answer Key at the end of the lesson, and review when necessary.

7. Complete any of the Additional Activities (Experiential Exercise and Questions for Exploration) that interest you or that are assigned by your instructor.

Overview

Marketing is one of the two basic functions performed by all organizations; the other function is production of a good, service, or idea. In performing these two functions, organizations create **utility**, the want-satisfying power of a good, service, or idea. The production function is responsible for converting raw materials and components into finished goods and services, creating form utility. Marketing is responsible for creating the three other types of utility: time utility, or making goods and services available when consumers want them; place utility, making goods and services available where consumers can buy them; and ownership utility, transferring title to the good or service when it is bought.

Today, **marketing** can be defined as the "process of planning and executing the conception, pricing, promotion, and distribution of ideas, goods, services, organizations, and events to create and maintain relationships that satisfy individual and organizational objectives." This definition has evolved in the last half of the twentieth century.

In order to compete, companies must continually search for the most efficient manufacturing sites and most lucrative markets for products. This global economy is expanding annually at about 4 percent. As standards of living rise, especially in Europe and Asia, customer demand for the latest goods and services increases. Expanding outside the U.S. market gives domestic companies access to almost 6 billion international customers.

The current definition of marketing and marketing's role in business is considerably different from that of earlier eras. A **production orientation** characterized most businesses up until the mid-1920s. With this orientation, businesses focused their efforts on producing quality products that they believed would "sell themselves." As production methods improved significantly between 1925 and the early 1950s, businesses had more products to sell and began to adopt a **sales orientation**, in the belief that consumers must be persuaded to buy a product. Even in this era, however, marketing was considered subordinate to production, engineering, and other departments. The Depression of the 1930s, which severely limited personal income and the demand for goods and services, led many businesses to place increased importance on marketing, a trend that was interrupted by World War II and the shortage of goods and services.

Following the end of the war, marketing resumed growing in importance. The era was characterized by an expanding **buyer's market**, with an abundance of goods and services. Businesses developed a strong **consumer orientation**, in which they first determined unmet consumer needs and then created products to satisfy those needs. Businesses had realized that goods and services not only had to be produced and sold, they had to be *marketed*. This realization was accompanied by the emergence of the **marketing concept**, a companywide consumer orientation with the objective of achieving long-run success. During the 1990s, organizations are concentrating on long-term, value-added relationships with suppliers and consumers. Today's marketers realize that marketing efforts must center on **relationship marketing,** the development, growth, and maintenance of long-term, cost-effective exchange relationships with individual customers, suppliers, employees, and other partners for mutual benefit. A few companies, however, suffer from what Theodore Levitt has called **marketing myopia**, defining their business too narrowly and thus hampering their ability to be fully consumer oriented.

The marketing strategy employed by most businesses today begins with identification of a **target market**, a group of people toward whom a firm will market its products. Once the target market is identified, marketers focus on the **marketing mix**, the combination of product strategies, pricing strategies, distribution strategies, and promotional strategies, that will satisfy that market.

Development of a **product strategy** encompasses all the decisions related to developing the correct good or service for the target market. Product strategy includes decisions about brand names, trademarks, package design, warranties, and customer service.

Pricing strategy involves setting a price that will be accepted by the target market and provide a profit for the producer. This strategy must consider consumer expectations, production costs, markups by wholesalers and other channel members, competitors, and legal constraints.

The **distribution strategy** covers all the decisions necessary for getting the product to the target market. It includes selection of methods for transporting goods and identification of the best marketing channels to handle the goods.

Promotional strategy is, perhaps, the most creative and exciting part of the marketing mix. Promotional strategy involves discussions on how best to communicate information about goods or services to the target market and to persuade consumers to buy the product. Promotional strategy includes advertising, sales promotion, and personal selling.

In making decisions about each of these four strategies, the marketer must be constantly alert to the five external environments—competitive, political-legal, economic, technological, and social-cultural—that can significantly influence the product and demand for that product.

Marketing has become an increasingly competitive endeavor. To survive and thrive in this environment, marketers are paying particular attention to techniques for enhancing **customer satisfaction**. Special emphasis is being placed on quality in all aspects of production and marketing to ensure that the good, service, or event meets or even exceeds the customer's needs and expectations. Today, concern for customer satisfaction influences every aspect of the marketing process.

As the new century approaches, we are entering into a new era of technological advances that are revolutionizing marketing, creating new industries and products. Two key developments of this technology era are interactive marketing and the Internet.

In **interactive marketing,** the customer controls the information received from a marketer through various channels—CD-ROM disks, e-mail, interactive 800 phone numbers, virtual reality kiosks, and the Internet. The challenge for marketers is to develop new strategies based on interactive marketing techniques to build lasting customer relationships.

The **Internet** is a global network that allows anyone with access to a personal computer send and receive images and data anywhere. On the Internet, customers can access the **World Wide Web,** an interlinked collection of easily accessible information sources.

To market their businesses, companies use online techniques such as interactive brochures, virtual storefronts, information clearinghouses, and customer service tools.

Interactive brochures range from simple electronic flyers to multimedia presentations. The **virtual storefront** takes the interactive brochure one step further, allowing customers to view and order merchandise. Information clearinghouses provide detailed product information, including questions and answers, online conferences, and discussion groups. The Web also acts as a customer service tool, allowing customers to order catalogs and place service orders. As the Web evolves, marketers need to explore its capabilities and learn to use it effectively as an extension of other communications media.

Strategic alliances, or partnerships that create competitive advantages, are increasing as companies find benefits from collaborative relationships. Some popular forms of strategic alliances are the affinity credit card program, co-marketing, and licensing arrangements.

Marketing is not an inexpensive activity. Most estimates of marketing costs indicate that those costs account for about 50 percent of the total cost of the average product. Although marketing is not directly involved in the physical production of goods or provision of services, it does perform eight essential functions: buying, selling, transporting, storing, standardization and grading, financing, risk taking, and securing market information.

In recent years, several well-known businesses have been involved in allegations of unethical conduct. As a result, more than half of all major corporations now offer ethics training to employees, and many firms take steps toward environmental protection, community contributions, and improved working conditions. These programs often result in improved customer relationships, increased employee loyalty, marketplace success, and improved financial performance.

Marketing is not an abstract, theoretical science. It is a collection of case histories, rules of thumb, concepts, and principles, all of which have validity because they work in the "real world." Marketing managers, unlike economists, will probably never be awarded Nobel prizes for complex mathematical models. Rather, "prizes" are awarded in the marketplace, where the product and its marketing strategy are presented and the consumer is the judge. Marketers are awarded their prizes in the form of objectives that are met and in profits that increase.

Video Program Notes

The video program for this lesson focuses on Walt Disney Productions. This corporation illustrates one definition of marketing: satisfying the needs and wants of a chosen consumer segment. Disney's chosen consumer segment originally was families and, as Walt Disney expressed it, "the child in each of us." You will see how Disney's marketing mix is based on corporate objectives and tempered by environmental forces. Toward the end of the program, you will learn how Disney established a new unit, Touchstone Pictures, to respond to changing consumer tastes and appeal to new audiences. *Splash* was the first movie produced by Touchstone. Since that time, Touchstone has released numerous movies, some targeted directly at adult audiences.

As you watch the video program, consider the following questions:
1. What is Disney selling?
2. How are the various Disney products promoted?
3. Were Disney's early films consumer oriented or product oriented?
4. How has Disney used marketing research?
5. Who are Disneyland's competitors?
6. Why did Disney embark on ventures such as television in the 1950s and cable television and Touchstone Productions in the 1980s?

7. How does merchandise licensing serve as a source of income and production?

Learning Objectives

After completing your study of this lesson, you should be able to:

1. Define the following terms as they relate to the marketing process:

buyer's market	production orientation
consumer orientation	product strategy
continuous improvement	promotional strategy
customer satisfaction	quality
distribution strategy	relationship marketing
exchange process	sales orientation
Internet	seller's market
interactive marketing	strategic alliance
marketing	target market
marketing audit	technology
marketing concept	total quality management
marketing mix	utility
marketing myopia	value-added
PDCA cycle	virtual storefront
pricing strategy	World Wide Web

2. Explain how marketing creates utility through the exchange process.

3. Describe the evolution of marketing during the four eras in the history of marketing.

4. Describe the elements of a marketing strategy and the environmental characteristics that influence strategy decisions.

5. Explain the universal functions performed by marketing.

6. Explain the relationship between value, customer satisfaction, and quality.

7. Describe the contribution of total quality management to the development of a successful marketing strategy.

8. Explain the changes in the marketing environment due to technology and relationship marketing.

9. Explain three reasons for studying marketing.

10. Explain the relationship between ethical business practices and marketing success.

Review Activities

Key Concepts

> Identify each of the following basic marketing concepts by writing the letter of the appropriate term in the blank next to the corresponding description.
>
> a. seller's market   f.   marketing concept
>
> b. production orientation   g.   marketing myopia
>
> c. marketing   h. sales orientation
>
> d. marketing mix   i.   exchange process
>
> e. buyer's market   j.   target market

_____ 1. process of planning and executing the conception, pricing, promotion, and distribution of ideas, goods, services, organizations, and events to create and maintain relationships that satisfy individual and organizational objectives

_____ 2. companywide consumer orientation with the objective of achieving long-run success

_____ 3. business philosophy that emphasizes efficiency in producing a quality product

_____ 4. problem of defining the business too narrowly and not taking a marketing orientation

_____ 5. blending of the marketing strategy elements to satisfy chosen consumer segments

_____ 6. situation in which fewer goods and services are available than potential consumers

_____ 7. situation in which more goods and services are available than potential consumers

_____ 8. assumes consumers will resist purchasing nonessential goods and services and that personal selling and advertising are needed to convince them to buy

_____ 9. two or more parties giving something of value to each other to satisfy perceived needs

_____ 10. group of people toward whom a firm markets goods, services, or ideas designed to satisfy specific needs or wants

---

Identify each of the following types of utility by writing the letter of the appropriate term in the blank provided.

a. place utility	c. form utility
b. time utility	d. ownership utility

_____ 11. utility created when the business firm converts raw materials into finished goods and services

_____ 12. utility created when the marketer makes goods and services available when consumers want to purchase them

_____ 13. utility created when the marketer makes goods and services available at locations convenient to consumers

_____ 14. utility created when title to goods or services is transferred to the consumer at time of purchase

Identify each of the following terms related to marketing strategy by writing the letter of the appropriate term in the blank provided.

a. distribution strategy
b. pricing strategy
c. product strategy
d. promotional strategy

_____ 15. strategy that involves the activities and institutions that will move a good or service from the producer to the final consumer

_____ 16. strategy that involves advertising, sales promotion, and personal selling to communicate with and persuade potential customers

_____ 17. strategy that involves setting justifiable and acceptable prices of goods and services to the ultimate consumer

_____ 18. strategy that involves decisions about package design, brand names, warranties, trademarks, product life cycles, positioning, and new-product development

Identify each of the following terms related to customer-focused quality by writing the letter of the appropriate term in the blank provided.

a. value-added
b. marketing audit
c. quality
d. PDCA cycle
e. customer satisfaction
f. continuous improvement
g. total quality management

_____ 19. the degree of excellence or superiority of an organization's goods and services

_____ 20. process of constantly studying and improving work activities

_____ 21. increased worth of a good or service as a result of added features, enhanced customer service, or other improvements in the marketing mix

____ 22. an effort to involve all employees in continually improving products and work processes

____ 23. ability of a good or service to meet or exceed a buyer's needs and expectations

____ 24. continuous improvement process of planning, doing, checking, and acting

____ 25. thorough evaluation of an organization's marketing philosophy, goals, policies, tactics, practices, and results

Completion

> Fill each blank in the following paragraphs with the most appropriate term from the list of completion answers below. A term may be used once, more than once, or not at all.
>
> | | | |
> |---|---|---|
> | buyer's | industrial | risk-taking |
> | buying | long-run | sales |
> | conception | marketing | securing marketing |
> | consumer | marketing audit | information |
> | continuous | marketing mix | seller's |
> | improvement | myopia | selling |
> | customer | needs | short-run |
> | customer | ownership | standardization |
> | satisfaction | PDCA cycle | and grading |
> | distribution | physical | storing |
> | environmental | distribution | target market |
> | exchange | place | time |
> | exchange process | pricing | transporting |
> | exchanges | product | value-added |
> | facilitating | production | want-satisfying |
> | financing | promotion | wants |
> | form | quality | |

1. Assume that you and another student have started a monthly newsletter. The purpose of the newsletter is to serve as an independent source of community news. You have purchased a personal computer and desktop publishing software to create

the newsletter. The process of gathering information, composing articles, entering the text into the computer, and creating a layout is mainly a _____ function. These activities are part of creating _____ utility. By hiring someone to deliver finished newsletters and selling them on consignment through local supermarkets, you have created _____ utility. By ensuring that the newsletter is delivered to readers on the first of the month, you are creating _____ utility. You are in charge of contacting potential customers. You talk to people to determine who wants or needs an independent newsletter and how much they are willing to pay. In addition, after a sale is made, the newsletter becomes the property of the purchaser. The activity in which you are involved results in _____ utility.

2. The foundation for the creation of utility is the designing and marketing of _____ goods, services, and ideas.

3. Marketing is the process of planning and executing the _____ , _____ , _____ , and _____ of ideas, goods, services, organizations, and events to create and maintain relationships that satisfy individual and organizational objectives.

4. The essence of marketing is the _____ , in which two or more parties give something of value to each other to satisfy felt _____ .

5. Effective marketing converts _____ for such items as food, clothing, and shelter into _____ .

6. The four eras in the history of marketing are, in sequence, the _____ era, the _____ era, the _____ era, and the _____ era.

7. A firm that first produces a product and then hires someone to sell it is probably _____ oriented.

8. If more goods and services are available than are demanded, a _____ market is said to exist.

9. A firm that has increased its production is probably in a _____ market.

10. The marketing concept is the companywide orientation that assumes a firm's goals are _____ satisfaction and _____ profits.

11. Management that defines the scope of the business too narrowly may fail to recognize that the purpose of its business is to satisfy specific wants and needs of customers. Such a narrow view of the marketplace is called marketing _____.

12. The marketing efforts of a firm consist of many types of activities, all related to satisfying the needs of the _____. These activities are known as _____ variables.

13. The marketing mix consists of four strategies: _____, _____, _____, and _____.

14. A firm's decision about a new product and how it will be packaged is part of the _____ strategy.

15. A firm's decision to deliver its products with trucks and use retail stores to sell to consumers is part of the _____ strategy.

16. The decision to use television advertisements instead of a direct-mail campaign is part of the _____ strategy.

17. The decision to reduce the selling price of a product is part of the _____ strategy.

18. The framework within which marketing strategies are planned consists of five _____ dimensions.

19. Marketing costs in relation to the overall costs of goods and services are estimated to be about 50 percent. These costs cover a wide range of functions performed by marketing. These functions may be grouped into three categories: _____, _____, and _____.

20. The exchange function encompasses the two functions of _____ and _____.

21. The physical distribution function includes the function of _____ and _____.

22. The facilitating functions performed by marketing are _____, _____, _____, and _____.

23. A company will probably not be successful if it fails to provide the same level of _____ and _____ as its competitors.

24. TQM focuses first and foremost on the _____.

25. When a good or service has something of personal significance to the customer, it is said to be _____.

26. Because customers' needs, wants, and expectations are constantly changing, one approach to enhancing customer satisfaction is known as _____. This approach may use a process known as the _____.

27. The XYZ firm has just hired a new vice president of marketing. One of her first requests is a written report of everything the firm is doing in marketing and why the activities are being done. The report must cover philosophy, goals, policies, tactics, practices, and results. The vice president has requested a _____.

Self-Test

Select the best answer.

1. Marketing is best defined as
   a. the creation of form utility, time utility, place utility, and ownership utility.
   b. exchange activities in a subsistence economy.
   c. carefully producing a quality product and then selling it to all consumers.
   d. the planning and execution of the conception, pricing, promotion, and distribution of ideas, goods, services, organizations, and events to create and maintain relationships that satisfy individual and organizational objectives.

2. The marketing concept emphasizes
   a. marketing managers who run the company.
   b. a product orientation.
   c. achievement of short-run profits.
   d. companywide consumer orientation.

3. The marketing mix consists of each of the following activities **EXCEPT**
   a. producing the product.
   b. planning the product.
   c. blending personal selling, advertising, and sales promotion.
   d. setting prices.

4. The approach to marketing that assumes that consumers are resistant to purchasing most goods or services is the
   a. sales orientation.
   b. product orientation.
   c. consumer orientation.
   d. marketing orientation.

5. Since World War II, most businesses have adopted
   a. a product orientation.
   b. marketing myopia.
   c. a sales orientation.
   d. the marketing concept.

6. Trademarks and brands are part of
   a. promotional strategy.
   b. pricing strategy.
   c. product strategy.
   d. distribution strategy.

7. By making goods available at a convenient location, marketing creates
   a. form utility.
   b. time utility.
   c. place utility.
   d. ownership utility.

8. A sales-oriented business is one that downplays its product strategy in favor of its

   a. service strategy.
   b. channels strategy.
   c. promotional strategy.
   d. pricing strategy.

9. When a marketing manager formulates the strategies of product, distribution, promotion, and pricing to satisfy certain consumer segments, he or she is developing the

   a. marketing mix.
   b. strategic plan.
   c. consumer orientation.
   d. marketing concept.

10. The eight universal marketing functions can be grouped into the three categories of

   a. buying, selling, and facilitating.
   b. exchange, physical distribution, and facilitating.
   c. exchange, transporting, and risk taking.
   d. selling, physical distribution, and financing.

11. The true measure of quality is

   a. products that are completely free of defects.
   b. increased corporate profits.
   c. satisfied customers.
   d. capturing the majority of customers.

12. In quality-conscious companies, customer satisfaction is

   a. mainly the concern of the marketing department.
   b. shared equally by production and marketing departments.
   c. mainly the concern of senior management.
   d. the concern of all employees.

13. The first step in increasing customer satisfaction is usually to

   a. analyze the record of production defects.
   b. compile feedback from customers.
   c. identify the target market.
   d. train the sales force and others who have direct contact with customers.

14. To fix quality problems, U.S. manufacturers spend about
    a. 10 percent of sales dollars.
    b. 25 percent of sales dollars.
    c. 40 percent of sales dollars.
    d 55 percent of sales dollars.

15. Online techniques to market businesses include
    a. virtual storefronts.
    b. interactive brochures.
    c. information clearinghouses.
    d. all of the above.

16. A nontraditional concept of marketing which focuses on long-term relationships with suppliers, employees, customers, and other partners is known as
    a. relationship marketing.
    b. global marketing.
    c. target marketing.
    d. interactive marketing.

Applying Marketing Concepts

Jack Musconi, a track-and-field coach at Western University, opened a sporting-goods store. The store, located near the Western campus, specializes in tennis and jogging equipment and carries all major brands. In addition to selling new tennis and jogging equipment, Musconi provides several services such as restringing tennis rackets.

In a recent interview, Musconi explained his business strategy: "I'm mainly concerned with satisfying the sporting needs of the students, faculty, and staff at Western University. Generally, I stock the products and brands that they ask for, as long as I can get those products and make a profit on their sales. I've had to stop dealing with some manufacturers, such as Freebas, because they've acted very independent, delivering running shoes more than six months after they were ordered. Some of the products I stock are purchased from wholesalers because we order in small quantities. Most of our orders are shipped to us by United Parcel Service (UPS). This ensures that we get the product in a week or less after placing the order, without incurring an exorbitant freight bill.

"My major advertising is done in the school newspaper, where I usually offer students a discount or some free product, like a pair of shoestrings, if they buy a minimum amount. My sales force consists of three college students and me. The sales personnel are required to charge all customers the same price for a certain item. The price is generally comparable to those offered by competitors. I feel it's necessary to be competitive because several other stores nearby offer comparable products or even the same brands. Overall, I've made enough to pay the bills and make a 10-percent return on my investment. My major concern is that my marketing costs seem to be too high; they're running about 25 percent of the selling price of my goods."

1. Restringing tennis rackets at Musconi's sporting-goods store creates
   a. form utility.
   b. place utility.
   c. ownership utility.
   d. time utility.

2. Newspaper advertising and a small sales force are part of Musconi's
   a. promotional strategy.
   b. pricing strategy.
   c. product strategy.
   d. distribution strategy.
   e. target market strategy.

3. Musconi's distribution strategy includes
   a. wholesalers.
   b. student discounts.
   c. free delivery to customers.
   d. UPS and wholesalers.

4. Musconi's pricing strategy includes
   a. charging all customers the same price for a certain item.
   b. prices comparable to those of competitors.
   c. student discounts.
   d. free products in conjunction with minimum purchases.
   e. all of the above.

5. Musconi's product strategy is best described as
   a. stocking the lowest-cost products available.
   b. selling the highest-quality products.
   c. offering customers the products they want.
   d. selling only nationally known brands.

6. Jack Musconi appears to have adopted
   a. the marketing concept.
   b. marketing myopia.
   c. a product orientation.

7. From Musconi's point of view, the Freebas Company may have adopted
   a. the marketing concept.
   b. marketing myopia.
   c. a product orientation.

8. Musconi's sporting-goods store faces
   a. a seller's market.
   b. a buyer's market.
   c. an open market.
   d. a closed market.

9. Compared to the national average, Musconi's marketing costs are
   a. higher.
   b. lower.
   c. about the same.

10. By locating his store near his market and customers, Musconi created
   a. ownership utility.
   b. place utility.
   c. time utility.
   d. product utility.

Additional Activities

Experiential Exercise

The purpose of this exercise is to broaden your understanding of marketing by comparing the definitions of marketing provided by managers of organizations operating in your community.

- Interview three-to-five people to find out how they define marketing. These people can be managers of restaurants, insurance companies, department stores, not-for-profit institutions, manufacturing companies, financial institutions, college bookstores, or any other organization. Ask them to define marketing. You should also ask them about their organizations, the markets they serve, and their goods or services, so that you can better understand their concept of marketing.

- Make a chart recording the results of your interviews. Include in your chart the following categories: name of person interviewed, title, name of organization, and definition of marketing.

- What are the major differences between the definitions you collected and the textbook definition? Some hints for finding differences in the definitions include examining which elements of the marketing mix are omitted, the role of consumers in the marketing definitions of those interviewed, and the role of production.

Questions for Exploration

Conceptual

In terms of broad generalizations, we can highlight two conflicting approaches within a firm: the creative entrepreneurial approach, which is willing to go with instincts, take extreme risks, and be creative; and the managerial approach, which relies on data, tries to control or offset risk, and prizes orderliness. Which approach should predominate in a commercial venture and why?

Practical

The video program attributed much of Disney's early success to Walt Disney himself. Following his death, the Disney empire was not consistently successful. What do you think Walt Disney supplied to the business that a host of trained managers did not? What is the current situation at Disney?

Answer Key

Key Concepts				
	1. c	8. h	14. d	20. f
	2. f	9. i	15. a	21. a
	3. b	10. j	16. d	22. g
	4. g	11. c	17. b	23. e
	5. d	12. b	18. c	24. d
	6. a	13. a	19. c	25. b
	7. e			

Completion

1. production, form, place, time, ownership
2. want-satisfying
3. conception, pricing, promotion, distribution (any order)
4. exchange process, needs
5. needs, wants
6. production, sales, marketing, technology
7. production
8. buyer's
9. seller's
10. consumer, long-run
11. myopia
12. target market, marketing-mix
13. product, distribution, promotion, pricing (any order)
14. product
15. distribution
16. promotion
17. pricing
18. environmental
19. exchange, physical distribution, facilitating (any order)
20. buying, selling (either order)
21. transporting, storing (either order)
22. standardization and grading, financing, risk taking, securing marketing information (any order)
23. customer satisfaction, quality (either order)
24. customer
25. value-added
26. continuous improvement, PDCA cycle
27. marketing audit

Self-Test				
	1. d	5. d	9. a	13. b
	2. d	6. c	10. b	14. b
	3. a	7. c	11. c	15. d
	4. a	8. c	12. d	16. a

Applying Marketing Concepts			
	1. a	5. c	8. b
	2. a	6. a	9. b
	3. d	7. c	10. b
	4. e		

I sleep so much better at night, knowing that America is protected from thin pickles and fast ketchup.
—Senator Orrin Hatch, "On the Record," *Time* (Dec. 14, 1981), p. 60.

2

Marketing Decisions

Assignments

For the most effective study of this lesson, we suggest that you complete the assignments in the following sequence:

1. Read the study guide Overview (Lesson Notes and Video Program Notes) and the Learning Objectives for this lesson.

2. Read *Contemporary Marketing Wired,* 9th edition, Chapter 3, "The Marketing Environment, Ethics, and Social Responsibility," pages 78-100. (The balance of the chapter will be assigned in a later lesson.)

3. View "The Road to Success: A Case Study in Marketing Decisions" video program.

4. Review the textbook assignment for this lesson.

5. Complete the Review Activities (Key Concepts and Completion), Self-Test, and Applying Marketing Concepts for this lesson.

6. Check your answers against the Answer Key at the end of the lesson, and review when necessary.

7. Complete any of the Additional Activities (Experiential Exercise and Questions for Exploration) that interest you or that are assigned by your instructor.

Overview

Marketing decisions are not made in a vacuum. Outside environments influence decisions about product, price, channels of distribution, promotion, and all other marketing activities. The five principal environments that marketers must consider are the competitive, the political-legal, the economic, the technological, and the social-cultural. Often, these external forces are beyond the direct control of the marketer, but in some instances, marketers can influence these forces through **environmental management**. The process of collecting information about the outside marketing environment in order to identify and interpret possible trends is called **environmental scanning.**

The **competitive environment** involves three types of competition: (1) marketers of directly competitive products, (2) marketers of products that can be substituted for one another, and (3) marketers competing for the consumer's purchasing power. Among the ways that a firm can influence this environment are introduction of new products with technological advances, joint ventures, mergers and acquisitions, price changes, customer service, use of the Internet, and promotional campaigns. Development of a competitive marketing strategy begins by considering whether the firm should compete. If the answer is positive, the firm must then identify the markets in which it should compete and develop a method for competing. For example, by using a **time-based competition** strategy, marketers develop and distribute goods and services faster than competitors.

The **political-legal environment** comprises all the federal, state, and local laws and interpretations of laws that require firms to operate under competitive conditions and to protect the rights of consumers. Marketers can try to control the political-legal environment by influencing the public and legislative bodies through advertising, political action committees, and lobbying. The newest frontier of government regulation is investigating ways to police the Internet and online services for such things as fraud, deceptive advertising, and invasion of privacy. Consumer interest groups have skyrocketed during the past 25 years, operating at national, state, and local levels.

The **economic environment** directly influences consumer spending and purchasing decisions. In considering the impact of the economic environment, marketers must be aware of the basic business cycle and which stage (prosperity, recession, depression, recovery) the economy is in at any given time. Other elements of the economic environment include inflation, unemployment, income, and resource availability. Marketers must also monitor the economic environments of other nations. Although the overall economic environment is difficult to influence, marketers can develop strategies that respond to the changes in consumer demand that characterize different economic environments.

Discoveries in science, inventions, and innovations resulting from research and development can significantly alter the **technological environment** in which a firm operates. Products can become obsolete or be vastly improved or made less expensive. Innovations in technology also create new industries. For example, the success of the Internet has resulted in new types of software firms, interactive advertising agencies, and job categories. Marketers must be knowledgeable about the technological environment in order to find new products to introduce and ways to increase productivity and operating efficiency or improve customer service and consumer satisfaction.

Of all the environments, the **social-cultural environment**, which consists of the relationship between marketing and society and its culture, is perhaps the most dynamic. Society's values are constantly changing, along with demographic shifts in the population and growing cultural diversity, especially in the United States. Marketers must be ever-alert to these changes because they determine, to a large extent, what goods and services consumers want and what they will—and will not—accept in the way of advertising. The social-cultural environment is even more influential in making international marketing decisions. An important element in the social-cultural environment is **consumerism**, which is a social force that exerts legal, moral, and economic pressure on business and government in order to aid and protect the buyer.

Video Program Notes

The video program for this lesson examines how Mitsubishi Motor Sales of America responded to environmental uncertainties when operating in a "foreign" market—the United States of America. Among the environments that most influenced Mitsubishi were the political-legal, economic, and competitive. In the political-legal environment, Mitsubishi was faced with import quotas at a time when the company needed to expand its model line in order to compete with other automobile manufacturers. Economically, Mitsubishi was affected by a severe recession when it first entered the market. In the competitive environment, Mitsubishi faced several major challenges. One of the most basic was establishing name recognition for Mitsubishi and creating a distinctive image for Mitsubishi cars in the minds of consumers.

As you watch the video program, consider the following questions:

1. What were some of the characteristics of the economic environment when Mitsubishi first entered the U.S. market?

2. What were some of the political and legal variables that Mitsubishi faced?

3. As shown in the video program, is Mitsubishi's car design center product oriented or consumer oriented?

4. How does Mitsubishi adapt its cars to the social-cultural environment in the United States?

5. Which environments led Mitsubishi to expand its product line to include the lower-priced Mirage?

6. How does Mitsubishi use marketing research to ensure its products are offered for sale where consumers want to purchase them?

7. What role do the car magazines (the "buff books") play in Mitsubishi's sales promotion strategy?

8. Key members of Mitsubishi's channel of distribution are dealers. What are some of the ways Mitsubishi tends to the interests of its dealers?

9. How does Mitsubishi use its advertising to reinforce product strategy and consumer awareness of the Mitsubishi name?

10. How does the company accommodate intercultural differences in management?

Learning Objectives

After completing your study of this lesson, you should be able to:

1. Define the following terms as they relate to marketing decisions:

competitive environment	environmental scanning
consumerism	political-legal environment
consumer rights	social-cultural environment
demarketing	technological environment
economic environment	time-based competition
environmental management	

2. Describe the competitive environment and explain the steps marketers take to develop competitive strategies.

3. Describe how government and other groups regulate marketing activities and how marketers can attempt to influence the political-legal environment.

4. Describe the economic forces that affect marketing decisions and consumer buying power.

5. Explain how the technological environment can affect a firm's marketing activities.

6. Describe the social-cultural environment and its influence on marketing.

Review Activities

Key Concepts

> **Identify each of the following concepts by writing the letter of the appropriate term in the blank next to the corresponding description.**
>
> a. competitive environment   g. economic environment
> b. political-legal environment   h. technological environment
> c. consumerism   i. demarketing
> d. environmental management   j. social-cultural environment
> e. time-based competition   k. environmental scanning
> f. consumer rights

_____ 1. process of reducing consumer demand for a good or service to a level that the firm can supply

_____ 2. characterized by laws that require firms to operate under competitive conditions and that protect consumer rights

_____ 3. achievement of organizational objectives by predicting and influencing external environments

_____ 4. strategy of developing and distributing goods and services more quickly than competitors

_____ 5. includes the rights to choose freely and to be safe

_____ 6. includes recession, inflation, and other business fluctuations

_____ 7. discoveries in science, inventions, and innovations that affect marketing decisions

_____ 8. interactive process that occurs in the marketplace among producers

_____ 9. consists of the marketer's relationships with society and its culture

_____ 10. a force that exerts legal, moral, and economic pressure on business and government

_____ 11. gathering information about the external marketing environment to identify and interpret potential trends

Completion

1. The five different environments that influence marketing strategies are _____ , _____ , _____ , _____ , and _____ .

2. The importance of the marketing environments can be exemplified by consideration of the actions taken against marketers who ignore consumers' desires. For example, legislation may be instituted against a marketer who produces a product that is considered harmful. The resulting legislation then becomes part of the _____ environment.

3. Similarly, as a result of unemployment during a recession, consumers may be unable to buy a marketer's products. Consequently, marketing activities are influenced by the _____ environment.

4. The effect that inventions, innovations, and discoveries in science have on marketing decisions is known as the _____ environment.

5. The way that consumers react to different products and marketing strategies is affected by such variables as population growth, changes in demographics, and shifts in values. These are all part of the _____ environment.

6. The competitive environment includes three different types of competition. The most direct competition is between makers of _____ products. Another type of competition is between products that can be _____ for one another. All firms compete with each other because they are competing for consumers' _____ amount of discretionary buying power.

7. Pro-Max, a manufacturer of sporting goods for professionals, has the capital to expand its business into backpacking goods. Its chief marketers are asking if Pro-Max should get into this new line, and, if it does, which lines it should go after first and how it should position itself in the market. Each of the above questions relates to developing a _____ strategy.

8. One of the environments that affects marketing consists of all laws that affect marketing behavior. This is referred to as the _____ environment.

9. Government regulation in the United States has gone through four phases. During the first phase, the regulations were principally _____. In the second phase, laws were directed toward protecting _____. The third phase focused on laws protecting _____. The fourth phase encourages competition through _____.

10. The federal agency that has the broadest powers to influence marketing activities is the _____.

11. Among the techniques marketers can use in trying to control the political-legal environment are _____, _____, and _____.

12. The business cycle, inflation, unemployment, income, and resource availability are factors that directly influence consumer buying power and marketing strategies. These factors are part of the _____ environment. Marketers must also monitor the _____ economic environment.

13. The business cycle consists of four stages. Consumers are most willing to buy in times of _____. Consumers are least willing to buy during a _____. Consumers usually avoid buying luxury items and focus on basic, low-cost items during a

_____. The fourth stage, characterized by consumers' ability but reluctance to buy, is known as _____.

14. A shrinkage in supply of widely used resources, such as energy, results in changes in consumer behavior. To help alleviate an energy crisis and other resource shortages, marketers may have to encourage consumers to reduce their demand, a process known as _____.

15. When members of the general public exert pressure on businesses by threatening to boycott a product or to bring suit against a company, they are demonstrating _____.

16. In 1962, President John F. Kennedy stated four consumer rights. Those rights are the right to choose freely, be _____ , be _____ , and be _____.

Self-Test

| Select the best answer. |

1. The competitive environment
   a. does not apply to high-priced items such as those produced by the Cadillac division of General Motors.
   b. is becoming less important in the United States.
   c. includes all firms that are competing for a limited amount of discretionary purchasing power.
   d. does not include sales made in foreign markets.
   e. does not depend on the marketer's competitive strategy.

2. If marketers encourage consumers to reduce their demand for a product to a level that can reasonably be supplied, they are practicing
   a. the marketing concept.
   b. demarketing.
   c. price fixing.
   d. illegal activities.

3. In considering the social-cultural environment, marketers look at male and female consumers and young and old consumers as
   a. similar markets.
   b. the same as they were 10 years ago.
   c. distinct markets.
   d. being different, but the differences are unimportant.

4. Lobby groups are attempts made by individual firms and trade associations to control the
   a. competitive environment.
   b. political-legal environment.
   c. economic environment.
   d. social-cultural environment.

5. At the federal level, the agency that has broadest powers to influence marketing activities is the
   a. Interstate Commerce Commission.
   b. Consumer Products Safety Commission.
   c. Federal Trade Commission.
   d. Environmental Protection Agency.

6. The historical cyclic pattern of the economy is
   a. depression, recession, prosperity, recovery.
   b. prosperity, recession, depression, recovery.
   c. recession, recovery, depression, prosperity.
   d. depression, recovery, recession, prosperity.

7. Discretionary income
   a. is about the same in both young and old consumers.
   b. is of little value to marketers.
   c. is generally higher among older people.
   d. refers to the amount of money people spend on food and clothing.

8. The consumerism movement is part of the
   a. political-legal environment.
   b. economic environment.
   c. competitive environment.
   d. social-cultural environment.

9. In developing a competitive strategy, the first question a firm must answer is:
   a. In what markets should we compete?
   b. Should we compete?
   c. How should we compete?
   d. How much will it cost to compete?

10. Sales of a five-pound portable television set dropped drastically after the firm failed to react to a competitor's introduction of a less-expensive, one-pound model that offered more features. This firm is a victim of the
    a. social-cultural environment.
    b. marketing environment.
    c. technological environment.
    d. economic environment.

Applying Marketing Concepts

Kathy Jackson manufactured and marketed a motor-oil additive that was supposed to lengthen the life of an automobile engine and improve gas mileage. Her problems started when she was unable to produce enough of the product to satisfy the demand. Then, a government-agency investigation led to widely publicized charges that Jackson's product did not double gas mileage as her advertising claimed. Another government suit followed because Jackson had sold her product to an automotive retail chain at a lower price than she charged independent retailers. This suit was dropped when Jackson showed that it had cost less to manufacture and distribute the product to the larger retailer than to other retailers. However, the courts upheld the government's charge about Jackson's advertisements, and she was required to advertise that the product did not double gas mileage.

Matters worsened when three Japanese firms marketed a substitute product for half the price Jackson charged. These lower-priced substitutes were favorably received by consumers, who were experiencing rising prices in the general economy.

While Jackson had managed to weather the government investigations and the Japanese substitutes, a consumer boycott of her product ended her business. The boycott resulted because laboratory studies showed the fumes from her product caused cancer in rats.

In retrospect, Jackson feels that she never should have tried to go into business because the environment is stacked against the entrepreneur.

> **Select the best answer.**

1. Jackson had problems with which of the following environments?
   a. economic
   b. political-legal
   c. competitive
   d. social-cultural
   e. all of the above environments

2. The economic condition that existed when the Japanese substitutes entered the market is called
   a. inflation.
   b. demarketing.
   c. depression.
   d. recession.
   e. recovery.

3. The consumer boycott experienced by Jackson is part of the
   a. competitive environment.
   b. economic environment.
   c. political-legal environment.
   d. social-cultural environment.

4. The Japanese firms that produced similar products are part of the
   a. competitive environment.
   b. economic environment.
   c. political-legal environment.
   d. social-cultural environment.

5. Jackson's biggest marketing error was probably that she
   a. didn't charge enough for her product.
   b. attempted to sell a product for which there was no consumer need.
   c. didn't adapt her marketing strategies to environmental conditions.
   d. entered the marketplace too late.

Additional Activities

Experiential Exercises

1. The purpose of this exercise is to broaden your understanding of the effect of the political-legal environment on the marketing activities of businesses. The assignment consists of using secondary sources to study a case involving the marketing efforts of a company or companies.

   Select a recent legal case involving the marketing activities of a company or companies. Possible sources to use in locating current cases include *Business Periodicals Index, Antitrust and Trade Regulation Report, FTC Reporter, Trade Regulation Reporter, The Antitrust Bulletin*, and the "Legal Departments" section of the *Journal of Marketing*. Try to select a case that has received considerable coverage in the literature.

   - Using available published information about the case, determine what marketing activities were involved. Was the case related to product strategy? pricing strategy? distribution strategy? promotional strategy?

   - What laws or rules possibly were being violated by the company?

   - Who was being harmed by the actions of the company? Was it competition, consumers, or some other members of the public?

   - What remedy, such as fines, imprisonment, or corrective advertising, was required in the case?

- What impact do you think this case and the remedies required will have on the company or companies involved? Will they conduct business the same as before, alter some of their marketing practices, or go out of business altogether?

2. This exercise will help you develop an appreciation of the effect of competition on marketing activities of companies in the personal computer industry.

   Gain a general understanding of the personal computer industry by going to the reference section of your college or university library and examining *U.S. Industrial Outlook* (U.S. Department of Commerce) and Standard and Poor's *Industry Survey*. You may take a look at other published sources, including *Business Week, Wall Street Journal,* and some of the many periodicals directed toward computer buyers and users, to gain an understanding of this industry. Another good source is *c/net News* on the World Wide Web.

   - Who are the major competitors in this industry?

   - What actions have the major competitors taken in the last year or so that adversely affected the performance of other companies? Which dimensions of the marketing mix have they used? Have they changed product, promotion, distribution, or price?

   - What firms, besides other computer manufacturers, should also be considered competitors? Remember that the textbook definition of competition suggests all firms competing for the same discretionary purchasing power should be included as part of the competition. Think of the product from the consumer's point of view: What might consumers consider as a substitute for computers?

   - Based on what you have learned, do you feel the personal computer industry has an expanded view of competition or a myopic one—one that tends to ignore any firms selling different products?

Questions for Exploration

Conceptual

According to the textbook, "Business cannot meet all consumer demands and still generate the profits necessary in order to remain viable." To what extent do you agree or disagree with this statement? How much should a business do to meet the demands arising from consumerism?

Practical

The video program for the lesson portrays Mitsubishi as a marketing success. In your opinion, was Mitsubishi successful in dealing with the environmental factors that existed in the U.S. marketplace? If yes, how? If no, why? What else could Mitsubishi have done?

Answer Key

Key Concepts			
	1. i	5. f	9. j
	2. b	6. g	10. c
	3. d	7. h	11. k
	4. e	8. a	

Completion

1. competitive, political-legal, economic, technological, social-cultural (any order)
2. political-legal
3. economic
4. technological
5. social-cultural
6. similar, substituted, limited
7. competitive
8. political-legal
9. antimonopoly, competitors, consumers, deregulation
10. Federal Trade Commission
11. advertising, political action committees, lobbying (any order)
12. economic, international
13. prosperity, depression, recession, recovery
14. demarketing
15. consumerism
16. informed, heard, safe (any order)

Self-Test			
	1. c	5. c	8. d
	2. b	6. b	9. b
	3. c	7. c	10. c
	4. b		

Applying Marketing Concepts

1. e
2. a
3. d
4. a
5. c

Interdependence re-creates the world
in the image of a global village.
—Marshall McLuhan

3

International Marketing

Assignments

For the most effective study of this lesson, we suggest that you complete the assignments in the following sequence:

1. Read the study guide Overview (Lesson Notes and Video Program Notes) and the Learning Objectives for this lesson.

2. Read *Contemporary Marketing Wired,* 9th edition, Chapter 4, "Global Dimensions of Marketing," pages 114-149.

3. View "A Hunger for Pesos/A Yen for Dollars: A Case Study in International Marketing" video program.

4. Review the textbook assignment for this lesson.

5. Complete the Review Activities (Key Concepts and Completion), Self-Test, and Applying Marketing Concepts for this lesson.

6. Check your answers against the Answer Key at the end of the lesson, and review when necessary.

7. Complete any of the Additional Activities (Experiential Exercises and Questions for Exploration) that interest you or that are assigned by your instructor.

Overview

Lesson Notes

International marketing is one of the most exciting areas of marketing today. Growing numbers of U.S. firms are expanding into overseas markets in Eastern Europe, Asia, and elsewhere, and the United States has become a target market for firms around the world. Foreign trade can have a significant impact—either positive or negative—on a nation's economy. For example, each billion dollars of exports supports about 14,200 jobs. Today, more than 100,000 U.S. firms are involved in some level of international marketing.

Although marketing to foreign countries entails making the same basic decisions about product, price, promotion, and distribution that are made for the domestic market, the international marketplace has some distinctive characteristics that require special attention.

To operate successfully in foreign markets, marketing managers must pay special attention to the market's size and its buying power and to the buying behavior and the marketing practices in the host nation. Although many foreign markets are large in number, they may be quite limited in buying power. India, for instance, has a population of more than 800 million, but a per capita annual income of $480. Buyer behavior varies greatly among the nations of the world because of different customs, tastes, and living conditions. A product considered a necessity by most people in the United States might be viewed as a luxury by people living in a subsistence economy.

When evaluating a foreign market for possible entry, a firm considers first whether a demand for the goods or services exists and, if so, how the competition, if any, is currently meeting that demand. These basic considerations are followed by evaluation of the nation's economic environment, social-cultural environment, and political-legal environment, all of which can greatly influence marketing strategy.

In assessing economic factors, a firm will look at a nation's population size, per capita income, and stage of economic development.

Also important are the nation's communication systems, transportation networks, and energy facilities, which make up the **infrastructure**, and the **exchange rate**, which is the price of one nation's currency in terms of another country's currency.

Social-cultural factors that influence marketing in foreign countries include education, social values, religious attitudes, and language. Ignorance of these and other social-cultural factors can easily cause a product or promotional strategy to fail completely in a foreign market.

Political-legal factors can have a significant impact on marketing to foreign countries. Civil riots, revolutions, ethnic strife, governmental instability, and terrorism are just a few of the political events that can influence the feasibility of marketing a product in a foreign country. Legal regulations also must be considered in marketing in a foreign country. The United States has many **friendship, commerce, and navigation (FCN) treaties** with other countries. Countries may have laws governing advertising, promotion, and product features, as well as trade regulations, tax laws, and import/export requirements.

Nations may also have trade barriers, including tariffs, import quotas, embargoes, and exchange controls. A **tariff** is a tax levied against imported goods. Revenue tariffs are designed to generate income for the government of the nation importing the product. Protective tariffs are designed to raise the price of the imported product to be equal to or greater than the price of a similar domestic product. **Import quotas** limit the number of a particular product that can be brought into a country, and an **embargo** is a complete ban on the import of a particular product. **Exchange controls** regulate the privilege of international trade by controlling access to foreign currencies through a central bank or other agency. **Dumping** occurs when a marketer sells a product in a foreign country at a lower price than the producer's domestic market.

Since 1947, a 117-nation trade accord known as the **General Agreement on Tariffs and Trade (GATT)** has substantially reduced worldwide tariff levels in such areas as smaller farm subsidies and protection for patents; eventually, it will end import quotas on clothing and textiles. As a result of the GATT talks, the **World**

Trade Organization (WTO) was established. This organization oversees agreements, mediates disputes, and continues attempts to reduce international trade barriers. In 1993, the **North American Free Trade Agreement (NAFTA)** was approved, lifting trade restrictions among the United States, Canada, and Mexico, the world's largest free-trade zone.

Once a firm has decided that it should enter a foreign market, it has several methods of doing so: exporting, contractual agreements, and international direct investment. **Exporting** has the lowest level of risk and the least degree of control; international direct investment carries the highest risk and greatest control. In exporting, a firm simply sells its domestically produced goods and services in a foreign country.

One method of entering foreign markets that has several advantages is via a **contractual agreement** providing flexible alternatives to exporting. Types of contractual agreements include franchising, foreign licensing, subcontracting, and sponsorships. Foreign licensing, in which a firm allows a foreign country to produce and distribute its goods or use its trademark, patents, or processes, provides expertise in local marketing practices, access to local distribution channels, protection from legal barriers, and does not require capital outlay. Because of these advantages, foreign licensing is attractive to many firms.

In international marketing, a company may form a **joint venture**, in which the firm shares the risks, costs, and management of the foreign operation with one or more partners, who are usually citizens of the foreign country.

Because of the rapid growth in international business, some corporations have become **multinational corporations**, with significant operations and marketing activities outside their home country. Examples of U.S. multinational corporations are Exxon, IBM, General Motors, and Citicorp. Other multinational corporations include Mitsubishi, Timex, Seiko, and Siemens.

Regardless of the size of the firm or the degree of involvement in international trade, a firm that sells to foreign markets may choose between two alternative approaches in developing a marketing mix to reach the target market.

If a firm adopts a **global marketing strategy**, it uses the same marketing mix, with minimal variations, in all of its foreign markets. Most firms, however, adopt a **multidomestic marketing strategy**, in which they tailor their marketing mixes to match the specific target markets in each nation.

In developing product and promotional strategies, a firm can choose from several options. One strategy is **straight extension**, in which the home market product is introduced to a foreign market with the same promotional strategy. This strategy is followed by firms employing a global market approach. Other strategies are **product adaptation**, in which the product is modified, but the same promotional strategy is used; **promotional adaptation**, in which the product is the same, but the promotional strategy is modified; and **dual adaptation**, in which both the product and promotional strategy are modified. In **product invention**, a firm develops a completely new product and promotional strategy to take advantage of a special opportunity in a foreign market.

As in a firm's home market, distribution strategy and pricing strategy are also critical to the successful marketing of a product. In developing the correct distribution strategy, a firm must first understand the distribution system as it exists in the foreign country. In developing a pricing strategy, a firm must first understand the foreign country's competitive, economic, political, and legal constraints on pricing. Sometimes the only way a marketer can access foreign markets is through **countertrade**, in which products are bartered rather than sold for cash.

Video Program Notes

The video program for this lesson explores the international marketing activities of two different fast-food companies: Carl's Jr. and MOS Foods West. The program examines the particular challenges faced by each company and compares the two perspectives and philosophies. Carl's Jr., a U.S. company, views foreign countries as logical markets for expansion; MOS Foods West, a Japanese company, thinks the U.S. market has enormous potential for growth.

Carl's Jr. is a chain of fast-food restaurants that started in California in 1941. It expanded vigorously throughout the West Coast and Southwest and is now the sixth largest fast-food chain in the United States. Instead of expanding further throughout the United States, which company management felt was saturated with similar fast-food restaurants, Carl's Jr. decided to export its hamburger-based menu and restaurant concept around the Pacific Rim and into Canada and Mexico. Featured in the program is the first Carl's Jr. restaurant in Monterrey, Mexico, a large industrial city about 100 miles from the U.S. border. Although the restaurant is geographically not too distant from the United States, Carl's Jr. found extensive differences in consumer food preferences and eating patterns. The company's chief of international development explains how the Monterrey restaurant was adapted to reflect those cultural differences.

The story of MOS Foods West and its Mikoshi Japanese Noodle Houses in California provides an interesting contrast to the Carl's Jr. operation in Mexico. Sakurada, owner of MOS Foods West, had successfully adapted a U.S. food product, the hamburger, to the Japanese market and decided to reverse the process in introducing a typically Japanese food product into the U.S. market. The principal food offered in Mikoshi Japanese Noodle Houses is ramen, a variety of noodle that is an important part of the Japanese diet. Sakurada believed ramen and other Japanese noodles would be successful as a fast food with U.S. consumers because of the wide assortment of ramen-type products in U.S. supermarkets. The company tailored traditional Japanese recipes to appeal to U.S. consumers. In promoting the restaurants, the company stresses the healthful nature of the foods, the quality of ingredients, and the service provided in the restaurants. Representatives of the public-relations firm hired by MOS Foods describe the promotional and educational campaigns they have developed for Mikoshi Japanese Noodle Houses.

As you watch the video program, consider the following questions:

1. Why did Carl's Jr. and MOS Foods decide to expand beyond their home countries?

2. What social-cultural and political-legal factors have influenced the international marketing activities of Carl's Jr. and MOS Foods?

3. What is the level of involvement of Carl's Jr. with the restaurant in Mexico? What is the level of involvement of MOS Foods with Mikoshi Japanese Noodle Houses?

4. What problems has the infrastructure in Mexico created for Carl's Jr.?

5. Why does Carl's Jr. think it important to train foreign operators of Carl's Jr. restaurants in California?

6. Is Carl's Jr. exporting anything more than a restaurant concept and type of food?

7. Why does Carl's Jr. not invest directly in foreign operations?

8. Why does the management of Carl's Jr. think the foreign operators of its restaurants are critical to the success of the company's international operations?

9. How is a Mikoshi Japanese Noodle House different from a standard U.S. fast food restaurant?

10. Why did MOS Foods select California as the location for the first Mikoshi Japanese Noodle Houses?

11. What is the target market for the Mikoshi Japanese Noodle Houses?

12. Why does MOS Foods stress public relations instead of advertising to promote Mikoshi Japanese Noodle Houses?

13. What examples are shown in the program of how each company meets consumers' needs?

14. What is the difference between how each company views the U.S. market? What are the reasons for this difference?

15. What are each company's plans for expansion in the international market? What particular challenges might each company face with continued expansion?

16. What is each company's perspective on the international marketplace? In what way are the two perspectives different?

17. What type of product and promotional strategies has each company adopted?

Learning Objectives

After completing your study of this lesson, you should be able to:

1. Define the following terms as they relate to international marketing:

countertrade	infrastructure
dual adaptation	joint venture
dumping	multinational
embargo	corporation
exchange control	multidomestic
exchange rate	marketing strategy
exporting	North American Free
foreign licensing	Trade Agreement
franchising	(NAFTA)
friendship, commerce, and	product adaptation
navigation (FCN) treaty	product invention
General Agreement on	promotion adaptation
Tariffs and Trade (GATT)	straight extension
global marketing strategy	tariff
importing	World Trade
import quota	Organization (WTO)

2. Explain the influence of social-cultural, economic, and political-legal factors on a firm's international marketing activities.

3. Explain the differences between a global marketing strategy and a multidomestic marketing strategy.

4. Identify the various strategies for entering international markets.

5. Describe the marketing mix strategies used in international marketing.

6. Explain why the United States is attractive to foreign marketers.

Review Activities

Key Concepts

> Identify each of the following fundamental marketing concepts by writing the letter of the appropriate term in the blank next to the corresponding description.
>
> a. exporting
> b. importing
> c. exchange control
> d. import quota
> e. foreign licensing
> f. global marketing strategy
> g. General Agreement on Tariffs and Trade (GATT)
> h. friendship, commerce, and navigation (FCN) treaty
> i. joint venture
> j. multinational corporation
> k. tariff
> l. embargo
> m. dumping
> n. countertrade
> o. product invention
> p. infrastructure
> q. dual adaptation
> r. exchange rate
> s. promotion adaptation
> t. straight extension
> u. product adaptation
> v. multidomestic marketing strategy
> w. North American Free Trade Agreement (NAFTA)

_____ 1. tax levied against imported goods

_____ 2. trade restriction that limits the number of units of certain goods that can enter a country for resale

_____ 3. regulating trade among importing organizations by controlling access to foreign currencies

_____ 4. purchasing of foreign goods and services

_____ 5. complete ban on the import of specific products

_____ 6. practice of selling a product at a price in a foreign market that is lower than the price in the domestic market

_____ 7. use of a more-or-less standardized marketing strategy in foreign markets

_____ 8. form of exporting in which goods and services are bartered rather than sold for cash

_____ 9. when goods and services are produced domestically and sold outside the producer's country

_____ 10. agreement in which a firm shares the risks, costs, and management of a foreign operation with one or more partners who are usually citizens of the host country

_____ 11. agreement that deals with many aspects of trading relations among nations

_____ 12. firm with significant operations outside its home country

_____ 13. agreement in which a firm gives a foreign company the right to produce or distribute the firm's products in a foreign market

_____ 14. international trade agreement that has helped to reduce world tariffs

_____ 15. price of one nation's currency in terms of another country's currency

_____ 16. modification of a product for a foreign market

_____ 17. development of a new product and promotional strategy to take advantage of foreign opportunities

_____ 18. development of a different promotional strategy for an unmodified product for a foreign market

_____ 19. a nation's communication systems, transportation networks, and energy facilities

_____ 20. introduction of an unmodified product to a foreign market with the same promotional strategy used in the home market

_____ 21. modification of both product and promotional strategies for the foreign market

_____ 22. tailoring of a firm's marketing mix to match specific target markets in different nations

_____ 23. agreement intended to remove trade restrictions among Canada, Mexico, and the United States

Completion

> **Fill each blank in the following paragraphs with the most appropriate term from the list of completion answers below. A term may be used once, more than once, or not at all.**
>
> | | | |
> |---|---|---|
> | adaptation | General Agreement on | North American |
> | buyer | Tariff and Trade | Free Trade |
> | contractual | (GATT) | Agreement |
> | agreements | global | (NAFTA) |
> | distribution | importing | per capita |
> | dual | import quota | political-legal |
> | dumping | international | pricing |
> | economic | international direct | size |
> | embargo | investment | social-cultural |
> | exchange control | invention | stage |
> | exporting | joint venture | straight |
> | friendship, | marketing | extension |
> | commerce, and | marketing mix | tariff |
> | navigation (FCN) | multidomestic | trade |
> | treaties | nation | |

1. The two basic divisions of foreign trade are the selling of domestically produced goods and services in foreign countries, known as _____ , and the purchasing of foreign products and raw materials, known as _____.

2. Foreign markets differ substantially from the domestic U.S. market. Principal differences that must be examined by any firm considering entering foreign markets are in market _____ , _____ behavior, and _____ practices.

3. Marketing practices differ by country. A firm must understand these differences and take care to adapt the _____ to local markets.

4. The three principal factors that influence the environment for international marketing are _____ , _____ , and _____ .

5. Among the aspects a firm should consider in assessing the economic environment in a foreign country are the nation's _____ , _____ income, and _____ of economic development.

6. An important aspect of the political-legal environment for marketing in a foreign country is _____ barriers.

7. Trade barriers are an important consideration in international marketing. A tax on imported products is called a _____ and is used to protect local infant industries, to prevent dumping, and to raise funds for the government.

8. When a country wishes to allow imports of only a certain amount of goods from another country, it will set an _____ .

9. A trade barrier in which a country bans the importation of specific goods is called an _____ .

10. Sometimes a central bank or governmental agency regulates trade by controlling the access of foreign firms to foreign currency; this practice is known as _____ .

11. When a firm sells a product at a lower price in a foreign market than it sells for in the domestic market, the firm is engaging in _____ .

12. U.S. firms doing business abroad must be concerned with U.S. law, _____ law, and the legal requirements of the host _____ .

13. Certain trade agreements and various treaties have promoted international marketing. A trade accord that has brought about a general reduction in tariffs is the _____ . Trade agreements that relate to a wide range of international marketing practices are _____ .
An agreement that eventually will remove trade restrictions among Canada, Mexico, and the United States is the _____ .

14. Once a firm decides to enter a foreign market, it may choose from among three basic strategies for doing so: _____ , _____ , and _____ .

15. Firms actively seeking international markets may permit a foreign company to produce and distribute its merchandise by signing _____ agreements.

16. The risks, costs, and management of foreign production and marketing may be shared with a citizen of the host nation by forming a _____ .

17. When a firm uses essentially the same marketing strategy in both domestic and foreign markets, it is using a _____ marketing strategy. When a firm tailors its marketing strategy to specific segments of foreign markets, it is using a _____ marketing strategy.

18. International marketers can use any of several different product and promotional strategies in foreign markets. A typical strategy used by firms employing a global marketing strategy is the one-product, one-message _____ strategy.

19. When a firm modifies the product for a foreign market but uses the same promotional strategy, the firm is practicing product _____ .

20. When a firm does not change the product but develops a new promotional strategy, the firm is practicing promotional _____ .

21. When a firm changes both the product and the promotional strategy in a foreign country, the firm is practicing _____ adaptation.

22. When a firm takes advantage of unique opportunities in a foreign market by creating a new good or service and new promotional strategy, the firm is practicing product _____ .

23. In some foreign markets, transportation systems and warehousing facilities may be inadequate. Because of such problems, a firm entering a foreign market must pay particular attention to its _____ strategy.

24. To be successful in a foreign market, a firm must understand the host country's competitive, economic, political, and legal constraints on _____.

Self-Test

> **Select the best answer.**

1. An agreement in which a domestic firm permits a foreign company to produce or distribute the firm's goods in the foreign country is called
   a. the General Agreement on Tariffs and Trade (GATT).
   b. a friendship, commerce, and navigation (FCN) treaty.
   c. exchange control.
   d. foreign licensing.

2. An accord that has reduced tariffs is
   a. the General Agreement on Tariffs and Trade (GATT).
   b. the friendship, commerce, and navigation (FCN) treaty.
   c. exchange control.
   d. the Foreign Corrupt Practices Act.

3. Franchising is a type of
   a. exporting.
   b. quota.
   c. countertrade.
   d. contractual agreement.

4. A tax designed to keep out imported goods that would compete with domestic goods is a
   a. revenue tariff.
   b. revenue embargo.
   c. protective tariff.
   d. protective embargo.

5. If Japan sold motorcycles in the U.S. market more cheaply than it sold them in Japan, Japan would be engaged in
    a. a quota system.
    b. an embargo.
    c. dumping.
    d. fair trade.

6. When a Japanese car manufacturer changed its U.S. name from Datsun to Nissan so the firm would be known by the same name worldwide, Nissan was, to some degree, using
    a. exchange control.
    b. a global marketing strategy.
    c. foreign licensing.
    d. joint-venture marketing.

7. When a domestic firm purchases from a foreign firm and brings the product into the domestic firm's country, the domestic firm is
    a. dumping.
    b. importing.
    c. exporting.
    d. reevaluating.

8. To control imports of a certain product, a country may use
    a. quotas and dumping.
    b. tariffs and countertrade.
    c. quotas and tariffs.
    d. tariffs and dumping.

9. When goods produced domestically are sold outside the seller's own country, the firm is engaged in
    a. exporting.
    b. importing.
    c. dumping.
    d. exchange control.

10. When a nation prohibits a product from being imported, it is using
    a. a tariff.
    b. a boycott.
    c. a quota.
    d. an embargo.

Applying Marketing Concepts

Midway is a food-processing company located in the Midwest. The company's best-seller is a frozen, microwaveable sandwich made of sliced roast beef, cheese, and assorted vegetables and spices, marketed under the brand name of Beefwich.

Last year, Midway received an inquiry from an Australian graduate student, Arthur Bowles, who had tasted the Beefwich and believed that it would be a success in his homeland, where the citizens often eat a quick lunch consisting of the famous Australian meat pie. Bowles asked Midway for the rights to sole distribution of Beefwiches in Australia.

The company, realizing that a market of almost 18 million people is almost as big as the one they now serve, countered by offering to bring Arthur into the firm. After a brief training period, he would be sent to Australia to introduce the product to the market.

Further investigation by Midway into the Australian microwave food market proved interesting. While many Australians do own microwave ovens, early efforts by other U.S. food processors specializing in microwaveable meals met with resistance. The resistance came primarily because of the meager portions of meat and the poor quality of bread used in the U.S. sandwiches. As the executive of one firm said, "Australians are very fussy about bread; they will put almost anything in a sandwich—beans, spaghetti, and corn are not unheard of down under—but if the bread isn't top quality, they will not repurchase." Another executive said, "They have a sandwich called 'The Lot.' It has everything—pineapple, egg, meat, you name it. We just could not compete with that so we changed our product."

Armed with such information, Midway executives rethought their position. After all, why take a financial risk? Since Bowles seemed to have financial backing, they decided to let him have the rights to the Beefwich for seven years if he paid them a 15 percent royalty on sales.

1. Midway's level of involvement under Bowles' original proposal would be
    a. accidental exporting.
    b. foreign licensing.
    c. subcontracting.
    d. a direct investment.

2. Midway's level of involvement under the counterproposal made to Bowles would be
    a. accidental exporting.
    b. foreign licensing.
    c. subcontracting.
    d. a direct investment.

3. The major barrier to doing business in Australia mentioned by the executives interviewed was
    a. economic.
    b. cultural.
    c. trade restrictions.
    d. political.

4. The component of the marketing mix that presents the biggest challenge for firms entering the Australian fast-food market is
    a. distribution.
    b. price.
    c. product.
    d. promotion.

Additional Activities

Experiential Exercises

1. The purpose of this exercise is to help you understand the importance of imported products in the U.S. market. Visit a local department or discount store or supermarket.

   - Select twenty items at random and determine what manufacturing company produced each item. List the item, a description of the item, name of manufacturer, and country of manufacture.

   - What countries in the product lines you surveyed seemed to have best adapted their marketing mix to the U.S. market?

   - How many of the products are manufactured by multinational corporations based in the United States? (You may need to use library resources such as Standard and Poor's *Industry Surveys* to answer this question.)

2. This second exercise will help you to understand some of the problems encountered when firms enter the international marketplace.

   - Arrange a meeting with a representative of a firm that is engaged in marketing domestically and internationally. Discuss the differences between marketing in the United States and in at least one foreign country. Use the materials in the textbook to prepare a set of questions before you meet with the executive. Be sure to cover the strategic areas of product, price, distribution, and promotion, as well as the environmental variables (competition and economic, political-legal, and social-cultural factors). After your meeting, write a brief report on how the company you visited plans and implements its marketing strategy in foreign countries and how it has solved the problems it has encountered.

Questions for Exploration

Conceptual

There is rich anecdotal literature on the mistakes and embarrassments that occur when companies do business in foreign countries. These mistakes occur in spite of the ready existence of information, agencies, and people that could prevent such problems. Why, then, do companies have such problems moving into foreign markets? What could they do to avoid them?

Practical

MOS Foods promotional strategy emphasizes public relations and consumer education over traditional advertising. Do you think this promotional strategy is correct? If not, what promotional strategy would you suggest?

Answer Key

Key Concepts				
	1. k	7. f	13. e	19. p
	2. d	8. n	14. g	20. t
	3. c	9. a	15. r	21. q
	4. b	10. i	16. u	22. v
	5. l	11. h	17. o	23. w
	6. m	12. j	18. s	

Completion

1. exporting, importing
2. size, buyer, marketing
3. marketing mix
4. economic, social-cultural, political-legal (any order)
5. size, per capita, stage
6. trade
7. tariff
8. import quota
9. embargo
10. exchange control
11. dumping
12. international, nation
13. General Agreement on Tariffs and Trade (GATT); friendship, commerce, and navigation (FCN) treaties; North American Free Trade Agreement (NAFTA)
14. exporting, contractual agreements, international direct investment (any order)
15. foreign licensing
16. joint venture
17. global, multidomestic
18. straight extension
19. adaptation
20. adaptation
21. dual
22. invention
23. distribution
24. pricing

Self-Test			
	1. d	5. c	8. c
	2. a	6. b	9. a
	3. d	7. b	10. d
	4. c		

Applying Marketing Concepts	
	1. b
	2. c
	3. b
	4. c

Make three correct guesses consecutively and you will establish a reputation as an expert.

—Lawrence Peters

4

Planning and Forecasting

Assignments

For the most effective study of this lesson, we suggest that you complete the assignments in the following sequence:

1. Read the study guide Overview (Lesson Notes and Video Program Notes) and the Learning Objectives for this lesson.

2. Read *Contemporary Marketing Wired,* 9th edition, Chapter 5, "Marketing Planning and Forecasting," pages 160-187.

3. View "Great Expectations: A Case Study in Marketing Planning and Forecasting" video program.

4. Review the textbook assignment for this lesson.

5. Complete the Review Activities (Key Concepts and Completion), Self-Test, and Applying Marketing Concepts for this lesson.

6. Check your answers against the Answer Key at the end of the lesson, and review when necessary.

7. Complete any of the Additional Activities (Experiential Exercise and Questions for Exploration) that interest you or that are assigned by your instructor.

Overview

Planning can be described as anticipating future events and conditions and then arranging courses of action for achieving desired organizational objectives. **Marketing planning** is planning that relates to arranging courses of action for achieving marketing objectives. Marketing planning is one of the most important functions of a company.

Marketing planning can be classified into strategic planning and tactical planning. **Strategic planning** refers to adopting general courses of action, allocating resources, then initiating actions necessary to implement the plan. **Tactical planning** is the implementation of specific courses of action to achieve strategic plan objectives. Generally, upper management is concerned with strategic planning, and middle and supervisory management are concerned with tactical planning.

The firm's **marketing strategy** is the overall company program and marketing mix for choosing and satisfying a particular target market. The marketing strategy is designed to meet organizational objectives, which are based on the organization's **mission,** or statement of purpose.

An important step in the development of any marketing plan is evaluation of the company's resources and capabilities within the context of external factors. **SWOT** (strengths, weaknesses, opportunities, and threats) **analysis** is an especially valuable method for providing management with an assessment of the organization's internal and external environments. At certain times, the specific capabilities of a company may be exceptionally well suited to special needs of the market. Such an occurrence is referred to as a **strategic window**.

One planning tool used by large companies that produce and market many products to various markets is the **strategic business unit (SBU).** An SBU is a related group of businesses within a diversified firm, with its own managers, resources, objectives, and competitors. An SBU provides top management of the parent firm with a method of evaluating the success of various businesses.

Another planning tool is the **market share/market growth matrix.** The matrix provides a framework for a business to categorize the market share a product holds so management can move the product into long-term profitability or drop it from the product line. Business units can be cash cows, stars, dogs, or question marks.

A technique that rates SBUs according to the attractiveness of their markets and their organizational strengths is the **market attractiveness/business strength matrix.** Criteria for market attractiveness include market share, growth, size, future profitability, amount of government regulation, competition, the environment, as well as the organization's strengths and areas of competence.

Computers and electronic spreadsheets play an important role in marketing planning. By entering and manipulating marketing data, such as sales figures, projections, and trends, marketers can do a **spreadsheet analysis** to estimate the impact of various marketing conditions on marketing planning decisions.

Sales forecasting involves the numbers, dollars-and-cents side of marketing planning and is usually based on both statistical (quantitative) and subjective (qualitative) data. Short-run sales forecasts cover periods less than one year; intermediate forecasts cover one to five years; and long-run forecasts extend beyond five years.

Qualitative sales forecasting techniques include the **jury of executive opinion,** the **Delphi technique, sales force composites,** and **surveys of buyer intentions.** These methods respectively consider the expectations of top management, the opinions of outside experts, the estimates of the salesforce, and the reactions of consumers.

Quantitative sales forecasting techniques include **market test, trend analysis,** and **exponential smoothing.** Each of these methods makes use of past data.

Sales forecasting methods vary by industry and company. However, most begin by looking at the big picture (the general economy), then at the industry, and finally the firm, in what is called top-down forecasting. The **environmental forecast** centers on external events and influences that affect a firm's markets, such as consumer spending and saving patterns, balance-of-trade surpluses and deficits, government expenditures, and business investments. Bottom-up, or grass-roots, forecasting involves analyzing sales projections made by the frontline sales force. Forecasting sales for a new product is especially difficult, since no firm data (statistical or subjective) exist for the product.

Video Program Notes

The video program for this lesson explores the planning and forecasting challenges facing Looking Good and Pizza Hop, both student ventures from the University of Southern California's Entrepreneurial Program, and Laura Scudder's, a snack-food company. For each business, the video program demonstrates the purpose of planning and forecasting: to formulate a marketing mix that will satisfy selected consumer segments. Various strategies for marketing planning are examined, and the importance of an accurate sales forecast is stressed. For new businesses, planning and forecasting are an essential beginning; in existing businesses, they are an ongoing endeavor.

As you watch the video program, consider the following questions:

1. What sales forecasting methods were used by Looking Good, Pizza Hop, and Laura Scudder's?

2. What type of marketing strategy was being pursued by each of the businesses shown in the program?

3. What role does the business plan play in the development of a marketing strategy?

4. What had been the results of Laura Scudder's lack of a strategic growth plan?

5. What did Looking Good do to help focus on a long-range goal rather than quick short-term profits?

6. Why might Looking Good's calendar competition be different every year?

7. What factors thwarted Pizza Hop's attempts at accurate sales forecasting?

8. Why do some of the marketers in the program disagree on whether or not sales forecasting is a "shot in the dark"? Is it?

9. Why can sales forecasting be termed a self-fulfilling prophecy?

10. How does Looking Good survey buyer intentions in order to help ensure successful sales?

Learning Objectives

After completing your study of this lesson, you should be able to:

1. Define the following terms as they relate to marketing planning and forecasting:

Delphi technique	planning
environmental forecast	sales force composite
exponential smoothing	sales forecast
jury of executive opinion	spreadsheet analysis
market attractiveness/ business strength matrix	strategic business unit (SBU)
marketing planning	strategic planning
marketing strategy	strategic window
market share/market growth matrix	survey of buyer intentions
market test	SWOT analysis
mission	tactical planning
	trend analysis

2. Distinguish between tactical planning and strategic planning.

3. Outline the steps in the marketing planning process and explain how marketing plans differ at various organizational levels.

4. Describe how the strategic business unit concept, the market share/market growth matrix, spreadsheet analysis, and the market attractiveness/business strength matrix can be used in marketing planning.

5. Describe the major types of forecasting methods.

6. Explain the steps in the forecasting process.

7. Describe the concept of SWOT analysis and its four major elements: leverage, problems, constraints, and vulnerabilities.

Review Activities

Key Concepts

> **Identify each of the following planning and forecasting concepts by writing the letter of the appropriate term in the blank next to the corresponding description.**
>
> a. marketing strategy
> b. marketing planning
> c. strategic planning
> d. tactical planning
> e. strategic business unit (SBU)
> f. strategic window
> g. market share/market growth matrix
> h. planning
>
> i. Delphi technique
> j. market test
> k. environmental forecast
> l. sales forecast
> m. market attractiveness/ business strength matrix
> n. mission
> o. SWOT analysis

_____ 1. determining an organization's primary objectives, allocating resources, and taking courses of action necessary to achieve those objectives

_____ 2. anticipating the future and determining courses of action necessary to achieve organizational objectives

_____ 3. anticipating future events and determining activities necessary to achieve marketing objectives

_____ 4. broad-based economic forecast focusing on the impact of external factors on markets

_____ 5. overall company program for identifying a particular consumer market and satisfying it with a particular marketing mix

_____ 6. a group of related businesses in the same multiproduct firm with specific managers, resources, objectives, and competitors

_____ 7. sales forecasting method that seeks the opinions of experts outside the firm

_____ 8. estimate of a company's future sales for a specified period

_____ 9. portfolio analysis technique that rates SBUs according to the potential of the market and the organization's resources

_____ 10. limited time period during which the "fit" between the needs of the market and the abilities of a firm is optimal

_____ 11. specific activities necessary to achieve a firm's objectives

_____ 12. four-quadrant classification scheme—cash cows, stars, dogs, and question marks—for a firm's various businesses, based on market share and potential for market growth

_____ 13. forecasting method involving the introduction of a new product or marketing variable to a small market in order to assess consumer reactions

_____ 14. evaluation of a firm's strengths, weaknesses, opportunities, and threats

_____ 15. the essential purpose that differentiates a company from others

Completion

Fill each blank in the following paragraphs with the most appropriate term from the list of completion answers below. A term may be used once, more than once, or not at all.

adapt	market share	resources
composite	middle	risks
Delphi	mission	sales forecast
distribution	objectives	strategic
exponential	operating	strategic
feedback	opinion	business units
high	opportunities	strategic window
intentions	planning	strategy
low	plans	SWOT
market	pricing	tactical
marketing	product	top
marketing strategy	promotion	trend

1. Marketing success cannot be assumed, regardless of the quality of the products. To succeed, a firm must anticipate the future and determine the courses of action necessary for achieving organizational objectives. This conscious effort is called _____ . The marketing planning process focuses on decisions about product lines, pricing, promotion, and distribution in order to achieve _____ objectives.

2. Financial-services companies are examples of companies that use planning. The Prudential Insurance Company, for example, decided to expand its position from a marketer of life insurance for middle- and lower-income families to that of a marketer of a broad range of financial services for upper-income families as well. Its long-range plan included acquisition of Bache, a stock brokerage firm. This long-range plan was the result of _____ planning. The actual implementation of the strategic plan through the acquisition of other companies or addition of new products, such as insurance policies with higher rates of returns, involves _____ planning.

3. While strategic decisions such as those made by Prudential generally involve many members of the organization, the major responsibility for this critical activity is usually assigned to _____ management.

4. The marketing planning process encompasses a number of basic steps. The first step, defining the organization's _____ , is followed by determining organizational _____ . The next two steps are concurrent: assessing organizational _____ and evaluating environmental _____ and _____ . The following step is formulating a marketing _____ , and the last step is implementing through _____ plans. Throughout the marketing planning process, the organization uses _____ to monitor and _____ strategies.

5. When a company is comparing its strengths and weaknesses to external opportunities and threats, an especially useful planning tool is _____ analysis.

6. A limited period during which the key requirements of the market and the particular competencies of a firm best fit together is known as a _____ .

7. A company's overall program for selecting a particular target market and then satisfying consumers in that market through careful use of the elements of the marketing mix is its _____ .

8. Subsets of the overall marketing strategy are the four components of the marketing mix: _____ , _____ , _____ , and _____ .

9. A major challenge facing a large firm with many products and many divisions is maintaining a focus on the markets for its various products. The addition of new products may result in the creation of new divisions in the organization. It may be in the best interest of the firm to organize its divisions into SBUs, which stands for _____ .

10. One critical measure of performance is the percentage of a market controlled by a firm; this percentage is commonly referred to as the _____ .

11. "Cash cows" have _____ market share and _____ market growth potential.

12. "Stars" have _____ market share and _____ market growth potential.

13. "Dogs" have _____ market share and _____ market growth potential.

14. "Question marks" have _____ market share and _____ market growth potential.

15. Assessment of future market share depends on expected company sales relative to industry sales for the period. This estimate of company sales for a specified future period is known as a _____ .

16. Some typical qualitative sales forecasting techniques include the jury of executive _____ , the _____ technique, sales force _____ , and survey of buyer _____ .

17. Some typical quantitative sales forecasting techniques include _____ analysis, _____ test, and _____ smoothing.

Self-Test

| Select the best answer. |

1. Which of the following techniques are used in *quantitative* sales forecasting?
   a. sales force composite, trend analysis, exponential smoothing
   b. market test, trend analysis, exponential smoothing
   c. market test, Delphi technique, survey of buyer intentions
   d. jury of executive opinion, market test, sales force composite

2. Strategic planning is best described as
   a. long-range pricing decisions.
   b. determining primary objectives of an organization and adopting courses of action.
   c. implementation of tactical plans.
   d. day-to-day plans set by middle management and supervisory personnel.

3. Businesses are most likely to drop products that are
   a. cash cows.
   b. dogs.
   c. stars.
   d. question marks.

4. The *qualitative* sales forecasting technique that solicits the opinion of experts outside the firm is the
   a. jury of executive opinion.
   b. sales force composite.
   c. survey of buyer intentions.
   d. Delphi technique.

5. The major purpose of relationship marketing is to
   a. link the firm's marketing plans to environmental factors.
   b. develop cooperative associations with its suppliers.
   c. establish long-term, cost-effective links with individual customers.
   d. build up loyalty among its employees.

6. The first step in top-down forecasting is the
   a. study of environmental factors that influence specific industries.
   b. examination of general economic conditions.
   c. review of the firm's past and present market share.
   d. analysis of estimates provided by the firm's sales force.

7. A strategic window is a limited period during which a firm
   a. completely controls a market.
   b. can optimally meet a market's need.
   c. conducts extensive marketing planning.
   d. can produce a product most efficiently.

8. Tactical planning in marketing mostly involves decisions made by
   a. upper management.
   b. consumers.
   c. middle management and supervisory personnel.
   d. labor employees.

9. The percentage of a market controlled by a firm or its product is called
   a. strategic window.
   b. SBU.
   c. market concentration.
   d. market share.

10. Marketing planning can best be described as
    a. anticipating the future and determining the courses of action to achieve marketing objectives.
    b. sales forecasting.
    c. making a thorough, objective evaluation of an organization's marketing philosophy, goals, policies, tactics, practices, and results.
    d. analysis of quantitative and qualitative data to increase sales.

Applying Marketing Concepts

For over 20 years, We Cook for You has been producing frozen foods. The company's original line, Filling Foods, offers standard TV-dinner-type meals of such foods as fried chicken and French fries and beef stew and mashed potatoes. The Filling Foods line has performed quite well since it was first introduced, capturing and holding on to a large market share. The line was continuing to grow modestly and provided a substantial part of the company's cash flow.

Four years ago, the company introduced Meals for Gourmets, a specialty line of classic-cuisine entrees, such as coq au vin and boeuf bourguignon. Initially, the line did quite well, but after about two years, sales stagnated and then started to decline. We Cook for You's marketing manager analyzed the situation and found that the overall market for gourmet frozen entrees and the company's share of that market were declining.

Two years later, the company introduced Meals for Kids, a line of preservative- and additive-free wholesome meals, including spaghetti and meatballs and macaroni and cheese, that children could cook in the microwave in less than 10 minutes. Meals for Kids quickly captured a large market share, and sales had continued to increase, in spite of the entry of competing lines into the market. Meals for Kids was also generating substantial income for the company, although the marketing department was spending a considerable amount of money to ensure continued growth of the line.

We Cook for You's latest entry into the market is Good for You, a line of low-fat, high-fiber, all-natural meals, built around such entrees as skinless chicken breasts, fish, and lean cuts of beef, accompanied by whole-wheat pasta, brown rice, broccoli, and carrots. The Good for You line has been in national distribution for one year. The company has received a great deal of favorable response from consumers about the product, but the line has not yet captured a significant share of what some marketing experts say is a rapidly growing market.

Select the best answer.

1. According to market share/market growth analysis, the Meals for Kids line is a
   a. cash cow.
   b. star.
   c. dog.
   d. question mark.

2. Using a market share/market growth matrix as a guide, the Filling Foods line appears to be a
   a. dog.
   b. star.
   c. cash cow.
   d. question mark.

3. We Cook for You's new line of low-fat, high-fiber meals
   a. probably won't go anywhere and should be discontinued as soon as possible.
   b. should be classified as a question mark and be carefully nurtured and marketed.
   c. is already a star and should be marketed as such.
   d. will become a cash cow before it becomes a star.

4. If you had to drop one of the Meals for You product lines, you would drop
   a. Good for You because the market is uncertain and the risk too great.
   b. Filling Foods because that market is about to decline, and the company should direct its resources to other lines.
   c. Meals for Kids because sales have plateaued and will soon decline.
   d. Meals for Gourmets because of the declining share of a declining market.

Additional Activities

Experiential Exercise

The purpose of this exercise is to help you to improve your understanding of marketing planning and the role of the marketing audit in the planning process. You are asked to assess the marketing efforts of a business of your choice. (You may want to review the section on "The Marketing Audit" in textbook Chapter 2, page 64, and Figure 2.10, "A Sample Marketing Audit Outline," pages 63-64.)

Choose a business, such as a manufacturer or retailer, to study. The firm may be chosen on the basis of proximity to your school or home and willingness of the firm's management to tell you about its marketing planning process. Alternative sources of firms to study are published accounts of the strategies used by national or international firms. Possible sources of information include *Business Week, Forbes, Fortune,* and the *Wall Street Journal.*

Gather information about your chosen company and its marketing effectiveness. Use your information to answer the questions that follow, and then prepare a report on your findings.

- On a scale of 1 (lowest rating) to 5 (highest rating), how would you rate the effectiveness of the marketing planning of this company?

- What, if anything, appears to be lacking in the marketing planning of this firm?

- On a scale of 1 to 5, how would you rate the company on each of the following aspects of marketing effectiveness?

    integrated marketing organization
    adequate marketing information
    strategic orientation
    operational efficiency

- Briefly describe the marketing planning process in this organization.

    Who is responsible for the planning?

    How often is the planning done in the organization?

    How is the effectiveness of marketing plans evaluated? How often?

Questions for Exploration

Conceptual

Does marketing planning increase or diminish creativity? Explain and cite examples.

Practical

What strengths and weaknesses did you see in the way that Robert Swartz, owner of Pizza Hop, made use of forecasting, strategy, and planning for his pizza business?

Answer Key

Key Concepts	1. c	5. a	9. m	13. j
	2. h	6. e	10. f	14. o
	3. b	7. i	11. d	15. n
	4. k	8. l	12. g	

Completion		
	1. planning, marketing	10. market share
	2. strategic, tactical	11. high, low
	3. top	12. high, high
	4. mission, objectives; resources, risks, opportunities; strategy, marketing; feedback, adapt	13. low, low
		14. low, high
	5. SWOT	15. sales forecast
	6. strategic window	16. opinion, Delphi, composite, intentions
	7. marketing strategy	17. trend, market, exponential
	8. product, pricing, distribution, promotion (any order)	
	9. strategic business units	

Self-Test	1. b	5. c	8. c
	2. b	6. b	9. d
	3. b	7. b	10. a
	4. d		

Applying Marketing Concepts	1. b	3. b
	2. c	4. d

*Get the facts, or the
facts will get you.*
—Thomas Fuller

5

Marketing Research

Assignments

For the most effective study of this lesson, we suggest that you complete the assignments in the following sequence:

1. Read the study guide Overview (Lesson Notes and Video Program Notes) and the Learning Objectives for this lesson.

2. Read *Contemporary Marketing Wired,* 9th edition, Chapter 6, "Marketing Research and Decision Support Systems," pages 196-222.

3. View "Prophesy: A Case Study in Market Research" video program.

4. Review the textbook assignment for this lesson.

5. Complete the Review Activities (Key Concepts and Completion), Self-Test, and Applying Marketing Concepts for this lesson.

6. Check your answers against the Answer Key at the end of the lesson, and review when necessary.

7. Complete any of the Additional Activities (Experiential Exercises and Questions for Exploration) that interest you or that are assigned by your instructor.

Overview

For marketing managers, the most critical task is decision making, and **marketing research** can supply the relevant information, analysis, and suggestions for possible actions that can greatly facilitate that task.

Today, advances in computer technology and programs help marketing professionals to analyze vast amounts of data quickly and accurately. Many marketing managers are assisted on a daily basis by information they receive from a **marketing information system** (MIS). An MIS is a planned computer-based system that provides a continuous flow of information relevant to a manager's specific decisions and areas of responsibility. A portion of an MIS is a **Marketing Decision Support System** (MDSS), which is an interactive communication network that links the marketing decision maker with pertinent databases and analysis tools.

Data mining is the process of searching customer files to find patterns. Once marketers identify patterns and connections, the information can be used to predict the effectiveness of their marketing strategies.

Marketing research most often focuses on matching new products with potential customers, assessing the performance of existing products and refining and improving current products. Types of marketing research activities are scanning, risk assessment, and monitoring. Marketing research projects usually follow a well-defined six-step process: (1) defining the problem, (2) conducting exploratory research, (3) formulating a hypothesis, (4) creating a research design, (5) collecting data, and (6) interpreting and presenting the findings.

The first step, defining the problem, is essential to performing meaningful marketing research. A clear definition of the problem enables the marketing researcher to gather the correct information quickly and accurately.

In **exploratory research,** the marketing researcher discusses the problem with sources inside the firm and wholesalers, retailers, and customers outside the firm. The researcher also examines existing information pertaining to the problem, including company records and the sales and profits of competing products. In examining company records, the researcher may do a **sales analysis,** an in-depth evaluation of a firm's sales, or a **marketing cost analysis,** an evaluation of such items as selling costs, distribution costs, and promotion costs. Financial statements are also useful in identifying financial issues that influence marketing. Exploratory research further refines the definition of the problem.

Once exploratory research has been completed, the researcher formulates a **hypothesis**—a tentative explanation of the problem being studied, which includes a statement about the relationship among the variables and the basis on which to test the explanation.

The hypothesis is the foundation on which the **research design** can be developed. The design is a master plan for conducting the research project and specifies the types of data to be collected, which is the next step of marketing research.

Data can be either primary or secondary. **Primary data** include all information that is collected for the first time during the research project. **Secondary data** include previously existing matter. Internal secondary data refer to a company's sales records, marketing costs, and similar items. External secondary data can be obtained from computerized databases, the federal government, trade associations, advertising agencies, marketing research firms, and online sources.

Sampling, or selecting people to be studied, is an important part of collecting primary data because the choice of respondents and questions can directly affect the research results. The group of people to be studied is called the **population (universe),** and the data collected on the population is called a **census.** Samples can be either **probability** or **nonprobability samples.** Types of probability samples include **simple random, stratified,** and **cluster samples.** Types of nonprobability samples include **convenience samples** and **quota samples.**

When secondary data are not suitable, the researcher must collect primary data. The three major methods used to collect primary data are observation, surveys, and controlled **experiments.** The newest observation method used by marketers is virtual reality. A popular survey method is the use of **focus groups,** in which 8 to 12 people gather to discuss a specific topic. Other types of surveys are conducted by mail, via fax, or online. Each of these methods of data collection has different strengths and weaknesses in terms of time, cost, difficulty of implementation, and appropriateness to a given type of marketing problem.

The final step in marketing research is interpreting and presenting the findings of the research project. Marketing researchers must be especially careful to present their findings in clear, concise, non-technical language so that marketing managers will be able to incorporate the findings into the marketing decision process.

Video Program Notes

The video program for this lesson examines some of the major techniques used by market research firms to gather data. The firm in this case study is ASI Market Research, and much of the program focuses on the work ASI has done for the Disney Channel to help the Disney Channel in making decisions that will optimize its position with consumers.

Among the research techniques used in the work for the Disney Channel are focus groups, telephone surveys, and Preview House screenings of proposed programming. Other techniques shown in the program are magazine advertising research and minimart test facilities.

Throughout the video program, representatives of ASI and the Disney Channel comment on the purpose of marketing research, stressing that the research is not an end in itself but a tool to be used by marketing managers in making decisions about marketing strategy. It is also an ongoing process as important today as it was when the Disney Channel was first trying to establish itself on cable systems.

As you watch the video program, consider the following questions:

1. What marketing problems did the Disney Channel seek to solve with the help of ASI?

2. What are some examples of primary data collection techniques used by ASI?

3. Why was the focus group considered "qualitative" rather than "quantitative"?

4. What types of marketing research information are collected at Preview House?

5. Why are cable channels used to test-market programs for the Disney Channel?

6. What kind of information was being gathered from the magazine advertising tests? For which marketing decisions would this information be most useful?

7. What is the value of the minimart tests?

8. How does the management of the Disney Channel view the role of research in marketing decision making?

9. What does ASI management feel is the role of marketing research in corporate decision making?

10. What steps in the marketing research process are shown in the program?

Learning Objectives

After completing your study of this lesson, you should be able to:

1. Define the following terms as they relate to marketing research:

census	marketing research
cluster sample	nonprobability sample
convenience sample	population (universe)
data mining	primary data
experiment	probability sample
exploratory research	quota sample
focus group	research design
hypothesis	sales analysis
marketing cost analysis	sampling
Marketing Decision Support System (MDSS)	secondary data
	simple random sample
marketing information system (MIS)	stratified sample

2. Describe the development of the marketing research function and its major activities.

3. List and explain the steps in the marketing research process.

4. Explain the different sampling techniques used by marketing researchers.

5. List the types and sources of primary and secondary data.

6. List the methods used by marketing researchers to collect primary data.

7. Explain the challenges of conducting marketing research in global markets.

8. Explain the contributions of Marketing Decision Support Systems to the marketing decision process.

Review Activities

Key Concepts

Identify each of the following fundamental marketing research concepts by writing the letter of the appropriate term in the blank next to the corresponding description.

a. marketing research
b. sales analysis
c. marketing cost analysis
d. secondary data
e. primary data
f. marketing information system (MIS)
g. exploratory research
h. census
i. focus group
j. experiment
k. hypothesis
l. research design

m. cluster sample
n. data mining
o. convenience sample
p. population (universe)
q. probability sample
r. nonprobability sample
s. Marketing Decision Support System (MDSS)
t. quota sample
u. sampling
v. stratified sample
w. simple random sample

_____ 1. collection and use of information in marketing decision making

_____ 2. computer-based system designed to provide a continuous flow of pertinent information for use in making marketing decisions

_____ 3. evaluating costs of such marketing items as selling, billing, and advertising to determine the profitability of certain products, customers, or territories

_____ 4. data collected for the first time during a marketing research study

_____ 5. previously published data

_____ 6. a detailed breakdown of sales by territories, sales representatives, products, or consumers

_____ 7. a tentative explanation about a specific event

_____ 8. preliminary limited search for possible causes of a marketing problem

_____ 9. collection of data from all possible sources in a population

_____ 10. group meeting of eight to twelve individuals to discuss a subject of interest to the marketing researcher

_____ 11. scientific investigation in which results of test groups are compared to those of control groups

_____ 12. arbitrary sample in which most standard statistical tests cannot be applied to the collected data

_____ 13. master plan for conducting marketing research

_____ 14. sample in which every member of the population has a known chance of being selected

_____ 15. nonprobability sample based on readily available respondents

_____ 16. probability sample in which geographic areas are selected

_____ 17. total group the researcher wants to study

_____ 18. searching customer files to detect patterns that affect marketing decisions

_____ 19. interactive communication network that links a decision maker with relevant databases

_____ 20. probability sample in which every item in the relevant universe has an equal opportunity of being selected

_____ 21. probability sample constructed in such a way that the total sample includes randomly selected subsamples

_____ 22. nonprobability sample divided so that different segments are represented in the total sample

_____ 23. selection of survey respondents or other research participants

Completion

Fill each blank in the following paragraphs with the most appropriate term from the list of completion answers below. A term may be used once, more than once, or not at all.

analysis	internal	quota
characteristics	known	research
control	marketer	results
convenience	marketing	sales
data	marketplace	sample
decisions	nonprobability	secondary
design	observation	share
expensive	outside	slow
experiment	personal	survey
exploratory	population	target market
external	potential	telephone
focus	primary	test
focus group	probability	time
hypothesis	problem	

1. Marketing research is the collection and use of information in marketing decision making. It is an information function that links the _____ and the _____.

2. The marketing research process consists of six specific steps. The first step is defining the _____ , which is followed by conducting _____ research. The third step is formulating a _____ , and the fourth step is creating a research _____. The last two steps are collecting _____ and interpreting and presenting the _____ information.

3. Defining the problem is an important first step in marketing research because it helps the researcher to _____ on just the information necessary for solving the problem.

4. The second step, exploratory research, usually involves collecting _____ data and exploratory interviews with persons _____ the firm.

5. A particularly valuable source of information during exploratory research is an organization's _____ records. An in-depth evaluation of a firm's sales in order to obtain meaningful information from accounting data is known as sales _____.

6. Another source of internal information that can be used in the exploratory research step is the firm's selling costs and warehousing, advertising, and delivery expenses. Evaluation of these items is known as _____ cost analysis.

7. On the basis of exploratory research, the researcher should be able to make a tentative explanation of the situation being studied. This statement about the relationship among variables, which also implies methods for testing the relationship, is known as a _____.

8. The means for testing the hypothesis are structured into a master plan for conducting the investigation, which is known as the research _____.

9. Data used in testing the hypothesis can come from two sources. Data from previously published sources are known as _____ data. Data collected for the first time during a marketing research study are known as _____ data.

10. Secondary data consist of two basic types: _____ data and _____ data. Secondary data collected on the population is a _____ ; the U.S. Census is one of the most-used sources.

11. Secondary data were originally gathered and reported for purposes other than those currently being considered by the marketing researcher. Despite time lags and differences in research purposes, secondary data should be considered prior to conducting original research and generating new primary data. Secondary data are sometimes preferred over primary data because their collection is less _____ and takes less _____.

12. If secondary data do not provide the desired information, the only alternative is to use _____ data.

13. The three primary methods the researcher has for gathering primary data are _____ , _____ , and controlled _____ .

14. The most widely used method of collecting primary data is the _____ method.

15. An inexpensive and quick way of conducting a survey is through _____ interviews. The best way of obtaining detailed information is the _____ interview. These interviews, however, are expensive and _____ to conduct. A popular technique used to gather information, in which eight to twelve people are brought together and asked to discuss a particular topic, is known as a _____ .

16. By using the Internet, marketing researchers can go _____ to conduct surveys and even focus groups.

17. The least-used method of marketing research is the _____ .

18. In a controlled experiment, the researcher manipulates a _____ group and compares the _____ with those of a _____ group that was not manipulated.

19. Sampling is frequently used in gathering primary data. In selecting respondents for a sample, it is important that the sample respondents accurately reflect the _____ .

20. The total group to be studied is called the _____ , or universe. A representative group of the universe is a _____ .

21. The two classifications of samples are _____ samples and _____ samples.

22. In a probability sample, every member of the population has a _____ chance of being selected.

23. A nonprobability sample is arbitrary, and standard statistical tests cannot be applied to the data. One type of nonprobability sample is based on the selection of readily available respondents and is known as a _____ sample. Another type of nonprobability sample is divided so

that different groups are represented in the total sample and is known as a _____ sample.

24. The marketing information system (MIS) is a planned, computer-based system designed to provide a continual flow of relevant information for use in making marketing _____.

Self-Test

> **Select the best answer.**

1. The critical task of the marketing manager is
   a. planning and implementing marketing research.
   b. developing an effective marketing information system.
   c. interpreting research results.
   d. making effective decisions to solve problems and prevent future problems.

2. The first task of the marketing researcher conducting a research investigation is to
   a. conduct exploratory research.
   b. define the problem or opportunity.
   c. do a sales and cost analysis.
   d. plan a research design.

3. The purpose of a sales analysis is to
   a. eliminate accountants' jobs.
   b. assess the profitability of sales territories.
   c. determine the trend of a company's market share.
   d. help assess the sales performance of individual sales territories, salespeople, products, and customers.
   e. put the marketing concept into action.

4. Compared to primary data, secondary data have the advantage of being
   a. less expensive to collect.
   b. up-to-date.
   c. classified in a useful way.
   d. more relevant.

5. Marketing information systems
    a. provide an orderly flow of information.
    b. are needed by companies that have marketing research departments.
    c. use secondary and primary data.
    d. include all of the above.

6. Marketing cost analysis requires a new way of classifying accounting data. This new approach requires that accounts be classified
    a. arbitrarily.
    b. functionally.
    c. traditionally.
    d. randomly.

7. A principal benefit of marketing research is that it provides
    a. simplification of complex marketing problems.
    b. historical information for summary reports.
    c. condensation of internal and external data.
    d. information for decision making.

8. Internal data are usually available to an organization in the form of
    a. accounting and financial data.
    b. internal audits of the marketing department.
    c. reports from trade associations.

9. A thorough breakdown and in-depth evaluation of sales is known as a sales
    a. report.
    b. analysis.
    c. forecast.
    d. plan.

10. To determine the profitability of particular customers, territories, or product lines, a firm performs
    a. a market analysis.
    b. a marketing cost analysis.
    c. a marketing survey.
    d. marketing research.

Applying Marketing Concepts

Andy Stewart, marketing research analyst for Cleanware Corporation, was asked to find out why Superclean, a heavy-duty industrial cleaning compound, wasn't doing as well as expected and to report his findings in three weeks.

First, he gathered primary data from all of the 5,000 customers who had bought Superclean in the past year to determine why more firms weren't making repeat purchases. After reviewing bids from three external marketing research companies, he chose the Natural Research Corporation because its bid was the lowest.

Stewart directed the research company to design and conduct the study of all customers without contacting any Cleanware management personnel. After the primary research study was commissioned, Stewart talked with Cleanware's sales force and wholesalers to determine the cause of the decline in sales of Superclean. Finally, he reviewed the records that were available in the company's marketing information system. These records included breakdowns of sales and marketing costs for Superclean in each sales territory. The following table shows the results of the analysis of these records.

	Territory							
	East		West		North		South	
	(Dollar amounts in thousands)							
	Actual	Quota	**Actual**	Quota	**Actual**	Quota	**Actual**	Quota
Sales	**$500**	$400	**$300**	$200	**$400**	$300	**$600**	$500
Cost of sales	**300**		**180**		**120**		**180**	
Gross margin	**200**		**120**		**280**		**420**	
Marketing expenses	**400**	120	**90**	60	**240**	90	**500**	150
Contribution of each territory	**($200)**		**$ 30**		**$ 40**		**($ 80)**	

> **Select the best answer.**

1. Of the ways listed below, the best way for the marketing research company to gather the information Stewart wanted from customers in three weeks would be
    a. observation.
    b. telephone interviews.
    c. personal interviews.
    d. focus groups.
    e. a mail survey.

2. The sales and cost analysis suggests
    a. sales in all territories were below expectations.
    b. the East was the only problem market.
    c. marketing expenses were above expected levels in all territories.
    d. the sales force was incurring excessive travel and entertainment expenses.
    e. customers do not like Cleanware products.

3. Stewart decided to do primary research before a sales and cost analysis. His decision was based on the conclusion that answers about the causes of Superclean's problems could be obtained from
   a. dealers.
   b. customers.
   c. the sales force.
   d. government publications.
   e. company management.

4. The results of Stewart's investigation should be
   a. discarded.
   b. reviewed by management and then discarded.
   c. added to Cleanware's marketing information system for future use.
   d. acted on immediately.

5. Stewart chose the Natural Research Corporation because it
   a. was the least expensive.
   b. had the desired expertise.
   c. was intellectually detached.
   d. was a subsidiary of the Cleanware Corporation.
   e. had done many similar projects for other companies.

6. Stewart was following accepted marketing research practices when he decided to collect primary data before secondary data.
   a. true
   b. false

7. A census of customers was taken.
   a. true
   b. false

8. To remain objective, outside marketing research organizations should conduct research projects without talking to the users of the research information.
   a. true
   b. false

9. Very few organizations purchase outside marketing research services.
   a. true
   b. false

10. Cleanware Corporation should not need marketing research if its marketing information system is effective.
    a. true
    b. false

Additional Activities

Experiential Exercises

1. This exercise was developed to broaden your understanding of how marketers can use the marketing research process to gain an understanding of their markets.

   Assume you are considering opening a new business near your college or university that would be directed primarily toward college students. Select a restaurant, coffeehouse, bookstore, video rental store, sports club, hair salon, sporting goods store, or similar business.

   - Determine the number of students who might be in the market for your goods or services by researching college publications, such as admissions reports, or by interviewing records personnel. This number may include all students or just part of the student body, depending on the target market for your business.

   - Using a telephone directory, student newspaper advertisements, and other sources, including observation, determine the names and locations of firms currently providing the goods or services you plan to market to college students. List the competitors and their locations.

- What do you think are the marketing strengths and weaknesses of these competitors? For each competitor, prepare a chart like the following:

Marketing Mix Element	Strengths	Weaknesses
Product		
Price		
Distribution		
Promotion		

- Interview at least five students who would be in the market for your goods or services to determine where they go to buy the products your business will sell; what they like about the places where they now buy; and what they don't like about these competitive businesses.

- Based on your research, do you feel there is sufficient evidence of business potential to support a more formal marketing research project, or do you think your evidence indicates there is no need for another business of this type and no more research can be justified?

2. The purpose of this second exercise is to show the different types and relative value of marketing information available for a retail area. It will help you distinguish the differences between primary and secondary research and recognize that the value of information in making decisions must be weighed against the cost of obtaining that information.

You are the owner of a chain of women's specialty stores. You are interested in the possibility of opening four new stores in a city of 600,000 that is located 800 miles from your current concentration of fourteen stores. You know nothing about the area except that it seems to be a good place for expansion. You contact a marketing research firm in the area in order to obtain information about the city, about your competition, and so on. The firm offers you the information given in Table 1, which includes both primary and secondary research projects and related costs.

Table 1

Research Project	Cost	Type (P/S)	Rank (1-10)
List of the gross sales figures of all current women's specialty stores in the area for the past two years.	$ 400		
Map of the area showing major traffic routes, current shopping centers and types of stores, and location of department and women's specialty stores.	$1,500		
Color-coded map of the area showing residential and commercial property values.	$1,000		
Telephone survey of 500 randomly selected households in the area; designed to determine the familiarity of consumers with your store name, interest in specialty stores of this type, and awareness of other specialty stores and their advertising.	$5,000		
Demographic breakdown of the area by sex, age, gross income, education, disposable income, family size, and occupation.	$2,000		
Mail survey of 300 readers of female-oriented magazines, questioning the readers about their awareness of styles, need for complete services in specialty women's clothing, amount of money spent annually on clothes, frequency of patronage of specialty shops.	$5,000		
Report of fifteen-year summary of economic trends of the area, shopping centers, occupations, disposable income, clothing sales, and specialty shops.	$1,800		
Focus-group report of twelve people concerning attitudes toward prices of clothing and specialty shops, services expected, appropriate atmosphere, type of salespeople, and seasonal changes.	$2,800		
List of all organizations, clubs, nightclubs, restaurants, and specialty stores that cater to the in crowd and their managers' names.	$ 800		
List of all current retail space openings in the area, with price per square foot, turnover rate for those spots and for shopping centers, population within one square mile, and income ranges, housing values, occupations, ages, and family sizes.	$2,400		

- In Table 1, indicate what type of research you feel each project would provide (P = primary and S = secondary).

- Using a scale of 1 to 10 (10 being most important), rank each research project in the order of its importance to the process of making decisions about the new market area.

- If you were limited to spending the following dollar amounts in obtaining the information in Table 1, which of the research projects would you purchase?

Dollar Amounts	Projects to Do
$ 4,000 maximum	
$ 8,000 maximum	
$12,000 maximum	
$16,000 maximum	

Questions for Exploration

Conceptual

"American industry's growing dependence on marketing research has led to a decrease in innovation in new products and services and an increase in 'new' products and services that are merely incremental modifications of existing products and services."

Do you agree or disagree with this statement? Why?

Practical

External marketing research often depends on "self-report" data in which the respondent tells the researcher about his or her own feelings, reactions, intentions, and opinions.

Discuss some of the reasons self-report data might not be dependable, and suggest ways in which the data could be made more reliable.

Are focus groups as shown in the program a good technique for learning what individuals think about a product? If not, why not?

Answer Key

Key Concepts				
	1. a	7. k	13. l	19. s
	2. f	8. g	14. q	20. w
	3. c	9. h	15. o	21. v
	4. e	10. i	16. m	22. t
	5. d	11. j	17. p	23. u
	6. b	12. r	18. n	

Completion

1. marketer, marketplace
2. problem, exploratory, hypothesis, design, data, research
3. focus
4. internal, outside
5. sales, analysis
6. marketing
7. hypothesis
8. design
9. secondary, primary
10. internal, external (either order), census
11. expensive, time
12. primary
13. survey, observation, experiment (any order)
14. survey
15. telephone, personal, slow, focus group
16. online
17. controlled experiment
18. test, results, control
19. target market
20. population, sample
21. probability, nonprobability (either order)
22. known
23. convenience, quota
24. decisions

Self-Test			
	1. d	5. d	9. b
	2. b	6. b	10. b
	3. d	7. d	
	4. a	8. a	

Applying Marketing Concepts			
	1. b	5. a	8. b
	2. c	6. b	9. b
	3. b	7. a	10. b
	4. c			

Some people are curiously afraid to even dream
of owning a product that is outside their life-style.

—Dr. Emanuel H. Demby

6

Consumer Behavior I

Assignments

For the most effective study of this lesson, we suggest that you complete the assignments in the following sequence:

1. Read the study guide Overview (Lesson Notes and Video Program Notes) and the Learning Objectives for this lesson.

2. Read *Contemporary Marketing Wired*, 9th edition, Chapter 8, "Consumer Behavior," pages 264-279. (The balance of the chapter will be assigned in the next lesson.)

3. View "Driving Passions: A Case Study in Understanding Consumer Behavior" video program.

4. Review the textbook assignment for this lesson.

5. Complete the Review Activities (Key Concepts and Completion), Self-Test, and Applying Marketing Concepts for this lesson.

6. Check your answers against the Answer Key at the end of the lesson, and review when necessary.

7. Complete any of the Additional Activities (Experiential Exercise and Questions for Exploration) that interest you or that are assigned by your instructor.

Overview

Lesson Notes

Buyer behavior refers to customers and businesses who make purchasing decisions. Two general forces determine the character of **consumer behavior:** personal influences from within the consumer and interpersonal determinants from the environment. These two forces are important both separately and in combination. This lesson focuses on some of the key personal and interpersonal influences on consumer behavior; the next lesson focuses on how the marketer seeks and uses a knowledge of consumer behavior to shape the promotion element of the marketing mix.

One way to explain consumer behavior is in terms of **needs** and **motives.** A need is the lack of something useful. For example, a family without a bathroom in the home could be said to need an in-house facility. If people consider a need relatively unimportant, it may not affect their behavior at a given time. Conversely, if consumers become convinced that their needs are important, they will be moved to act. The need then becomes directed by a motive.

Two important ways that marketers explain motivation are by examining consumers' self-images and by considering their types of needs. When people assess their self-images and feel they are too distant from their ideal selves, they may be moved to act.

Maslow's hierarchy of needs suggests, however, that people first emphasize the satisfaction of physiological needs and will consider safety, social/belongingness, esteem, and self-actualization needs only after these basic needs are at least partially satisfied. People may not be concerned with trying to achieve their ideal selves until the need for self-actualization becomes activated.

One of the most important interpersonal influences on consumer behavior is the social group. Social groups influence an individual's needs, motives, perceptions, and attitudes. Each group expects its members to conform with certain **norms:** the values, attitudes, and behaviors appropriate for the group. The influence of the group on an individual depends on the individual's **status** and **role** in the group. Group influence is greatest for products that are easily identifiable and socially conspicuous.

Social class and reference groups are other types of interpersonal influence. **Social class** is determined by occupation, source of income, education, family background, and dwelling area. Often, groups influence an individual's buying decisions more than he or she realizes. The impact of groups on individual behavior is known as the **Asch Phenomenon. Reference groups** are those people with whom an individual identifies and orients his or her behavior.

Family and culture are two other sources of interpersonal influence on consumer behavior. Family influence changes as the family's stage in the family life cycle changes. Other factors are also involved; for example, the working status of women affects their purchasing role in the family.

Culture is a social force that encompasses numerous **subcultures** and groups. It comprises learned values, tastes, and other meaningful symbols and includes beliefs regarding a diverse number of objects and experiences, as well as preferences, including religion, food, personal appearance, and success.

An understanding of the personal influences on the consumer, such as needs and self-image, and interpersonal influences, such as family, reference groups, and culture, enables the marketer to develop and deliver goods and services that are truly needed and desired by consumers. When such products are available, both consumers and marketers are winners.

Video Program Notes

The video program for this lesson introduces the forces that influence individual consumer behavior. By using a single example—the automobile—the program illustrates why people buy and why they do not buy. The program demonstrates how an individual's self-image and Maslow's hierarchy of needs can be used to explain buying behavior. The program also explores other consumer behavior concepts that can affect the marketing mix, including social class and subculture.

As you watch the video program, consider the following questions:

1. Why do marketers consider automobiles as more than transportation?

2. How do people use cars to satisfy each of the needs identified by Maslow—and what are the implications for marketers?

3. A motorcycle is used to illustrate self-actualization. What other needs in Maslow's hierarchy might it fulfill?

4. How cognizant of his own buying motives is the artist who drives the '57 Cadillac? Why?

5. What are some examples of how people use their automobiles to attempt to influence the way other people feel about them?

6. What social influences affect the purchase of vehicles such as the Peugeot station wagon and VW bus?

7. What roles do social groups, such as fraternities and sororities, play in a group member's selection of a car?

8. How are children influenced in their selection of a vehicle?

9. How do marketers use the concept of "opinion leader" to see their products?

10. How do class and cultural background affect the purchase decision?

Learning Objectives

After completing your study of this lesson, you should be able to:

1. Explain the following terms as they relate to consumer behavior:

Asch phenomenon
buyer behavior
consumer behavior
culture
motive
need

norm
opinion leader
reference group
role
status
subculture

2. Identify three categories of interpersonal influences on consumer behavior.

3. Define culture and subculture and give examples of how they influence consumer behavior.

4. Describe and give examples of social influences on consumer behavior.

5. Describe and give examples of family influences on social behavior.

6. Identify the levels of Maslow's hierarchy of needs and describe their relevance to marketing.

Review Activities

Key Concepts

> **Identify each of the following concepts of consumer behavior by writing the letter of the appropriate term in the blank next to the corresponding description.**
>
> a. consumer behavior   g. opinion leader
> b. buyer behavior   h. reference group
> c. need   i. role
> d. Asch phenomenon   j. culture
> e. motive   k. subculture
> f. status   l. norm

_____ 1. values, beliefs, preferences, and tastes passed from one generation to the next

_____ 2. group with which an individual identifies to the point where it directs a standard of behavior

_____ 3. acts of individuals to obtain and use goods and services, including the decision processes that precede and determine these acts

_____ 4. discrepancy between a desired state and an actual state

_____ 5. relative position of an individual within a group

_____ 6. groups within a larger group that have distinct modes of behavior and values

_____ 7. influence of a group on an individual's purchase decision, often without the individual's conscious awareness

_____ 8. inner state that directs a person toward satisfying a felt need

_____ 9. behavior that members of a group expect from an individual within that group

_____ 10. individual who serves as an information source for members of a group

_____ 11. process by which consumers make purchase decisions

_____ 12. values, attitudes, and behaviors considered appropriate by a group for its members

Completion

Fill each blank in the following paragraphs with the most appropriate term from the list of completion answers below. A term may be used once, more than once, or not at all.

after	family	purchase
attitudes	identified	reference group
before	image	safety
behavior	income	self-
car	interpersonal	self-actualization
chair	motive	self-image
conspicuous	occupation	social belongingness
culture	opinion leaders	society
education	personal	subcultures
esteem	physiological	values

1. Marketers view consumer behavior as mental and physical processes carried out to obtain and use goods and services. A narrow view of consumer behavior is to examine only the actual _____ . This view overlooks events that come _____ and _____ the purchase act.

2. The two types of forces that determine consumer behavior are _____ and _____ influences.

3. An example of an interpersonal influence that may affect the consumer's behavior is the _____ group in which the individual is born and raised.

4. People will frequently alter their behavior so that their friends will view them differently or they can become more like what they want to be. As a result, the individual's _____ image influences consumption _____ .

5. If a person feels a need to buy new clothing in order to achieve the ideal self-image, he or she perceives some tension or an aroused need. The aroused need that serves as the driving force behind the consumer's behavior is a _____.

6. Maslow classified human needs into categories. These types of needs are arranged in a hierarchy according to how they exert their influence. The first level of needs is _____ needs, such as the need for food and water.

7. Besides physiological needs, other needs on Maslow's hierarchy, from second to fifth level, include _____ , _____ , _____ , and _____ .

8. If a husband and wife decide to buy a large car because they believe it can withstand a crash better than a small car, they are motivated by what Maslow might call a _____ need.

9. A teenager may buy a motorcycle in order to join a motorcycle club. According to Maslow's hierarchy, the need the teenager is trying to satisfy is the _____ need.

10. A person may have satisfied a variety of needs, but not the need to develop his or her fullest potentialities and capacities. This highest-level need is the need for _____ .

11. Groups can influence an individual's behavior even if the individual is not a formal group member. A group with which an individual identifies, one that he or she uses for standards of performance, is called a _____ .

12. Group influence depends on the characteristics of the product. Group influence is greatest if the item can be _____ by others and is _____ .

13. Social class is primarily determined by _____ , _____ , family background, and dwelling area.

14. It is difficult to determine what social class a family earning $50,000 a year is in because _____ is not a primary determinant of social class.

15. Not all members of a group have an equal influence on other members. Some members are respected and their opinions are sought. These trendsetters are called _____ .

16. In the United States, we may say that the purpose of food is nourishment and the ideal appearance is one of slender youthfulness. These society-wide values represent part of the U.S. _____ .

17. Culture is defined as the _____ , beliefs, _____ , and tastes that are handed down from generation to generation.

18. Within a culture, several variations of cultural traditions, mores, and customs may exist. These variations are known as _____ and may represent distinct market segments.

Self-Test

1. Consumer behavior includes
   a. purchasing goods and services.
   b. asking friends about alternatives that might satisfy consumer needs and wants.
   c. dissatisfaction with a purchase.
   d. arousal of a need for a product.
   e. all of the above factors.

2. A woman who purchases an item at a Tupperware party, even though she doesn't think she needs the item, is an example of
   a. the Asch phenomenon.
   b. consumer learning.
   c. opinion leadership.
   d. cognitive awareness.

3. An aroused need is
   a. a perception.
   b. an attitude.
   c. a motive.
   d. a cue.

4. For a reference group to influence a person's buying behavior, the
   a. person must belong to the group.
   b. group must have opinion leaders.
   c. product being purchased must be owned by all members of the group.
   d. product being purchased is most likely one that can be seen by others.
   e. person must have daily contact with the group.

5. With regard to family roles,
   a. husbands and wives do not share any buying roles.
   b. children do not influence the purchase of their clothing.
   c. children often become experts on major family purchases.
   d. most people are members of only one family during their lifetimes.

6. In making decisions about such products as can openers and brooms, there is no real reference group influence because the products are
   a. purchased by only one member of the family.
   b. priced relatively low.
   c. inconspicuous and ordinary.
   d. used by only one member of the family.

7. A reference group would **LEAST** influence the purchase of a
   a. sweater.
   b. car.
   c. computer.
   d. dishwashing detergent.

8. Of the following determinants, the one that is **NOT** a primary determinant of a person's social class is
   a. education.
   b. income.
   c. family background.
   d. occupation.

9. Maslow's hierarchy of needs includes all of the following needs **EXCEPT**
   a. physiological needs.
   b. esteem needs.
   c. personal needs.
   d. social needs.
   e. safety needs.

10. People who serve as information sources and tend to set trends are known to marketers as
    a. reference-group leaders.
    b. style setters.
    c. opinion leaders.
    d. heads of households.

Applying Marketing Concepts

Jane Mason, a recent graduate of the MBA program at Midstate University, was so successful in her first marketing job at AP&T, a national manufacturer of consumer products, that she moved rather quickly into middle management. Her recent experiences with her car, a 1991 Ford, were less rewarding. Numerous problems with the engine and transmission of the car convinced her that it was not worth fixing again, and she decided to buy a new car.

After talking to friends at work, Mason become convinced that she should buy a Toyota Camry. Several had one or said they knew others who had one. Her father had recommended that she buy a Saturn because he thought it a more dependable car. After several days of reading advertisements and reviewing *Consumer Reports*, she decided on the Camry.

Next, Mason had to decide where to buy the car, because three local dealers sold it. During the following week, she studied the ads of the three local Toyota dealers. All three were advertising price reductions for end-of-the-model-year clearance. Mason's attention focused on the $2,000 price reduction offered by Select Motors; the $500 price reduction offered by the two other dealers was not even competitive.

She subsequently bought a blue Camry from Select Motors and drove to her father's house, intent on convincing him that she had made the right decision. Unfortunately, the new car stalled five miles from her destination and she had to call her father for assistance. Mason suffered considerable doubt about her purchase.

Select the best answer.

---

1. Mason's decision to buy the Toyota, perhaps to fit in with her friends, helped her satisfy her
    a. physiological needs.
    b. safety needs.
    c. social/belongingness needs.
    d. esteem needs.
    e. self-actualization needs.

2. If Maslow's theory of needs applies to Mason, she also has at least partially satisfied
   a. her physiological needs.
   b. her safety needs.
   c. her social needs.
   d. all of the above needs.
   e. none of the above needs.

3. Friends who set the standards Mason used in selecting a car can be classified as her
   a. opinion leaders.
   b. social class.
   c. reference group.
   d. subculture.

4. The opinion leader in Mason's buying process was
   a. a friend at work.
   b. her father.
   c. the car salesman.
   d. not identified.

5. Mason's need became a motive because of
   a. dissatisfaction with her Ford.
   b. peer pressure to buy a Toyota.
   c. family pressure to buy a Chevrolet.
   d. internal dissatisfaction with self-image.

Additional Activities

Experiential Exercise

The purpose of this exercise is to show that, in part, a consumer's behavior, patronage, and consumption habits are based on personal fears and the desire to avoid fear-inducing situations. You will be asked to identify some common fears and phobias of consumers and describe goods or services that could aid them in alleviating their fears.

People naturally try to avoid the things they fear. Fear, both real and imaginary, and avoidance have both plagued and helped humanity. While we wisely avoid touching hot stoves, it is common for builders to eliminate the number *13* from floors or rooms, because of the connotation of bad luck. For the same reason, some U.S. pet shops refuse to sell black cats. Some restaurants do not put salt on the tables unless a customer requests it. Fear and superstition strongly motivate people, including consumers.

Excessive fear can be partially alleviated through the use of some goods or services that help people avoid or counteract the possible outcome of the fear (rabbits' feet, triple door locks, wall safes, insurance, and similar products ease some types of fear for many people). Marketers continually try to help consumers with practical, functional ways of overcoming disabling fears. Devising goods and services that help reduce fear is not too different from making new products appease people's appetite for food.

- Name five fears that you feel are fairly common in our society. They do not have to be technical or clinically recognized. What goods or services might help overcome those fears?

- Define the following extreme fears, or *phobias*. What good, service, or environment could marketers provide to consumers to alleviate these phobias?

acrophobia	myophobia	pathophobia
agoraphobia	mysophobia	pyrophobia
claustrophobia	nyctophobia	triskaidekaphobia

Questions for Exploration

Conceptual

Are people basically hermits who interact only to acquire material welfare? Or are they social creatures who interact for reasons other than their material welfare? Choose a point of view, argue your case, and indicate its implications for marketing.

Practical

The video program for this lesson focuses on the consumer and the automobile. What other type of good or service could have been used to illustrate Maslow's hierarchy of needs and self-image theories? Do you feel that marketers should rely more, or less, on psychological concepts and theories in developing a practical marketing mix?

Answer Key

Key Concepts			
	1. j	5. f	9. i
	2. h	6. k	10. g
	3. a	7. d	11. b
	4. c	8. e	12. l

Completion

1. purchase, before, after
2. interpersonal, personal (either order)
3. family
4. self-, behavior
5. motive
6. physiological
7. safety, social/ belongingness, esteem, self-actualization
8. safety
9. social/belongingness
10. self-actualization
11. reference group
12. identified, conspicuous
13. occupation, education (either order)
14. income
15. opinion leaders
16. culture
17. values, preferences (either order)
18. subcultures

Self-Test		
	1. e	6. c
	2. a	7. d
	3. c	8. b
	4. d	9. c
	5. c	10. c

Applying Marketing Concepts		
	1. c	4. d
	2. d	5. a
	3. c	

The young householder has one trait that endears him to a broad range of businesses: He needs what he needs right now, today.

—Edward L. Grubb

7

Consumer Behavior II

Assignments

For the most effective study of this lesson, we suggest that you complete the assignments in the following sequence:

1. Read the study guide Overview (Lesson Notes and Video Program Notes) and the Learning Objectives for this lesson.

2. Review *Contemporary Marketing Wired*, 9th edition, Chapter 8, "Consumer Behavior," pages 279-291.

3. View "Breaking through the Clutter: A Case Study in Understanding Consumer Behavior" video program.

4. Review the textbook assignment for this lesson.

5. Complete the Review Activities (Key Concepts and Completion), Self-Test, and Applying Marketing Concepts for this lesson.

6. Check your answers against the Answer Key at the end of the lesson, and review when necessary.

7. Complete any of the Additional Activities (Experiential Exercise and Questions for Exploration) that interest you or that are assigned by your instructor.

Overview

Lesson Notes

The previous lesson examined how consumer behavior is shaped by personal forces (those from within the consumer) and interpersonal forces (those from the consumer's environment). This lesson examines how the marketer seeks and employs knowledge of target consumers in order to shape the promotion element of the marketing mix.

Segmentation of markets based primarily on demographic characteristics often understates the impact motivations, perceptions, attitudes, and reference groups have on consumer behavior. People who are the same age, earn the same amount of income, and share other demographic characteristics do not necessarily exhibit the same behavior.

The variations in seemingly similar, demographically segmented consumers become more evident if viewed in terms of buying behavior. This view considers the act of purchasing a good or service as only one part of the decision process. The marketer broadens the definition of consumer behavior to include all the acts of individuals in obtaining and using goods and services, including the mental processes and physical actions that occur from the time a potential consumer recognizes a need until he or she has consumed a product and evaluated its performance.

Perception is another concept marketers use to explain the meaning consumers attribute to incoming stimuli. The attributed meaning depends on the characteristics of both the stimuli and the person receiving them. The marketer's concern with perception focuses on understanding the **perceptual screen,** the processes by which consumers filter out some stimuli and how they interpret the stimuli that are received. The marketer's objective is to "break through the clutter."

In **subliminal perception,** stimuli such as advertisements are introduced to consumers at the subconscious level; however, stimuli may not be strong enough or introduced for a long enough time to gain the attention of, let alone influence, the receiver. Subliminal advertising is also ineffective with groups of people, as wide variations are observed in individual perceptual thresholds.

The marketer realizes that consumers will probably not buy a product if they evaluate it as inferior to other brands or if for any reason they have an unfavorable attitude toward the product. Consumer **attitudes** are defined as a person's evaluations, feelings, or tendencies to act toward some object or idea. Once the nature of consumer attitudes is determined, marketers usually realign the marketing mix so that the target market is satisfied, because revision of the marketing mix is generally easier than changing the attitudes of consumers. The consumer's **self-concept,** or picture of himself or herself, affects consumer behavior, as well.

However, the behavior of buyers can be changed through the process of **learning** and includes **drives** or stimuli that impel action. In effect, the marketer attempts to "teach" the consumer a new behavior (buying the product) by providing **cues** (such as a newspaper ad). The marketer hopes that the customer's satisfaction with the product will result in **reinforcement** of the buying behavior—and win a steady customer.

Buying behavior can be described as a six-stage decision process: problem or opportunity recognition, search, evaluation of alternatives, purchase decision, purchase act, and postpurchase evaluation. During the search, the consumer considers an **evoked set,** or number of brands, before buying. In choosing among the alternatives, the consumer considers a product's features, or **evaluative criteria.** In the last stage, the consumer may experience anxiety, or **cognitive dissonance,** once a purchase has been made. By understanding this process, the marketer can develop a marketing mix that influences consumer behavior and supports a consumer's satisfaction with the purchase.

Video Program Notes

The video program for this lesson explores how marketers gain an understanding of consumers and what motivates consumers to buy. Starting with the idea that the marketer is selling a product for which there is a need, the program deals with concepts of perception, attitude, consumer self-concept, and cognitive dissonance. And—through the work of psychologist Renee Fraser of Kenyon and Eckhardt and Bob Abel of Robert Abel and Associates (advertising firms)—the program reveals how professional advertisers develop and use their knowledge of consumer behavior, attitudes, and perceptions in the creation of persuasive advertising.

As you watch the video program, consider the following questions:

1. Why would an advertising agency employ a full-time psychologist?

2. Why are advertisers willing to pay for psychographic research?

3. What reasons explain why some ads work better than others?

4. How are focus groups, in-depth interviews, and field trips used to develop consumer profiles?

5. How do marketers use advertisements to deal with "cognitive dissonance"?

6. Why is humor used in some advertisements for subjects, such as insurance, that are not humorous?

7. Why do marketers measure consumer reaction to finished advertisements?

Learning Objectives

After completing your study of this lesson, you should be able to:

1. Explain the following terms as they relate to consumer behavior:

attitude | learning
cognitive dissonance | perception
cue | perceptual screen
drive | reinforcement
evaluative criteria | self-concept
evoked set | subliminal perception

2. Identify perceptions, attitudes, learning, and self-concept as personal determinants of consumer behavior and describe the influence of each on purchasing decisions.

3. List the three components of attitude and identify techniques for changing consumer attitudes.

4. List the components of the learning process as they relate to consumer behavior.

5. Outline the steps involved in the consumer decision process.

6. Describe the conditions under which cognitive dissonance is likely to occur and methods that marketers use to reduce it.

Review Activities

Key Concepts

> **Identify each of the following consumer behavior terms by writing the letter of the appropriate term in the blank next to the corresponding description.**
>
> a. attitude g. self-concept
> b. perception h. reinforcement
> c. subliminal perception i. cognitive dissonance
> d. learning j. evoked set
> e. drive k. evaluative criteria
> f. cue l. perceptual screen

_____ 1. number of brands a consumer actually considers before making a purchase decision

_____ 2. postpurchase anxiety, sometimes referred to as "buyer's remorse"

_____ 3. the meaning a person attributes to incoming stimuli received through the five senses

_____ 4. a person's enduring favorable or unfavorable evaluations, emotional feelings, or action tendencies toward some object or idea

_____ 5. receipt of information at the subconscious level

_____ 6. changes in behavior as a result of experience

_____ 7. any strong stimulus that impels action

_____ 8. reduction in drive that results from an appropriate response

_____ 9. an object that determines the nature of the response to a drive

_____ 10. one's multifaceted picture of oneself

_____ 11. price, brand name, and other criteria the consumer considers in making a choice among alternatives

_____ 12. filtering process through which messages must pass

Completion

> **Fill each blank in the following paragraphs with the most appropriate term from the list of completion answers below. A term may be used once, more than once, or not at all.**
>
> | | | |
> |---|---|---|
> | affective | evaluative | reinforcement |
> | attitude | evoked | responses |
> | cognitive dissonance | hearing | sight |
> | consumer attitudes | individual | smell |
> | cues | perceptions | stimulus |
> | discrepancy | perceptual | subliminal |
> | drives | problem | taste |
> | evaluate | product | touch |

1. Marketers send stimuli to potential consumers. The meaning people attribute to these stimuli depends on their experiences, attitudes, beliefs, and other influencing forces. This variation in the understanding of the stimuli reflects variation in _____ .

2. Perception is the meaning a person attributes to stimuli received through the senses of _____ , _____ , _____ , _____ , and _____ .

3. A person's perception of an object results from the interaction of two types of factors: _____ and _____ factors.

4. Some stimuli are not received at all. This unreceived information fails to penetrate the consumer's _____ screens.

5. Advertising designed to reach the receiver by aiming *below* the conscious level of awareness is _____ advertising.

6. A person's evaluations, feelings, and tendencies in regard to some object or information are known as _____ .

7. A person's feelings and emotional reaction to an object are the _____ component of attitude.

8. If marketers discover that consumers do not like their brand, they can attempt either to change _____ or change the _____ .

9. Learning depends on _____ such as thirst, _____ such as advertisements, _____ such as purchasing a can of Pepsi, and _____ such as pleasant taste and thirst-quenching refreshment.

10. According to current theory, the consumer decision-making process starts when a _____ exists between an individual's current state of affairs and desired state of affairs.

11. Once a problem is recognized, the consumer looks for goods or services to satisfy the need. The brands considered as feasible alternatives are called the consumer's _____ set.

12. The brands considered as feasible alternatives are judged on the basis of price, style, or any other _____ criteria that the consumer chooses to use.

13. The decision-making process does not end with the purchase of a product. After the purchase, the consumer will _____ the purchase and the resulting satisfaction. If postpurchase doubt occurs, the consumer experiences _____ , which he or she subsequently attempts to reduce.

Self-Test

1. Perception is the result of interaction of
   a. needs and motives.
   b. stimulus and individual factors.
   c. learning and attitudes.
   d. the real self and the ideal self.

2. The receipt of incoming information at a subconscious level is termed
   a. subliminal perception.
   b. subhuman perception.
   c. subcutaneous perception.
   d. learning.

3. Of the following components, the one that is **NOT a** component of attitude is
   a. affective.
   b. semantic.
   c. behavioral.
   d. cognitive.

4. One way that a marketer might attempt to change the *behavioral* component of attitude is to
   a. use subliminal advertising.
   b. provide new information to the customer.
   c. give out free samples.
   d. use advertisements to persuade the consumer.

5. The meaning that each person attributes to incoming stimuli received through the five senses is
   a. perception.
   b. attitude.
   c. learning.
   d. self-concept.

6. The consumer decision-making process includes all of the following steps **EXCEPT**
   a. evaluation of alternatives.
   b. postpurchase evaluation.
   c. search.
   d. cognitive dissonance.

7. When an advertiser makes a special effort to assure customers they have made the right choice, the advertiser is attempting to overcome
   a. the Asch phenomenon.
   b. consumer learning.
   c. consumer attitude.
   d. cognitive dissonance.

8. In self-concept theory, the way individuals view themselves is known as the
   a. self-image.
   b. looking-glass self.
   c. real self.
   d. ideal self.

9. One way that a marketer might attempt to change the *affective* component of attitude is to
   a. give out free samples.
   b. relate the use of the product to desirable consequences for the user.
   c. provide new information about the product's features.
   d. use subliminal advertising.

10. A marketer might attempt to change the *cognitive* component of consumer attitude by
    a. providing new information about the product's features.
    b. relating desirable benefits of using the product.
    c. giving out free samples.
    d. using celebrity endorsements.

Applying Marketing Concepts

Ted Thomas is a grinding-machine operator in a local factory not far from the small three-bedroom home where he lives with his wife, five-year-old daughter, and eight-year-old son. He recently received an inheritance when a relative died. Although the inheritance was modest, it provided enough money for Ted to make what was for him a major purchase. After analyzing all his wants and desires, he narrowed the decision to two choices: he would either buy a Yamaha 400cc motorcycle or make a large down payment to purchase a 27-foot Winnebago motor home.

Owning a motorcycle would enable him to join a local motorcycle touring club. He missed biking, which he used to do before he was married, and he would enjoy getting together with members of the club. Several of Ted's friends from work belonged to the club, including his boss. He liked the idea of getting away on the weekends, and getting to know his boss "couldn't hurt." However, his wife frowned when he mentioned the motorcycle and said he had better get the motor home instead—at least she would not worry about him being injured or killed.

Owning a motor home, on the other hand, would enable the whole family to get away for the weekend and give his kids an opportunity to get out into nature and away from the smoggy city. Ted decided to buy a motor home. When he went to look at recreational vehicles at the RV center to see what was available, he thought a small Winnebago would be in his price range. At the RV center he also saw Pace Arrow and Southwind motor homes. Finally, he bought a 31-foot Pace Arrow because of all the equipment and accessories it had. Although the motor home cost more than he planned to spend, he thought the larger size and completely equipped kitchen would make camping trips more enjoyable for his wife and children.

Less than two weeks later, after taking his family in the motor home on a weekend trip to a nearby national forest, Ted was reflecting on his purchase and beginning to have second thoughts. His children had not liked the trip at all. His daughter had a nightmare about a bear attacking the motor home, and his son complained about missing his favorite cartoons on Saturday morning. His wife was still trying to get over how much the monthly payments would be to pay off the balance owed on the motor home.

> **Select the best answer.**

1. The most important interpersonal influence on Ted was
   a. social class.
   b. reference group.
   c. culture.
   d. family.

2. Ted's postpurchase doubt is called
   a. cognitive dissonance.
   b. status loss.
   c. subliminal perception.
   d. psychotic imbalance.

3. The brands of motor homes thought of first by Ted are known as the
   a. evoked set.
   b. reference group.
   c. subgroup.
   d. evaluative set.

Additional Activities

Experiential Exercise

The purpose of this exercise is to help you improve your understanding of consumer behavior by examining the process you used in making a recent purchase. Select a significant purchase, such as clothing, car, sound system, computer, or other major item, that you have made recently. Use this purchase experience to answer the following questions:

- What brought you to recognize the need for this item?

- What sources of information did you use to determine the alternatives available to satisfy your needs?

- What were the different brands of the product you considered before you made the purchase?

- What factors led you to buy this brand over the others? Was it price, quality, size, performance, color, or something else?

- Where did you buy the product? What criteria led you to buy from that place?

- Did you have any cognitive dissonance after this purchase? Do you wish, for example, that you had purchased a different brand, from a different store, or had postponed your purchase altogether?

Now, assume you are a marketer of the type of product you purchased. If you wished to market your product to consumers who behaved as you did, what would you include in your marketing mix? (Marketing mix includes price strategy, product strategy, promotional strategy, and distribution strategy.)

Questions for Exploration

Conceptual

Do marketers study consumer behavior in order to meet the needs and wants that already exist? Or do marketers study consumer behavior in order to alter consumers' needs and wants to fit the desires of the producer? What is the actual practice? What should the practice be? Give some examples.

Practical

Not only must advertisements break through the clutter, they must do so with the advertiser's message. Too often advertisers feel that consumers love their ads but can't remember their products. Do you feel the TransAmerica Insurance advertisement shown in the video program for this lesson was successful at "breaking through the clutter" and in conveying TransAmerica's message? Why?

Answer Key

Key Concepts			
	1. j	5. c	9. f
	2. i	6. d	10. g
	3. b	7. e	11. k
	4. a	8. h	12. l

Completion

1. perceptions
2. sight, hearing, touch, taste, smell (any order)
3. individual, stimulus (either order)
4. perceptual
5. subliminal
6. attitude
7. affective
8. consumer attitudes, product
9. drives, cues, responses, reinforcement
10. discrepancy
11. evoked
12. evaluative
13. evaluate, cognitive dissonance

Self-Test		
	1. b	6. d
	2. a	7. d
	3. b	8. a
	4. c	9. b
	5. a	10. a

Applying Marketing Concepts	
	1. d
	2. a
	3. a

*. . . elements in the industrial and consumer marketing
mixes are as different as silicon chips and potato chips.*
—James D. Hlavack

8

Business/Industrial Marketing

Assignments

For the most effective study of this lesson, we suggest that you **complete the
assignments in the following sequence:**

1. Read the study guide Overview (Lesson Notes and Video Program
   Notes) and the Learning Objectives for this lesson.

2. Read *Contemporary Marketing Wired,* 9th edition, Chapter 9, pages
   294-327, "Business-to-Business Marketing" and Chapter 10, pages
   347-358, "Buyer-Seller Relationships in Business-to-Business Markets"
   and "Links Between Buyers and Sellers in Business-to-Business
   Markets."

3. View "Skyfox: A Case Study in Industrial Markets" video program.

4. Review the textbook assignment for this lesson.

5. Complete the Review Activities (Key Concepts and Completion),
   Self-Test, and Applying Marketing Concepts for this lesson.

6. Check your answers against the Answer Key at the end of the lesson,
   and review when necessary.

7. Complete any of the Additional Activities (Experiential Exercise and
   Questions for Exploration) that interest you or that are assigned by your
   instructor.

Overview

Lesson Notes

Business-to-business marketing refers to organizations that purchase goods and services to support production of other goods and services or daily company operations or for resale. The business market consists of the **commercial market,** individuals, and organizations that acquire goods and services for use in production; **trade industries** such as retailers and wholesalers, who acquire goods for resale to others; government organizations, which primarily purchase products in order to provide some sort of public benefit or service; and institutions such as colleges, churches, and other not-for-profit organizations.

Although most market segmentation is done for consumer markets, a small amount is done for business markets. In addition to geographic segmentation, two other approaches used in segmenting business markets are customer-based and end-use application. **Customer-based segmentation** divides a business market into homogeneous groups based on product specifications identified by buyers for organizations. **End-use application segmentation** divides a business market into homogeneous groups based on how different business purchasers will use a product.

The business market is distinguished from the consumer market because of the different types of demand that call for different marketing responses. These major types of demand are **derived demand** (demand linked to demand for a consumer product of which it is a component), **joint demand** (demand linked to another product necessary for use of the first product), volatile demand (immense variability in demand), and demand created by inventory adjustments (changes in inventory policy by purchasing organizations). Innovative, or just-in-time (JIT) inventory policies, involve cutting inventory to a minimum and receiving goods as needed. Sometimes JIT leads to **sole sourcing,** buying a firm's entire stock of a product from one vendor. In **outsourcing,** goods and services formerly produced in-house are acquired from outside.

The business market has several distinct characteristics: it is concentrated geographically, it has a relatively small number of buyers, it emphasizes more intense relationships between **buyers** and sellers than consumer relationships, and, in comparison to the consumer decision process, business buying is more complex.

Business buying usually involves more time, people, and specialized buying procedures than does consumer purchasing. The concentrated business market makes access through a professional sales force economically feasible.

Business buyers frequently select suppliers on the basis of service, certainty of supply, and efficiency of the products they supply. Systematic purchasing procedures are common in business markets. All those who participate in business buying are referred to as the **buying center**, and they play various roles: users, gatekeepers, influencers, deciders, and buyers.

In developing marketing strategies for the business market, marketers must also be familiar with the different kinds of organizational buying situations. The most complex situation is **new-task buying,** a unique situation in which an organization carefully analyzes all aspects of the buying process. Two other buying situations are the **straight rebuy**, in which an organization repurchases a satisfactory good or service, and the **modified rebuy**, in which an organization reevaluates available options before repurchasing a good or service. In **reciprocity**, a controversial practice in a number of organizational buying situations, purchasing preference is extended to suppliers who are also customers.

Two analysis tools that help professional buyers make purchase decisions are **value analysis,** a study of a purchase's components to determine a cost-effective way to acquire it, and **vendor analysis,** an ongoing evaluation of a supplier's performance in certain areas.

One segment of the business market, the government, is especially formalized in its purchasing processes. This government segment generally requires competitive **bids,** or written sales proposals, from producers in response to tightly drafted bid **specifications** describing needed items in detail. Buyers may consult online catalogs that help them compare products from competitors.

Other markets include institutions and international markets, which often practice **remanufacturing** or restoring of worn-out products. **Global sourcing** is the practice of contracting to buy goods and services from suppliers worldwide.

Video Program Notes

The video program for this lesson focuses on the Skyfox Corporation. This unique industrial producer manufactures aircraft from existing parts and sells them to large markets, such as governments. The program shows how Skyfox's marketing strategy minimizes many of the drawbacks of selling to the government, such as excessive paperwork, bureaucracy, and needless regulations. This program also details how the industrial market segment was identified and how Skyfox shaped its marketing mix to take advantage of legal, economic, and competitive environments.

As you watch the video program, consider the following questions:

1. Who are Skyfox's customers?

2. Despite its emphasis on production, what makes Skyfox market oriented?

3. Why did Skyfox locate in Mojave?

4. With what types of goods does Garrett Turbine supply Skyfox?

5. How does Garrett Turbine experience both joint demand and derived demand?

6. What are some of the problems that Skyfox experiences in trying to sell to foreign government markets?

7. What is Skyfox's pricing strategy?

8. What role does publicity play in Skyfox's promotional strategy?

Learning Objectives

After completing your study of this lesson, you should be able to:

1. Explain the following terms as they relate to business-to-business marketing:

bid	outsourcing
business-to-business marketing	reciprocity
	remanufacturing
buying center	sole sourcing
commercial market	specifications
customer-based segmentation	Standard Industrial
derived demand	Classification (SIC)
end-use application	straight rebuy
global sourcing	supply (value) chain
joint demand	systems integration
modified rebuy	trade industries
multiple sourcing	value analysis
new-task buying	vendor analysis

2. Identify the major components and characteristics of the business market.

3. Describe the primary approaches to segmenting business-to-business markets.

4. Describe major influences on business buying behavior.

5. Explain the buying center concept and describe the roles of buying center participants.

6. Describe the types of organizational buying situations and list the steps in the organizational buying process.

7. Describe the challenges of marketing to government, institutional, and international buyers.

8. Describe the major differences between consumer and business-to-business marketing.

Review Activities

Key Concepts

> Identify each of the following concepts of business-to-business marketing by writing the letter of the appropriate term in the blank next to the corresponding description.
>
> a. commercial market
> b. reciprocity
> c. trade industries
> d. buying center
> e. customer-based segmentation
> f. derived demand
> g. joint demand
> h. end-use application segmentation
> i. new-task buying
> j. sole sourcing
> k. multiple sourcing
> l. Standard Industrial Classification (SIC)
>
> m. bid
> n. specification
> o. systems integration
> p. value analysis
> q. vendor analysis
> r. straight rebuy
> s. modified rebuy
> t. global sourcing
> u. remanufacturing
> v. business-to-business marketing
> w. outsourcing

_____ 1. classification system the federal government uses to divide all types of business into broad industry groups

_____ 2. organizations that acquire goods and services for use in production or for resale

_____ 3. demand for business products linked to demand for consumer products

_____ 4. use of several vendors for purchase of supplies

_____ 5. divides a business market into homogeneous groups based on product specifications provided by organizational buyers

_____ 6. divides a business market into homogeneous groups based on how different purchasers use a product

_____ 7. retailers, wholesalers, and other organizations that purchase goods for resale to others

_____ 8. use of a single vendor for purchase of goods and services

_____ 9. extension of purchasing preference to suppliers who are also customers

_____ 10. when a firm buys the same product again without reevaluating the purchase decision

_____ 11. occurs when demand for one business product depends on the demand for another business product

_____ 12. refers to everyone who participates in an organizational buying action

_____ 13. detailed description of needed good or service

_____ 14. written sales proposal required by law for most government purchases

_____ 15. an initial or unique buying situation requiring considerable effort on the decision maker's part

_____ 16. ongoing assessment of a supplier's performance in such areas as timely delivery and attention to special requests

_____ 17. study of the components of a purchase to determine the most cost-effective way to acquire an item

_____ 18. when a firm reevaluates available options before repurchasing the same good or service

_____ 19. centralization of the buying function

_____ 20. when goods and services formerly produced in-house are acquired from outside vendors

_____ 21. practice of contracting to buy goods and services from international suppliers

_____ 22. restoring worn-out products to like-new condition

_____ 23. purchase of goods and services to use in producing other goods and services

Completion

Fill each blank in the following paragraphs with the most appropriate term from the list of completion answers below. A term may be used once, more than once, or not at all.

bids	end-use	purchasing
business goods	excessive	regulations
buying center	expense items	resale
capital items	gatekeeper	shortages
commercial	geographically	Standard Industrial
customer-based	influencers	Classification (SIC)
demand	inventory	supply
depreciation	production	trade

1. The largest segment of the business market is the _____ market.

2. The business market is more concentrated _____ than the consumer market.

3. A purchase by an organization is considered part of the business market if the product purchased is to be used for _____ or _____ .

4. Firms that buy goods and services for production of other goods and services are called _____ markets. Wholesalers and retailers, on the other hand, purchase solely for resale and are part of the _____ industries.

5. Organizational buying behavior is complex. Within an organization, many persons may influence the purchase decision, and several sources of _____ may be used to ensure against _____ . In addition, the purchase process may be very systematic and include a _____ manager, who devotes all of his or her time and effort to determining needs, locating and evaluating alternative sources of supply, and making purchase decisions.

6. The purchasing manager is one player on an informal team that takes part in the business purchase. Collectively, this team is referred to as the _____ .

7. The flow of information to the members of the buying center is controlled by the _____ .

8. The participants in the buying center who affect the buying decision by supplying information for the evaluation of alternatives or by setting specifications are known as _____ .

9. Demand for business goods and services may swing dramatically, depending on the _____ for the consumer products, the demand for other _____ to be used jointly with the purchased item, and the adjustments in _____ by potential purchasers of business goods.

10. Segmentation of business markets may be based on geographic location, product, and end use. When marketers want to focus on a particular segment of the business market, they can use the federal government's system that separates all types of businesses into distinct industry groups. This system is called the _____ .

11. Two approaches to segmenting the business market are _____ segmentation and segmentation by _____ application.

12. Government makes up a sizable segment of the business market. This market has been characterized by practices such as requiring sellers to submit _____ .

13. Many marketers complain that the government requires _____ paperwork and compliance with needless _____ .

14. Long-lived business assets such as buildings and equipment that must be depreciated over time are known as _____ .

15. Goods and services such as office supplies that are used within a short time are known as _____ .

16. In today's global marketplace, companies may practice _____ , contracting to purchase goods and services from suppliers worldwide.

Self-Test

1. The largest part of the business market comprises
    a. commercial markets.
    b. trade industries.
    c. government.
    d. industrial distributors.

2. Persons who have formal authority to select a supplier and implement procedures for securing the good or service are known as
    a. deciders.
    b. users.
    c. buyers.
    d. gatekeepers.
    e. influencers.

3. In business buying,
    a. usually only one person in a firm controls buying.
    b. committees are seldom used for purchasing.
    c. many organizations use several sources of supply for the same product.
    d. few firms have purchasing managers.

4. Derived demand means the
    a. demand for consumer goods depends on the demand for business goods.
    b. demand for business goods depends on the demand for consumer goods.
    c. higher the price for consumer goods, the greater the demand for business goods.

5. The government market
    a. is part of the consumer market.
    b. is declining in size at the state and local levels.
    c. makes purchases on the basis of bids.
    d. does not use specifications of needed items.

6. The federal government has grouped industrial markets into broad categories known as the
   a. Standard Industrial Classification system.
   b. Industrial Marketing System.
   c. Census of Manufacturers.
   d. General Industrial Classification System.

7. A buyer who is satisfied with the quality of photocopier paper and who decides to continue buying the paper from the same supplier is an example of a
   a. modified rebuy.
   b. constant rebuy.
   c. new-task buy.
   d. standardized purchase.
   e. straight rebuy.

8. Systematic study of the components of a purchase to determine the most cost-effective way to acquire the item is known as
   a. specification.
   b. vendor analysis.
   c. product classification.
   d. value analysis.

9. A characteristic of commercial producers is that they buy products that are
   a. resold as is directly to the ultimate consumer.
   b. resold as is to other industries.
   c. used in producing a product.
   d. consumed.

10. The division of a business-to-business market into homogeneous groups based on product use is called
    a. customer-based segmentation.
    b. end-use application segmentation.
    c. geographic segmentation.
    d. demographic segmentation.

Applying Marketing Concepts

Jane Trussel, sales manager for Lane Electronics, recently failed to make two important sales. In the first case, Boring Airplane Company decided to buy from Lane's competitor, Aviation Dynamics Company, which has controlling interest in an airline company that buys all its airplanes from Boring. This failure to sell was very costly, considering Trussel's sales team made seven calls on Boring over a period of several months. In the second case, Lane Electronics lost a potential U.S. Air Force contract because a Japanese firm proposed to supply the product at a lower cost. The U.S. Air Force ignored Trussel's arguments that the Japanese product would cost substantially more to maintain than that of Lane Electronics.

> **Select the best answer.**

1. The case of Boring Airplane Company favoring Aviation Dynamics over Lane Electronics may have involved
   a. bribery.
   b. reciprocity.
   c. derived demand.

2. Why did Lane lose the Air Force contract?
   a. Lane's bid was too high.
   b. Lane's product quality was too low.
   c. Lane's suppliers were not stable.
   d. Lane was unable to provide needed service.

3. Lane had to submit a bid for the Air Force contract.
   a. true
   b. false

4. The demand of the Boring Company would be derived from the demand for transportation by air.
   a. true
   b. false

Additional Activities

Experiential Exercise

The purpose of this exercise is to familiarize you with the marketing of goods to the government. Visit the office of a government agency located near your campus. You may select from among federal, state, or local organizations. Some agencies whose offices might be convenient for you to visit could include the local school district; your local police or sheriff's department; or city, county, or state administrative offices. Once you have made an appointment to visit, tell your contact person that you would like to know how that organization buys its equipment and supplies. In your interview, cover the areas described below.

- Ask about the methods the organization uses to make a purchase. Is purchasing the job of an individual, a committee, or a higher agency?

- Ask about the process of requesting bids and getting contracts. Are there any special rules that apply to this agency?

- Ask about the "bid list." Does the agency have one and how is it used, if at all?

Following your interview, write a brief report of your findings.

Questions for Exploration

Conceptual

Which concept seems most influential in business markets: the law of supply and demand or the marketing concept? Why?

Practical

In the video program for this lesson, Skyfox seems to be very closely tied to the Garrett Corporation, the company that supplies new engines for Skyfox. What are the advantages of such dependencies? The disadvantages? What do you think that Skyfox can do to capitalize on the advantages and to overcome the disadvantages?

Answer Key

Key Concepts			
1. l	7. c	13. n	19. o
2. a	8. j	14. m	20. w
3. f	9. b	15. i	21. t
4. k	10. r	16. q	22. u
5. e	11. g	17. p	23. v
6. h	12. d	18. s	

Completion		
1. commercial	9.	demand, business goods, inventory
2. geographically		
3. production, resale (either order)	10.	Standard Industrial Classification (SIC)
4. commercial, trade	11.	customer-based, end-use
5. supply, shortages, purchasing	12.	bids
6. buying center	13.	excessive, regulations
7. gatekeeper	14.	capital items
8. influencers	15.	expense items
	16.	global sourcing

Self-Test	
1. a	6. a
2. c	7. e
3. c	8. d
4. b	9. c
5. c	10. b

Applying Marketing Concepts	
1. b	
2. a	
3. a	
4. a	

America has believed that in differentiation, not in uniformity, lies the path of progress.
—Louis D. Brandeis

9

Market Segmentation

Assignments

For the most effective study of this lesson, we suggest that you complete the assignments in the following sequence:

1. Read the study guide Overview (Lesson Notes and Video Program Notes) and the Learning Objectives for this lesson.

2. Read *Contemporary Marketing Wired*, 9th edition, Chapter 7, "Market Segmentation, Targeting, and Positioning" pages 226-255.

3. View "Gold in the Hills: A Case Study in Market Segmentation" video program.

4. Review the textbook assignment for this lesson.

5. Complete the Review Activities (Key Concepts and Completion), Self-Test, and Applying Marketing Concepts for this lesson.

6. Check your answers against the Answer Key at the end of the lesson, and review when necessary.

7. Complete any of the Additional Activities (Experiential Exercise and Questions for Exploration) that interest you or that are assigned by your instructor.

Overview

Lesson Notes

For a group to constitute a **market** for a product, the group, in addition to the willingness to buy, must also meet two other prerequisites. First, the people or the institutions composing the market must have the purchasing power to buy; second, they must have the authority to buy.

A basic division of markets is into those for **consumer products**, which are purchased by the ultimate consumer for personal use, and **business products**, which are produced by businesses and industries for use, either directly or indirectly, in producing goods and services for resale.

Beyond that basic division, however, markets can be further divided into market segments. In **market segmentation**, the total market is divided into relatively homogeneous groups that are thought to be interested in similar products based on such factors as geographic location, demographic characteristics, psychographic characteristics, or the consumer's relationship to a specific product. Market segmentation and identification and selection of specific target markets from among those segments are critical first steps in developing a marketing mix strategy for most products.

Geographic segmentation is one of the oldest forms of market segmentation. Geographic segmentation can be used to identify purchasing patterns and tendencies for particular products. Consumer tastes for particular foods, for example, may vary among different regions of the United States, and rural and suburban populations may purchase more of such items as gardening supplies than do urban dwellers.

There are three types of classification of geographic segmentation by urban data: a **Metropolitan Statistical Area (MSA)**, or freestanding urban population center; a **Consolidated Metropolitan Statistical Area (CMSA)**, in which major populations are concentrated; and a **Primary Metropolitan Statistical Area (PMSA)**, an urbanized county or counties with ties to nearby areas. Marketers can also use a **Geographic** information system (GIS) or map containing computerized data about consumers in a certain area.

Dividing consumer groups according to such variables as sex, age, income, occupation, education, household size, and stage in the family life cycle is known as **demographic segmentation**. It is the most common form of market segmentation.

In comparison to demographic segmentation, **psychographic segmentation** provides more detailed information about consumers by examining their **lifestyles**—how people actually live their lives. One technique for developing lifestyle profiles of consumers is through analyzing responses to **AIO statements,** which reflect the "activities, interests, and opinions" of respondents. Another system used in psychographic segmentation is **VALS™ 2,** which stands for "values, attitudes, and lifestyles." Psychographic segmentation can be especially useful in understanding and predicting consumer behavior.

The last major type of market segmentation is **product-related segmentation**, which divides a population into homogeneous groups based on the benefits consumers expect to derive from a product, on their usage rates for a product, or on their degree of brand loyalty. According to the **80/20 principle,** a large amount of a product's revenues come from a small amount of customers.

To reach a decision on which target market segments will ultimately be selected for a specific product, marketing managers follow a five-step process: (1) identifying segmentation bases, (2) developing relevant profiles for each segment, (3) forecasting market potential, (4) forecasting probable market share, and (5) selecting specific market segments.

Once target markets have been selected, strategies can be developed that will best match a product to the needs of particular target markets. Four basic strategies for reaching target markets are undifferentiated marketing, differentiated marketing, concentrated marketing, and micromarketing. **Undifferentiated marketing**, also known as mass marketing, is used by organizations that produce only one product and market it to all consumers using a single marketing mix. A **differentiated marketing** strategy is used by organizations that produce numerous products and use different marketing mixes to reach specific market segments. The third strategy, **concentrated marketing**, also known as niche marketing, directs all of an organization's marketing resources to a small segment of the total market. Finally, **micromarketing** involves targeting potential customers at a very basic level.

Once marketers have chosen a strategy, they must decide how to place the product in the minds of potential buyers. This strategy is known as **positioning,** and may include using a **positioning map** to illustrate how buyers perceive competing products.

Video Program Notes

The video program for this lesson examines how the Irvine Company, a land-development firm in southern California, successfully used market segmentation to develop and sell houses to diverse groups of home buyers. Special attention is also given to how the attraction of diverse types of homeowners was central to the company's goal of building complete communities ("new towns") on the 90,000-acre Irvine Ranch.

Market segmentation was critical to meeting the company's marketing and social objectives because it provided a structure for growth and guided the actual design of the various types of housing. The company originally tried using psychographic segmentation, but it was not too successful. The program explains how the company turned to gathering information directly from home buyers about their needs and wants and then combined those findings with basic demographic data to determine the types of houses to build. Interviews with homeowners from many of the distinct communities within Irvine illustrate how the company has been able to target specific age, income, and lifestyle segments of the market.

Although the Irvine Company was able to use market segmentation successfully, rapid escalation of home prices in the late 1970s eliminated many potential buyers from the market. Prices eventually stabilized, and the Irvine Company was able to return to its original marketing strategy. In recent years, as the city of Irvine has grown and the demographics of the residents changed, the Irvine Company added different types of housing to the mix, designed to be more compatible with the increasingly urban nature of the city and to satisfy the changing needs of its residents.

As you watch the video program, consider the following questions:

1. What role did population shifts play in the rising need for new housing?

2. What kinds of segmentation are used in marketing for new housing?

3. What were the benefits of segmentation for the Irvine Company?

4. Why was demographic segmentation more useful than psychographic segmentation to the Irvine Company?

5. What types of demographic segmentation are shown in the program?

6. Why did the Irvine Company attempt to appeal to a cross section of market segments?

7. What are some examples of how a home is designed for a particular market segment?

8. How did inflation and subsequent recession affect the Irvine Company's attempts at market segmentation?

9. What role did price (or the home buyer's ability to purchase) play in the Irvine Company's segmentation strategy?

10. How has the growth of the city of Irvine influenced the Irvine Company's marketing segmentation strategy?

Learning Objectives

After completing your study of this lesson, you should be able to:

1. Define the following terms as they relate to market segmentation:

   AIO statements
   business product
   cohort effect
   concentrated marketing
   Consolidated Metropolitan
      Statistical Area (CMSA)
   consumer product
   demographic segmentation
   differentiated marketing
   80/20 principle
   Engel's laws
   family life cycle
   geographic information
      system (GIS)
   geographic segmentation
   lifestyle
   market
   market segmentation
   Metropolitan Statistical
      Area (MSA)

   micromarketing
   positioning
   positioning map
   Primary Metropolitan
      Statistical Area
      (PMSA)
   product-related
      segmentation
   psychographic
      segmentation
   repositioning
   target market
   target market decision
      analysis
   undifferentiated
      marketing
   VALS 2

2. Identify the components of a market and describe the role of market segmentation in developing a marketing strategy.

3. Describe the criteria necessary for effective segmentation.

4. Identify each of the four bases for segmenting consumer markets.

5. Identify steps in the market segmentation process.

6. Describe alternative strategies for reaching target markets.

7. Summarize the types of positioning strategies and the purposes of positioning and repositioning products.

Review Activities

Key Concepts

Identify each of the following concepts of market segmentation by writing the letter of the appropriate term in the blank next to the corresponding description.

a. market
b. concentrated marketing
c. consumer product
d. family life cycle
e. Engel's laws
f. lifestyle
g. AIO statements
h. target market decision analysis
i. market segmentation
j. differentiated marketing
k. geographic segmentation
l. business product
m. demographic segmentation
n. undifferentiated marketing
o. psychographic segmentation
p. VALS 2
q. product-related segmentation
r. geographic information system (GIS)
s. Primary Metropolitan Statistical Area (PMSA)
t. Metropolitan Statistical Area (MSA)
u. Consolidated Metropolitan Statistical Area (CMSA)
v. 80/20 principle
w. positioning
x. micromarketing

____ 1. form of demographic segmentation that concerns the process of family formation and dissolution

____ 2. people or institutions with willingness to buy, purchasing power, and the authority to buy

____ 3. good or service purchased by a consumer for personal use

____ 4. theory that as family income increases, a smaller percentage goes for food, the percentage for housing and clothing remains constant, and a larger percentage is spent on other items, such as recreation or education

_____ 5. strategy that directs all of a firm's marketing resources toward serving a single segment of the market

_____ 6. responses dealing with the activities, interests, and opinions of consumers used in formulating psychographic segmentation

_____ 7. evaluation of potential market segments on the basis of relevant characteristics

_____ 8. the way people decide to live their lives, including family, job, social activities, and consumer decisions

_____ 9. process of dividing the total market into several homogeneous groups

_____ 10. dividing a market into segments based on characteristics of the consumer's relationship to the product

_____ 11. dividing a market into segments based on the behavioral and lifestyle profiles of consumers

_____ 12. using factors such as age, sex, and income to establish market segments

_____ 13. using population location as a basis for market segmentation

_____ 14. a psychographic segmentation system that reflects consumer resources and self-motivation

_____ 15. strategy used by firms that produce numerous products and market each product to a specific market segment with a different marketing mix

_____ 16. good or service purchased for use directly or indirectly in the production of other goods and services for resale

_____ 17. strategy used by firms that produce only one product and market it to all customers with a single marketing mix

_____ 18. targeting potential customers at a very basic level

_____ 19. computer-based maps that record several layers of data

_____ 20. concept that a few buyers can account for much of a product's sales

_____ 21. major urban area within an urban giant

_____ 22. includes two or more PMSAs

_____ 23. freestanding urban area with an urban center population of at least 50,000

_____ 24. marketing strategy aimed at distinguishing, in the consumer's mind, a good or service from that of the competition

Completion

Fill each blank in the following paragraphs with the most appropriate term from the list of completion answers below. A term may be used once, more than once, or not at all.

age	family	positioning
activities	geographic	potential
attributes	heterogeneous	product-related
authority	homogeneous	profiles
bases	household	psychographic
benefits	income	purchasing
brand loyalty	increases	regional
concentrated	interests	segments
constant	larger	sex
decreases	location	share
demographic	map	smaller
differentiated	micromarketing	undifferentiated
diffused	occupation	usage
education	opinions	

1. A market represents people and institutions who not only have a willingness to buy but who also have _____ power and the _____ to buy.

2. Market segmentation is the division of the total market into relatively _____ groups. The process of market segmentation requires identification of factors that influence _____ decisions.

3. Markets can be segmented in various ways. The four principal types of consumer market segmentation are _____ , _____ , _____ , and _____ .

4. Geographic segmentation divides an overall market on the basis of population _____ . Geographic segmentation is useful only when _____ preferences exist.

5. The most common approach to market segmentation is _____ .

6. Among the variables considered in demographic segmentation are _____ , _____ , _____ , _____ , _____ , _____ size, and stage in the _____ life cycle.

7. Within the broad category of demographic segmentation, one of the most often used methods is segmentation by _____ , which is related to purchasing power.

8. Engel's laws, which describe the impact of changes in household income on consumer spending behavior, state that, as family income increases, a _____ percentage of expenditures goes for food; the percentage spent on housing, household operations, and clothing remains _____ ; and the percentage spent on items such as recreation _____ .

9. In general, psychographic segmentation refers to profiles of consumers. The profiles are usually developed by analyzing consumers' responses to statements about their _____ , _____ , and _____ .

10. Product-related segmentation focuses on the _____ that people seek in a product, on the _____ rates for a product, and on the _____ that consumers feel toward an item.

11. In segmenting either a consumer or business-to-business market, marketing managers follow a five-stage process. The first step is to identify market segmentation _____; the second is to develop relevant _____ for each segment; the third is to forecast market _____; the fourth is to forecast probable market _____; and the fifth is to select specific market _____ .

12. In marketing its products to specific target markets, a firm can use one or more of four strategies: _____ marketing, _____ marketing, _____ marketing, and _____ .

13. A firm that produces only one product line and markets it to all customers with a single marketing mix is using _____ marketing.

14. A firm that produces numerous products and uses different marketing mixes for different market segments is using _____ marketing.

15. A firm that focuses its marketing resources on one segment of the market is using _____ marketing.

16. A firm that targets customers at a very basic level, such as a specific occupation, is using _____ .

17. Marketers use a _____ strategy to place a product in a certain position in the minds of prospective buyers. A positioning _____ shows how consumers view competing products.

Self-Test

> **Select the best answer.**

1. Markets require people, a willingness to buy, and
   a. purchasing agents.
   b. purchasing power.
   c. authority to buy.
   d. all of the above requirements.
   e. the requirements in b and c.

2. Proper classification of a product as a consumer product or a business product is based principally on who the purchaser is and the
   a. size of the purchase.
   b. reasons for buying the product.
   c. type of product purchased.
   d. income level of the purchaser.

3. Dividing the total market into several homogeneous groups is called
   a. market gridding.
   b. market segmentation.
   c. sorting out.
   d. planning the marketing mix.

4. Which of the following is **NOT** one of Engel's laws? As family income increases, the percentage of income spent on
   a. food decreases.
   b. household operations and housing remains about the same.
   c. clothing remains about the same.
   d. transportation and entertainment remains about the same.

5. The family life cycle is based on
   a. age and income.
   b. lifestyle.
   c. marital status.
   d. number and ages of children.
   e. age, marital status, and number and ages of children.

6. Segmenting markets into hedonists, don't wants, the weight conscious, and the moderates is an example of
   a. geographic segmentation.
   b. demographic segmentation.
   c. psychographic segmentation.
   d. benefit segmentation.

7. Casters on a rollaway bed are business goods to the furniture manufacturer. If you go to the hardware store and buy an identical replacement, the new caster is
   a. still a business good.
   b. a consumer good.
   c. a resale good.
   d. a replacement good.

8. Segmenting markets into youngsters, oldsters, and in-betweens is an example of
   a. geographic segmentation.
   b. psychographic segmentation.
   c. demographic segmentation.
   d. benefit segmentation.

9. One of the ways in which product-related segmentation divides a population into homogeneous groups is according to
   a. who benefits from the product.
   b. the benefits the end user expects from the product.
   c. the features and benefits inherent in the product.
   d. the percentages of the population who benefit from the product.
   e. the age, sex, and income level of those who benefit from the product.

10. A firm selling just one product is using
   a. undifferentiated marketing.
   b. concentrated marketing.
   c. differentiated marketing.
   d. either concentrated or undifferentiated marketing.

Applying Marketing Concepts

Kay Collins, product manager for Mary Lou Cosmetics, Inc., was trying to decide what action should be taken in response to a move by the firm's major competitor, Tashmir Cosmetics. Tashmir had just introduced a new product aimed at the over-65 market. For years, Mary Lou Cosmetics had been the only firm in this market and had not tried to develop products for any other market. Tashmir, on the other hand, had a broad line of cosmetic products aimed at several different markets: preteens, teens, and adults under 65. The new product for Tashmir was simply a new product aimed at a new target market.

Select the best answer.

---

1. The strategy being used by Mary Lou Cosmetics is
   a. undifferentiated marketing.
   b. differentiated marketing.
   c. concentrated marketing.

2. The strategy being used by Tashmir Cosmetics is
   a. undifferentiated marketing.
   b. differentiated marketing.
   c. concentrated marketing.

3. If Mary Lou Cosmetics decided to broaden its promotional activities to encourage preteens, teens, and adults under 65 to use its product, it would be employing a strategy of
   a. undifferentiated marketing.
   b. differentiated marketing.
   c. concentrated marketing.

Additional Activities

Experiential Exercise

The purpose of this exercise is to help you understand the importance of market segmentation studies in isolating and evaluating markets. You are asked to apply the four principal types of segmentation (geographic, demographic, psychographic, and product-related) to a local restaurant with which you are familiar.

- Indicate the site of your chosen restaurant on a map of the town or city.

- How far from the restaurant do you think most of the customers live?

Identify the following demographic characteristics of the restaurant's regular customers: age, family life cycle, education income.

- Do you think the psychographic profile of the regular customers is different from that of most other residents of the city or town? If the psychographic profile is different, how does it differ?

- Why do you think the regular customers choose to eat at this restaurant rather than at some other restaurant? Describe the influence, if any, of each of the following factors on the customers' choice of this restaurant: food, atmosphere, prices, location, and entertainment.

- Note why you feel the restaurant's marketing mix (price, promotion, product, distribution) fits, or fails to fit, the needs and wants of the regular customers.

Conceptual

"Segmentation is really a ludicrous exercise, since it ignores individuality and arbitrarily lumps people together."

Agree or disagree with the above comment. Argue your case and cite examples.

Practical

In the video program on market segmentation, representatives of the Irvine Company say they segmented the market as part of their developmental efforts. From the evidence you saw in the program, did they (a) actually use their knowledge of consumer segments to develop their housing plans or (b) develop the housing plans on their own and then simply use their knowledge of consumer segments to figure out which housing types they would sell to what people?

Answer Key

Key Concepts			
1. d	7. h	13. k	19. r
2. a	8. f	14. p	20. v
3. c	9. i	15. j	21. s
4. e	10. q	16. l	22. u
5. b	11. o	17. n	23. t
6. g	12. m	18. x	24. w

Completion

1. purchasing, authority
2. homogeneous, purchasing
3. geographic, demographic, psychographic, product-related (any order)
4. location, regional
5. demographic
6. sex, age, income, occupation, education (any order); household, family
7. income
8. smaller, constant, increases
9. activities, interests, opinions
10. benefits, usage, brand loyalty
11. bases, profiles, potential, share, segments
12. undifferentiated, differentiated, concentrated (any order); micromarketing
13. undifferentiated
14. differentiated
15. concentrated
16. micromarketing
17. positioning, map

Self-Test

1. e	5. e	8. c
2. b	6. c	9. b
3. b	7. b	10. d
4. d		

Applying Marketing Concepts

1. c
2. b
3. a

The underdog in many products . . . can pick and choose where it wants to hit the giant; the giant, by contrast, must defend itself everywhere.

—George H. Lesh, former president, Colgate-Palmolive Co.

10

Product Adoption

Assignments

For the most effective study of this lesson, we suggest that you complete the assignments in the following sequence:

1. Read the study guide Overview (Lesson Notes and Video Program Notes) and the Learning Objectives for this lesson.

2. Read *Contemporary Marketing Wired,* 9th edition, Chapter 11, "Product Strategy," pages 370-393.

3. View "All the Right Moves: A Case Study in Product Strategy" video program.

4. Review the textbook assignment for this lesson.

5. Complete the Review Activities (Key Concepts and Completion), Self-Test, and Applying Marketing Concepts for this lesson.

6. Check your answers against the Answer Key at the end of the lesson, and review when necessary.

7. Complete any of the Additional Activities (Experiential Exercises and Questions for Exploration) that interest you or that are assigned by your instructor.

Overview

Lesson Notes

In marketing, "product" does not refer to a purely tangible item or a specific service. It is, instead, a concept that encompasses all the features associated with the product. In this sense, a **product** is a "bundle of physical, service, and symbolic attributes designed to enhance consumers' want satisfaction."

Products are divided into two broad categories—consumer and business—determined primarily by how they are used. Consumer products are created to be used by the ultimate consumer. Business products are used directly or indirectly in producing other products. Both categories are further subdivided.

The classification of consumer products is based on consumer buying behavior and divides the products into three groups: convenience, shopping, and specialty.

Convenience products are goods and services that consumers purchase often, immediately, and without much effort. Food, shampoo, magazines, dry cleaning, and shoe repair are examples of convenience products. Convenience products are further subdivided into the categories of staples, impulse products, and emergency items. Staples include items such as milk, bread, and gasoline, the need for which is ongoing. Impulse items are unplanned purchases of products such as specialty foods and novelties; an ice cream cone or a souvenir T-shirt, for example. Emergency items are purchased because of an unexpected, urgent need and include items such as a visit to the dentist because of a toothache and the purchase of an elastic bandage for a sprained ankle. Because consumers seldom spend much effort in purchasing convenience products, manufacturers make such products widely available in supermarkets, drugstores, convenience stores, and vending racks.

Shopping products, the second type of consumer products, are those that are purchased only after the consumer has compared competing products in competing stores or sources on the basis of such features as price, quality, style, and color. Clothing, furniture, and appliances, tires, home repairs, and gardening maintenance are examples of shopping products. Consumers view such shopping products as dishwashers and refrigerators as essentially the same; these products are termed homogeneous. Other products such as furniture and many clothing items are considered essentially different and are termed heterogeneous. Because of the efforts made by buyers of shopping products, producers of such products use fewer locations than do producers of convenience products.

The last category of consumer products, **specialty products**, includes items with unique characteristics that cause the buyer to prize them and make a special effort to purchase them. Specialty products are usually expensive and often carry a prestigious brand name: Dior, Cartier, Rolex, Ferrari. Their availability is usually limited to a few outlets.

Classification of consumer products is helpful because different consumer behavior is associated with each type of product. However, the classification is not perfect. Many products fall in between categories, and not all consumers behave alike when buying the same product.

In comparison to the classification of consumer products, which is based on consumer buying behavior, the classification of business products is based on product use. Business products are grouped into six major types: installations, accessory equipment, component parts and materials, raw materials, supplies, and business services.

Installations include major capital items such as computer and telecommunications systems, heavy machinery, and cargo ships that are expensive and relatively long-lasting. These items are used in producing final products. A firm purchasing an installation item is usually more concerned about the product's efficiency and performance than its price.

Accessory items are also capital items and are used in producing final products, but they are less expensive and shorter-lived than installations. Hand tools, laptop computers, and cash registers are examples of accessory items. In purchasing these items, a firm is probably concerned with price as much as it is with features.

Component parts and materials are the finished items of one producer that become part of the final product of another producer. Zippers and buttons that become part of dresses, slacks, and other clothing, as well as microchips and spark plugs, are examples of component parts and materials.

Raw materials comprise both farm products and natural products. Like component parts and materials, raw materials such as cotton and copper become part of final products.

Supplies are items that are used in a firm's daily operation but do not become part of the final product. Supplies, or **MRO items,** include maintenance items (vacuums, cleaning supplies), repair items (gaskets, screws), and operating supplies (toner cartridges, fax paper).

The last category of business products is **business services**, which encompass the intangible products that firms buy to facilitate their activities and operations. Insurance and legal and security services are examples of business services.

Most firms offer customers a series of related products, or a **product line,** since growth potential is limited when it concentrates on only one product. For example, a product line which centers on the cosmetic industry may include skin cream, facial cleansers, and concealers. By developing complete product lines, firms are motivated in several ways: they have the desire to grow, they receive optimal use of company resources, and their position is enhanced in the market.

Successful consumer and business products pass through different stages in what is called the **product life cycle**. The four stages of this cycle are introduction, growth, maturity, and decline. In the **introductory stage**, the objective is to stimulate demand for the new product. In the **growth stage**, when sales are rising, competitors are likely to enter the market. The **maturity stage** is characterized by continued sales growth in the early part, followed by a plateau in total sales, and then the beginning of a drop, when supply of the product starts to exceed demand. Finally, in the **decline stage**, there is an absolute decline in sales of the product, and producers stop making the product and search for alternatives.

Although almost all products experience the product life cycle, certain marketing strategies can extend the product's life cycle by increasing the frequency of use of a product, increasing the number of users, finding new uses, and changing package sizes, labels, or quality of the product. A firm may continue to carry an unprofitable product to meet customer demand.

A **product mix** is a group of related products that are usually measured in terms of width, length, and depth. Width refers to the number of product lines offered; length refers to the number of products for sale; and depth refers to variations of each product. In a **line extension,** a marketer introduces a new product that is related to existing products in the product line.

Video Program Notes

The video program for this lesson shows how Carushka, an entrepreneur, has developed and marketed an innovative line of dance and exercise wear. This program illustrates the concept of product by showing how Carushka's products are much more than tangible goods. For her customers, her products have desirable symbolic attributes (stylishness, prestige). Carushka, by making her products long-lasting and comfortable and by listening to her customers, provides the additional attribute of service that enhances the value of this consumer product.

The program also explores the product life cycle and its impact on Carushka's business and the techniques she used to extend the life cycle. In the early years, Carushka's product was demanded by consumers who buy new products, which helped create more demand for the product; in the later years, her product became almost a mass-market item. Of particular interest is the story of how Carushka, whose original business experienced problems because of a downturn in the market, re-created her business in a form that she now feels she can control and that provides her with exceptional satisfaction.

As you watch the video program, consider the following questions:

1. How does the product life cycle of fashions, such as Carushka's body wear, differ from that of other products?

2. Who were the first purchasers of a new line from Carushka?

3. How did Carushka originally distribute her product line in order to reach target consumers? How and why did this later change?

4. What sales promotion activities did Carushka perform in place of advertising?

5. When Carushka expanded into department stores, did her product change from being a specialty good to a shopping good?

6. Why do purchasers of Carushka body wear feel that it is more than just a "useful outfit"?

7. Why did Carushka's attempt to expand her line into men's body wear (the "Travolta line") fail?

8. Why did doing business become more difficult when the body-wear product entered the growth stage?

9. How did entry into the "maturity stage" of body wear affect Carushka's product/service strategy?

10. How has Carushka recreated her business?

11. At what stage in the product life cycle is her new business?

12. How does Carushka distribute her products in her new business?

Learning Objectives

After completing your study of this lesson, you should be able to:

1. Define the following terms as they relate to product strategy and adoption:

    accessory equipment
    business service
    component parts
        and materials
    convenience product
    industrial distributor
    installation
    line extension
    MRO item

    product
    product life cycle
    product line
    product mix
    raw material
    shopping product
    specialty product
    supplies

2. Describe a broad view of products.

3. Identify the three classifications of consumer products.

4. Identify the six classifications of business products.

5. Explain the concept of the product life cycle and techniques for extending the cycle.

6. Explain why most firms develop lines of related products rather than marketing individual products.

7. Identify the major product mix decisions that marketers must make.

Review Activities

Key Concepts

> Identify each of the following product strategy terms by writing the letter of the appropriate term in the blank next to the corresponding description.
>
> a. product
> b. product life cycle
> c. product line
> d. product mix
> e. line extension
> f. convenience product
> g. shopping product
> h. specialty product
> i. accessory equipment
> j. business services
> k. supplies
> l. component parts and materials
> m. raw material
> n. MRO item
> o. installation
> p. industrial distributor

_____ 1. series of related products produced and marketed by a company

_____ 2. group of product lines and single products measured by width, length, and depth

_____ 3. typical path of products from introduction to growth and maturity to eventual decline

_____ 4. introduction of a new product that is closely related to other products in a firm's existing line

_____ 5. combination of physical, service, and symbolic characteristics designed to enhance the want-satisfaction of consumers

_____ 6. product that consumers purchase frequently, immediately, and with a minimum of effort

_____ 7. product bought by a consumer who is well aware of what he or she wants and is willing to make a special effort to obtain the good or service

_____ 8. product purchased by the consumer only after comparison with competing products on such bases as price, quality, style, and color

_____ 9. finished business products that become part of a final product

_____ 10. intangible products bought by firms to facilitate their production process and ongoing operations

_____ 11. capital items, less expensive and shorter-lived than installations, such as laptop computers and photocopying machines

_____ 12. wholesaling marketing intermediary who often handles small accessory equipment and operating supplies

_____ 13. expense items necessary to the firm's daily operation but not part of the final product

_____ 14. major capital item, usually relatively expensive and long-lived

_____ 15. regular expense item used in maintenance, repair, or operations

_____ 16. a farm product or natural product used in producing a final product

Completion

Fill each blank in the following paragraphs with the most
appropriate term from the list of completion answers below.
A term may be used once, more than once, or not at all.

accessory	decline	other
equipment	depth	physical
awareness	evaluation	price
business	expansion	raw materials
business services	frequency	service
consumer's wants	growth	shopping
changing	highest price	shopping product
component parts	installations	specialty
and materials	interest	specialty product
consumer	introductory	supplies
consumer adoption	length	symbolic
process	life cycle	trial
convenience	lowest price	ultimate
convenience	marketing	uses
product	maturity	value
decay	number	width

1. From the marketing point of view, a product is a combination
   of _____ , _____ , and _____ attributes
   designed to enhance the _____ .

2. For example, a consumer who buys an exercise outfit (a tangible
   product) is buying more than the fabric and thread from which
   the garment is made. The tangible product (the outfit) and
   what the product enables the consumer to do (to exercise or
   dance in comfort) are considered _____ attributes. The
   fact that the outfit has a prestigious brand name well thought
   of by the consumer's friends is a _____ attribute. The
   manufacturer's lifetime guarantee to replace the product if it
   wears out is a _____ attribute.

3. The two major categories of products are _____ products
   and _____ products.

4. Consumer products are destined for use by the _____ consumer. Business products are used in producing _____ products for resale.

5. The three subcategories of consumer products are _____ products, _____ products, and _____ products.

6. Consumers purchase some products with a minimum amount of time and effort. A soft drink purchased at the nearest vending machine would probably be considered a

   _____.

7. However, if the consumer purchasing a soft drink wanted only Jolt Cola and was willing to go to several places to find this particular brand, the purchase would best be described as the purchase of a _____.

8. Some products are purchased after the consumer has given careful consideration to the prices and quality of several competing products. An automobile that was purchased after comparing prices and various features of several competing makes of cars would be considered a _____.

9. Consumers may perceive certain types of shopping products to be relatively homogeneous in style, quality, and product characteristics. In shopping for these homogeneous products, consumers usually look for the product with the _____.

10. The six major types of business products are _____, _____, _____, _____, _____, and

    _____.

11. New ships purchased by a cruise line are business products classified as _____. Such a purchase is a major decision, and the purchaser is usually more interested in the product's efficiency and performance than in _____.

12. Capital items that are usually less expensive than installations are classified as _____. Firms purchasing these items are more _____ conscious than they are when purchasing installations.

13. The finished business products of one producer that become part of the final product of another producer are known as _____.

14. Farm products and natural products are the main components of the _____ category.

15. The "convenience products" of the business market are represented by _____. These items are used in a firm's daily operation but are not part of the finished product.

16. Intangible products bought by firms to facilitate their production and operational processes are known as _____.

17. A product passes through a series of stages from the time it is introduced to the time it is no longer marketed; these stages are referred to as the product's _____.

18. As sales volume begins rising rapidly and the firm begins making profits on a product, the product has entered the _____ stage.

19. When total industry sales decrease and innovations begin replacing a product, a product's life cycle is in the _____ stage.

20. When a product first appears on the market, it is said to be in the _____ stage.

21. When total industry sales begin to reach a peak and competing products become more alike, the product is in the _____ stage.

22. An understanding of the product life cycle can be used to plan marketing strategy for a product and to prolong a product's life cycle. Among the techniques that can extend the cycle are increasing the _____ of use, increasing the _____ of users, finding new _____ , and _____ package size, labels, or product quality.

23. A product mix is a group of related products that are usually measured in terms of _____ , _____ , and _____.

24. Most firms offer customers a _____ , or series of related products.

25. The introduction of a fat-free candy bar that is already successful in its original high-fat version is called a _____ .

Self-Test

Select the best answer.

1. The most complete definition of *product* is
   a. the physical product along with any services designed to meet buyer needs.
   b. the physical product along with any symbolic attributes the buyer may desire.
   c. the physical, service, and symbolic attributes designed to enhance the want-satisfaction of buyers.
   d. any good or service that buyers want.

2. Consumer products may be defined as goods and services
   a. made by consumers.
   b. destined for use by the ultimate consumer.
   c. used to make other goods and services that are bought by ultimate consumers.
   d. described by all of the above.

3. Consumer products may be subdivided into
   a. shopping products, supplies, and services.
   b. convenience products, shopping products, and supplies.
   c. specialty products, shopping products, and services.
   d. convenience products, shopping products, and specialty products.

4. Finished goods that become part of another manufacturer's finished product are called
   a. accessories.
   b. component parts and materials.
   c. supplies.
   d. installations.

5. In the business market, the "specialty products" are represented by
   a. component parts and materials.
   b. business services.
   c. installations.
   d. accessory equipment.

6. By developing complete product lines, firms
   a. have the desire to grow.
   b. receive optimal use of company resources.
   c. enhance their position in the market.
   d. are motivated by all of the above.

7. The typical path of products from introduction to eventual deletion is known as the
   a. consumer adoption process.
   b. product life cycle.
   c. diffusion process.
   d. product management cycle.

8. During the introductory stage of a product's life cycle, it is generally true that
   a. sales rise slowly.
   b. the company profits greatly.
   c. many competitors enter the market.
   d. most sales are to existing customers.

9. During the growth stage of a product's life cycle, it is generally true that
   a. sales grow slowly.
   b. profits hold steady.
   c. many competitors enter the market.
   d. most sales are to new customers.

10. During the maturity stage of a product's life cycle, it is generally true that
    a. sales rise rapidly.
    b. profits are at their peak.
    c. most sales are to older adults.
    d. most sales are to people who have used the product before.

11. A group of related products measured in terms of width, length, and depth is called a
    a. product mix.
    b. line extension.
    c. raw material.
    d. convenience product.

12. When a marketer introduces a new product that is related to existing products in the product line, it is called a
    a. product mix.
    b. line extension.
    c. raw material.
    d. convenience product.

Applying Marketing Concepts

Jo Munro, sales manager of Parker Brake, Inc., was going over sales figures for a new type of metallic disc brake pad her company had introduced three years earlier. Sales of the product had increased the two years following introduction, but were beginning to decline in the last quarter of the current year. Several competitors had introduced similar pads shortly after Parker's breakthrough and new product introduction. However, sales had continued to climb as Parker lowered prices during this last year, and total industry sales were continuing to increase but at a slower rate than the previous year.

> **Select the best answer.**

1. At what stage of the product life cycle is the product?
   a. introductory
   b. growth
   c. maturity
   d. decline

2. If Jo Munro concluded that the product was in the decline stage of its life cycle, she would be wrong because
   a. total industry sales are increasing.
   b. her competitor's sales are increasing.
   c. her firm's sales are decreasing.

Additional Activities

Experiential Exercises

1. The product life cycle consists of four stages: introduction, growth, maturity, and decline. For each stage of the life cycle, specify a consumer product currently in that particular stage. Briefly explain what characteristics of the market for the product led you to place it in that stage.

2. The purpose of this exercise is to help you understand how a product's life can be extended. You are asked to suggest ways to extend the product life cycle for a variety of products and to identify products that might have their lives extended through creative marketing.

One way a product's life can be extended is by finding new users for the product. For example, Johnson & Johnson promotes the use of its Baby Shampoo by women and men. Another way to extend a product's life is by finding new uses for the product. Arm and Hammer promoted a new use for its baking soda—to absorb refrigerator odors—and thus extended the product's life. A third way to extend a product's life is simply to promote greater use of the product, as Florida Orange Juice Growers did by emphasizing that orange juice is not just a breakfast drink—it's an anytime drink. And a product's life can be extended by making physical changes, such as Domino's Pizza did by introducing garlic-crunch and cheese-filled crusts.

- Suggest ways that the manufacturer might seek to extend the life of Ajax cleanser, Kool-Aid drink mix, and Laura Scudder's potato chips by promoting new uses, finding new users, promoting increased usage, and making physical changes.

- List three other products in their maturity stage and suggest how the marketers might extend their lives.

Questions for Exploration

Conceptual

Why do people adopt a new product when their lives were perfectly happy before that new product ever existed?

Practical

What was the central problem that Carushka faced in promoting adoption of her initial product (the striped leotard)? Evaluate her strategies in this area. What did she do well? What did she do poorly? What other techniques could she have used to promote her product?

Answer Key

Key Concepts				
	1. c	5. a	9. l	13. k
	2. d	6. f	10. j	14. o
	3. b	7. h	11. i	15. n
	4. e	8. g	12. p	16. m

Completion

1. physical, service, symbolic (any order); consumer's wants
2. physical, symbolic, service
3. consumer, business (either order)
4. ultimate, other
5. convenience, shopping, specialty (any order)
6. convenience product
7. specialty product
8. shopping product
9. lowest price
10. installations, accessory equipment, component parts and materials, raw materials, supplies, business services (any order)
11. installations, price
12. accessory equipment, price
13. component parts and materials
14. raw materials
15. supplies
16. business services
17. life cycle
18. growth
19. decline
20. introductory
21. maturity
22. frequency, number, uses, changing
23. width, length, depth (any order)
24. product line
25. line extension

Self-Test				
	1. c	5. c	8. a	11. a
	2. b	6. d	9. c	12. b
	3. d	7. b	10. d	
	4. b			

Applying Marketing Concepts	
	1. c
	2. a

Product testing should not be the basis for introducing a new product because 90% of the failures have had successful product test results.

—Richard H. Buskirk

11

New Products

Assignments

For the most effective study of this lesson, we suggest that you complete the assignments in the following sequence:

1. Read the study guide Overview (Lesson Notes and Video Program Notes) and the Learning Objectives for this lesson.

2. Read *Contemporary Marketing Wired,* 9th edition, Chapter 12, "Brand Management and New Product Planning," pages 396-425 and Chapter 10, pages 349-352, "Co-Marketing and Co-Branding."

3. View "Coming of Age: A Case Study in New Products/Brands" video program.

4. Review the textbook assignment for this lesson.

5. Complete the Review Activities (Key Concepts and Completion), Self-Test, and Applying Marketing Concepts for this lesson.

6. Check your answers against the Answer Key at the end of the lesson, and review when necessary.

7. Complete any of the Additional Activities (Experiential Exercise and Questions for Exploration) that interest you or that are assigned by your instructor.

Overview

Lesson Notes

A **brand** is a name, term, sign, symbol, design, or some combination identifying a firm's products. A brand's success can be measured in terms of **brand recognition, preference,** or **insistence** on the part of the consumer. A manufacturer may decide to use the same brand on a line of products (**family brand**) or use **individual brands** for each product. Some firms sell **generic products** that have no branding. For consumers who choose generic products, the symbolic quality, prestige, or security associated with buying a well-known brand is outweighed by the price advantages of the generic product.

Brands can be private, manufacturer's, family, or individual. A **manufacturer's brand** refers to a well-known producer of the brand, such as IBM or Xerox. **Private brands,** such as Sears Kenmore, are placed on products marketed by wholesalers and retailers. In **brand equity,** certain brand names increase the value of a product. By using differentiation, relevance, esteem, and knowledge, firms can increase brand equity. Because brand equity is so important, marketers hire a **brand manager** to plan and implement strategies that will lead to strong brand equity.

Before introducing a new product, a **brand name** identifying and promoting the product is usually selected. Good brand names must be easy to say, recognize, and remember. The brand name should also evoke positive associations for the consumer and should be legally protectable. Failure to consider all of these factors can harm the new product's chances of success. Often, brand names become descriptive **generic names,** such as nylon. A **trademark** is a brand that legally gives the owner exclusive access.

In most products, the package serves as much more than just the container for the product. In fact, the package is sometimes the most innovative aspect of a new product (for example, the aerosol can for shaving cream). A package protects the product; it can also be used to promote the product, suggest methods of use, and for providing convenience; and it must be cost-effective. In some cases, the package is reusable (for example, returnable bottles).

Another aspect of packaging is **labeling.** Consumer dissatisfaction over packaging and labeling in recent years has caused many firms to change the informational content and package size of certain products. Federal agencies have assumed a significant role in specifying the type and amount of information on package labels. They also regulate product safety and safety standards since manufacturers and marketers are responsible for **product liability.** The Consumer Product Safety Commission, with its authority to ban, recall, or redesign products, has emphasized the need to produce safe products. Labels also indicate products that are environmentally safe. The development of the **Universal Product Code (UPC)** has saved labor costs and improved inventory control.

Some brands become so popular that marketers use their names on new products in unrelated categories. This practice is known as **brand extension. Brand dilution** results when there are too many brand extensions. Increasingly, firms practice **brand licensing,** in which other companies pay firms to use the seller's brand names. In **co-branding,** two strong brand names are joined to sell a product.

Because new products can mean new business, introducing new products into a product line is important. A full, dynamic product line can improve a firm's sales, allow optimum use of resources, increase a firm's hold on the market, and ensure that the firm will not become a victim of product obsolescence. Management must continuously evaluate the firm's product line to determine whether products need to be added or deleted. Four strategies for new-product development are market penetration, market development, product development, and product diversification.

Just as products move through a cycle, consumers go through distinct stages in accepting a new product. The **consumer adoption process** has five stages: awareness (consumers learn of the product), interest (consumers seek information), evaluation (consumers consider the benefits), trial (consumers purchase to determine the product's usefulness), and adoption/rejection (if consumers are satisfied, they will buy again). People who buy new products as soon as they are available are **consumer innovators.** The acceptance of new products is called the **diffusion process.**

The adoption rate is usually determined by: relative advantage, compatibility, complexity, possibility of trial use, and observability. Understanding these characteristics can be valuable to the marketer in developing techniques to speed the adoption rate.

Four different organizational arrangements are typically used to develop new products effectively: new-product committees, new-product departments, **product managers,** and **venture teams.** Successful product development follows a pattern of idea generation, screening, business analysis, development, test marketing, and commercialization. Careful planning and use of **concept testing** and **test marketing** sometimes help reduce risks of new products.

Video Program Notes

The video program for this lesson shows how the Robert Mondavi Winery brought a new product to market and what decisions it made along the way. Before deciding to produce a product, Mondavi analyzes market opportunity. Following the new-product development process, major decisions are made about specific wines to produce and market. Each element of the marketing mix—product, price, distribution, and promotion—is fully considered by the Mondavi staff. New-product decisions on branding and packaging and labeling decisions help to shape marketing of the product. Federal and state regulations also play an important role in the new-product decision-making process.

As you watch the video program, consider the following questions:

1. Does the Robert Mondavi Winery tend to be production oriented or consumer oriented?

2. What does Mondavi do to maintain a high price/ high-quality relationship image for the consumer?

3. What accounted for the rapid growth in the white-wine market between 1970 and 1980?

4. What was the effect of renaming the Sauvignon Blanc, making it Fumé Blanc?

5. What are some of the methods Mondavi used to promote the Mondavi brand? Why doesn't the company advertise?

6. Toward what market segments does Mondavi target its brands?

7. How does Mondavi use "opinion leaders" as "ambassadors" for its brands?

8. At what stage of the product life cycle is white wine? Muscato D'oro? Low-alcohol wine?

9. What role does the bottle label play in winning new customers?

10. Why did Mondavi eliminate several wines from its product line?

Learning Objectives

After completing your study of this lesson, you should be able to:

1. Explain the following terms as they relate to new-product planning and development:

adoption process	generic name
brand	generic product
brand dilution	individual brand
brand equity	label
brand extension	manufacturer's brand
brand insistence	parallel
brand licensing	product development
brand manager	phased development
brand mark	private brand
brand name	product liability
brand preference	product manager
brand recognition	product positioning
cannibalization	task force
co-branding	test marketing
co-marketing	trademark
concept testing	Universal Product Code
consumer innovator	(UPC)
diffusion process	venture team
family brand	

2. Describe how firms develop strong identities for their products and brands.

3. Describe alternative strategies for developing new products and explain how firms determine strategies for success.

4. List and describe the stages in the new-product development process.

5. Explain the role of product identification—including brand, branding, brand management, and brand equity—in marketing strategy.

6. Explain the various organizational structures for new-product development.

7. Identify the determinants of a new product's rate of adoption and the methods for accelerating the speed of the adoption.

8. Outline the functions of the Consumer Product Safety Commission, and summarize the concept of product liability.

9. Relate the concepts of co-marketing and co-branding to relationship marketing.

Review Activities

Key Concepts

> Identify each of the following terms related to new-product development by writing the letter of the appropriate term in the blank next to the corresponding description.
>
> a. concept testing
> b. product manager
> c. venture team
> d. test marketing
> e. cannibalization
> f. task force
> g. phased development
> h. product positioning
> i. parallel approach
> j. universal product code (UPC)
> k. product liability
> l. label

_____ 1. traditional pattern of developing new products in an orderly series of steps

_____ 2. new-product development group comprised of specialists from different areas of the organization

_____ 3. concept that businesses are responsible for injuries and damages caused by their products

_____ 4. marking on a package that is read by optical scanners

_____ 5. interdisciplinary group on temporary assignment that works through functional departments

_____ 6. process that involves teams of people from different departments in the development of a new product from idea generation to commercialization

_____ 7. individual who is given complete responsibility for the marketing decisions for a specific product or product line

_____ 8. introducing a new product with a complete marketing campaign in a specific city or television coverage area

_____ 9. contains the brand name, product composition and size, and other information for the buyer of the product

_____ 10. buyer's perception of a product's attributes, use, quality, advantages, and disadvantages in relation to competing brands

_____ 11. occurs when a product diverts sales from another offering in the same product line

_____ 12. measuring consumer attitudes and perceptions of a product idea prior to actual development of the product

Identify each of the following concepts related to product identification by writing the letter of the appropriate term in the blank next to the corresponding description. Some terms may be used more than once.

a. family brand
b. manufacturer's brand
c. private brand
d. individual brand
e. generic product
f. generic name
g. brand extension
h. brand

i. trademark
j. brand recognition
k. brand preference
l. brand insistence
m. brand licensing
n. brand mark
o. brand name
p. brand equity

_____ 13. also known as a national brand

_____ 14. "Fresh 'n' Fruity"—a line of tropical fruit marketed by Northern Produce, a food wholesaler

_____ 15. brand name used for several products, such as Hunt's Ketchup, Hunt's Tomato Paste, and so on

_____ 16. brand name, such as Dove soap, that is used for just one product

_____ 17. food or household staple that is characterized by a plain label, little or no advertising, and no brand name; competes with branded items based on price

_____ 18. Sears Kenmore appliances that are made by Whirlpool

_____ 19. names such as cola, nylon, and aspirin

_____ 20. Tide or All or Bold or Fab

_____ 21. that part of a brand consisting of words or letters in a name used to distinguish a firm's offerings from those of competitors

_____ 22. ultimate stage in brand acceptance in which buyers will not accept substitute brands and will search extensively for the specific brand of good or service

_____ 23. stage of brand acceptance in which consumers choose a specific brand based on previous experience with the product, rather than competing brands

_____ 24. achieved when buyers can remember having seen or heard of a brand, but do not prefer it

_____ 25. name, term, sign, symbol, design, or some combination of these devices used to identify the products of one firm

_____ 26. brand that has legal protection exclusive to its owner

_____ 27. marketing strategy of using a popular brand name for a new-product entry in an unrelated product category

_____ 28. symbol or pictorial design used to identify a product

_____ 29. allowing another firm to use a brand name for a fee

_____ 30. added value a certain brand name gives to a product

Completion

> Fill each blank in the following paragraphs with the most appropriate term from the list of completion answers below. A term may be used once, more than once, or not at all.
>
> | | | |
> |---|---|---|
> | abandon | connotation | information |
> | brand | consumer adoption | innovators |
> | brand extension | process | legally |
> | brand insistence | continue | manufacturer's |
> | brand name | convenient | national |
> | brand preference | costs | new products |
> | brand recognition | customers | packaging |
> | business analysis | development | pilferage |
> | buyers | easy | private |
> | cannibalization | family | protect |
> | commercialization | generic | resources |
> | company | generic product | screening |
> | compatibility | idea generation | test marketing |
> | complexity | individual | vocalize |
> | concept testing | | |

1. When a new product is introduced, individual consumers must decide whether or not they will buy the product. The decision-making process involved in adopting a new product is referred to as the _____ .

2. The first consumers to adopt a new product are called consumer _____ .

3. Sometimes a firm unwisely introduces a new product that "eats up" sales that otherwise would have been made of a product already in the firm's line. This event is known as _____ .

4. The adoption rate is influenced by five characteristics of the new product: relative advantage, possibility of trial use, observability, _____ , and _____ .

5. Most firms attempt to spread operating costs over several related products in order to optimize use of company _____ and to reduce average _____ .

6. Another factor that influences new-product planning is the company's desire to exploit the product life cycle. Since every product eventually reaches the decline stage, a company with only one product faces eventual sales decline and extinction. Through exploitation of the product life cycle, a firm may avoid overall sales decline by continually introducing _____ .

7. The introduction of "new" products by a company does not necessarily mean products that have never appeared on the market. A new product may be defined as a product that is new to _____ or new to the _____ .

8. When management determines buyer reactions to a new product by marketing initially in a limited area, it is _____ .

9. The step in which a company converts a product idea into a physical product is known as _____ .

10. When management separates ideas for new products with potential from those that do not meet company objectives, it is _____ ideas.

11. The step in the new-product development process in which concepts for new products emerge is known as new-product _____ .

12. The step in new-product development in which the company conducts a detailed study of specific product ideas to determine potential, growth rate, and compatibility with company resources is known as _____ .

13. The step in which full-scale marketing of a new product takes place is called _____ .

14. In sequence, the six steps in new-product development are _____ , _____ , _____ , _____ , _____ , and _____ .

15. If a firm asks potential buyers to evaluate the product idea, the firm is using the technique of _____ .

16. At each stage prior to commercialization, management must choose among three available alternatives. Management can _____ the project, _____ to the next stage, or seek more _____ before proceeding.

17. All products must be given identities by the companies that are marketing them. Products are identified through the use of _____ names, symbols, and distinctive _____ .

18. A name, term, symbol, design, or some combination of these devices used to identify the product of a particular company is called a _____ . The part formed with words or letters should be easy to _____ . These words or letters are referred to as a product's _____ .

19. A brand should be acceptable to consumers. Brand acceptance may be measured in three stages. When consumers are aware that a brand exists but are not particularly predisposed to buy that brand, the brand has achieved the stage of _____ .

20. Some consumers will choose a particular brand if it is available. If it is not available, a substitute brand may be purchased. Choosing a particular brand, if available, is referred to as _____ .

21. When consumers become so convinced of a product's merits that they will accept no alternatives, a brand has reached the stage of _____ .

22. The degree of brand acceptance will depend on whether a good brand name is chosen. A good brand name is _____ to pronounce, recognize, and remember, has the right _____ , and is _____ protectable. Legal protection of a brand is lost if the brand name is ruled to be legally _____ .

23. If Yamaha Motorcycles decided to develop a line of sportswear and riding clothes for motorcyclists and to brand them Yamaha-Wear, the company would be practicing the strategy of _____ .

24. Brands may be classified as family brands or individual brands. Campbell's Vegetable Soup and Campbell's Pork and Beans are examples of the use of _____ brands.

25. Although Procter and Gamble markets several different detergents, such as Tide, Cheer, and Oxydol, each has its own brand name. This is an example of the use of _____ brands.

26. Some wholesalers and retailers offer their own brands of products that compete with the manufacturer's brands. These are called private brands. Manufacturer's brands

are sometimes called national brands. The Sears DieHard Battery would be called a _____ brand, while Honda's Accord would be called a _____ brand.

27. Some products do not rely on any branding identification; low prices are the primary appeal used to sell these products. A can of string beans with no brand name is an example of a _____ .

28. Package design is an integral part of product strategy. Packaging can_____ the product from physical hazards, encourage consumers to select the product from store shelves, or, like aerosol or pop-top cans, make it more _____ to use the product.

29. Packages have to meet the needs of retailers, who face losses from product theft. Products packaged with oversize cardboard backing can prevent _____ .

Self-Test

> **Select the best answer.**

1. The new-product development stage in which ideas with potential are separated from those not meeting company objectives is called
   a. test marketing.
   b. idea generation.
   c. business analysis.
   d. commercialization.
   e. screening.

2. A buyer's perception of a product's attributes, use, quality, advantages, and disadvantages is known as product
   a. positioning.
   b. recognition.
   c. preference.
   d. insistence.

3. The part of the new-product development process designed to determine consumer reaction to a product is called
   a. idea generation.
   b. concept testing.
   c. screening.
   d. business analysis.

4. The first step in developing a new product is
   a. commercialization.
   b. test marketing.
   c. idea generation.
   d. business analysis.

5. A name, sign, symbol, design, or some combination of these devices used to identify the products of one firm and to differentiate them from competitive offerings is a
   a. brand name.
   b. brand.
   c. product.
   d. label.

6. The highest stage of brand acceptance is brand
   a. preference.
   b. recognition.
   c. name.
   d. insistence.

7. The detailed study of specific product ideas to determine potential growth rate and compatibility with company resources is known as new-product
   a. commercialization.
   b. idea generation.
   c. business analysis.
   d. test marketing.

8. The part of the brand consisting of words or letters forming a name used to identify and distinguish the firm's offerings from those of competitors is known as the
   a. package.
   b. brand name.
   c. label.
   d. product.

9. The term "family brand" refers to
   a. one brand name used for several products made by the same firm.
   b. brand names that identify the family that started the business.
   c. brand names used by families.
   d. such brands as Cragmont sold exclusively by the Safeway supermarket chain.

10. Products known by their own brand name, such as Tide or Crest, rather than by the name of the manufacturer, are
    a. family brands.
    b. individual brands.
    c. generic brands.
    d. product brands.

11. The first group of customers to buy a new product is referred to as
    a. consumer innovators.
    b. consumer adopters.
    c. early adopters.
    d. leaders.

12. The stage of the consumer adoption process in which a consumer considers whether the product may satisfy a personal want is the
    a. interest stage.
    b. trial stage.
    c. awareness stage.
    d. evaluation stage.

Applying Marketing Concepts

The Sherwood Company has been making vitamins for the past fifty years. Originally, it developed and marketed a new high-potency vitamin C capsule containing ten times the normal daily requirement of this vitamin. Recently, Magnum Force, a manufacturer of weight-training equipment, joined Sherwood to develop a new line of fitness products combining a regime of exercise and vitamin supplements.

Select the best answer.

---

1. Each new product addition has carried the same brand name as the very first product: Sher C, Sher A, Sher B, and so on. This type of branding is an example of
   a. individual brands.
   b. family brands.
   c. private brands.
   d. generic brands.

2. Sherwood was recently approached by a large retail drug chain that wants to buy its vitamin E. The product would be marketed under the drug chain's name. This type of branding is an example of
   a. individual brands.
   b. family brands.
   c. private brands.
   d. generic brands.

3. The decision to develop the new line of products together is an example of
   a. brand extension.
   b. cannibalization.
   c. co-branding.
   d. product positioning.

4. If the Sherwood Company decided to market and evaluate Sher E in Sacramento, California, before going national, it would be using
   a. product testing.
   b. limited marketing.
   c. concept testing.
   d. test marketing.

Additional Activities

Experiential Exercise

The purpose of this exercise is to help you understand the requirements for package design, layout, eye appeal, and uniqueness that the marketer must consider in putting together a complete product image. You are asked to create a package for a new product with appropriate package information, incentives, visual appeal, key phrases, and color coordination, and to describe five factors that would affect the type and style of package design.

The package is frontline promotion. Its design and engineering are an art and a science. Building a safe, easily opened, properly sized, shelf-fitting, and durable package requires the most current engineering expertise. The color, layout, type, and graphic design of a package are put together properly only by the most creative and sensitive marketer. Each package must compete with a myriad of other products to attract the buyer's attention.

The buyer may have heard of or seen the product in mass media advertising, but unless the package on the shelf lives up to the buyer's expectations of visual appeal, freshness, attractiveness, and usefulness, the sale may well be lost. The package gives the buyer in-hand feedback, either negative or positive.

For this project, choose one of the following products:

- A family cereal called Mountain Nuggets—an all-natural product containing nuts and pieces of dried pears, lightly sweetened with molasses.

- A snack food called Tri-Pro, which has three times the protein of any other boxed snack food on the market.

- An instant dessert called Fudge a Little—a creamy, low-calorie dish with a bottom layer of brownies and a top layer of pudding.

- For the product you have selected, create an original package design. Cover an appropriately sized existing package (such as a box of breakfast cereal) with plain paper. Use colors, layout, type, and graphic designs to make an attractive package that would be likely to appeal to target customers. You may use cartoons, logos, photos, coupons, puzzles, or whatever you feel is appropriate for your package design. (*Suggestion:* Design each panel of the package separately, then paste it onto the box.)

Questions for Exploration

Conceptual

What is the difference between a new product and one that is merely an incremental adaptation of an existing product? For example, is a Mr. Coffee with a built-in digital clock different enough from a Mr. Coffee without a clock to be considered a new product? What are the implications for the marketing strategy?

Practical

If the Mondavi Winery were to use its product knowledge of wines to enter the new "alcohol-free" wine market or the "jug-wine" market, should it use the Mondavi family brand name? Why?

Answer Key

Key Concepts				
	1. g	9. l	17. e	25. h
	2. c	10. h	18. c	26. i
	3. k	11. e	19. f	27. g
	4. j	12. a	20. b	28. n
	5. f	13. b	21. o	29. m
	6. i	14. c	22. l	30. p
	7. b	15. a	23. k	
	8. d	16. d	24. j	

Completion

1. consumer adoption process
2. innovators
3. cannibalization
4. compatibility, complexity (either order)
5. resources, costs
6. new products
7. customers, company
8. test marketing
9. development
10. screening
11. idea generation
12. business analysis
13. commercialization
14. idea generation, screening, business analysis, development, test marketing, commercialization
15. concept testing
16. abandon, continue, information
17. brand, packaging
18. brand, vocalize, brand name
19. brand recognition
20. brand preference
21. brand insistence
22. easy, connotation, legally, generic
23. brand extension
24. family
25. individual
26. private, manufacturer's
27. generic product
28. protect, convenient
29. pilferage

Self-Test			
	1. e	5. b	9. a
	2. a	6. d	10. b
	3. b	7. c	11. a
	4. c	8. b	12. d

Applying Marketing Concepts		
	1. b	3. c
	2. c	4. d

You know you've bought a service and not a product when, after you've spent your money, you have nothing you can hold in your hand.

—George Spelvin

12

Services

Assignments

For the most effective study of this lesson, we suggest that you complete the assignments in the following sequence:

1. Read the study guide Overview (Lesson Notes and Video Program Notes) and the Learning Objectives for this lesson.

2. Read *Contemporary Marketing Wired,* 9th edition, Chapter 13, "Marketing of Services," pages 430-453.

3. View "Testing the Waters: A Case Study in Service Strategy" video program.

4. Review the textbook assignment for this lesson.

5. Complete the Review Activities (Key Concepts and Completion), Self-Test, and Applying Marketing Concepts for this lesson.

6. Check your answers against the Answer Key at the end of the lesson, and review when necessary.

7. Complete any of the Additional Activities (Experiential Exercise and Questions for Exploration) that interest you or that are assigned by your instructor.

Overview

Lesson Notes

Services account for about three-quarters of the U.S. gross domestic product. The marketing of services is similar to the marketing of goods in that the marketing-mix elements include service, price, distribution, and promotion. By using a **goods-services continuum,** marketers can easily see the differences between goods and services.

When marketing services, the marketer must first identify services that will satisfy chosen consumer segments. The service itself must be defined, and the marketer must successfully manage it through its life cycle and the consumer adoption process. The marketer must also determine how and where the service will be provided and how to make it accessible and available to potential consumers.

The marketer must also select appropriate pricing strategies for the services, or the different combinations of services and goods, offered to consumers. Price determination is typically made by totaling the cost of offering the service, the cost of promoting it, and the company's desired profit. Of course, this asking price must be tempered by external forces such as what the competition is charging and what the customer is willing to pay.

Although there are many similarities in marketing goods and services, there are also important distinctions. First, services can exist independent of any physical goods. This characteristic makes the service provider's reputation an important variable in the consumer adoption process. Because services are intangible, the promotion of a service is often more difficult than the marketing of a good. For this reason, creative promotion often plays a greater role in marketing services than in marketing goods.

The consumer often perceives services and the service provider as one entity. This makes reputation, image, and high customer-service standards essential to the success of the service firm.

Services are perishable; they cannot be stored. This fact makes it difficult to match the supply of services with the demand. A house painter cannot save the rainy days when he couldn't paint; a cruise ship cannot store empty cabins, entertainment, and food for later cruises. It is also difficult to standardize services.

Buyers of services are often more involved than buyers of goods in defining the services they buy. While goods are usually bought as is, services are often purchased after interaction between the service provider and the consumer. For example, magazine writers tailor articles to meet the needs of publishers; a vacationer may purchase a personalized vacation package from a wide range of choices offered by the travel agent. The communication between the buyer and the seller of services helps to define the service that will be purchased.

Services also have several variations in **service quality,** which is determined by five variables. They are: tangibles, reliability, responsiveness, assurance, and empathy. Sometimes **gaps,** or differences between expected service quality and perceived service quality, occur. Gaps include misperceptions, differences between intentions and the service itself, poor communications, and low standards. Most buyers perceive service quality during the **service encounter,** or the point of interaction between service providers and customers. Like producers of goods, economic, social-cultural, political-legal, technological and competitive forces vary for service firms, as well.

Part of a company's service strategy involves deciding whether to focus all efforts on a single service or to develop an entire line of related services. By offering a range of services, a company can improve its sales, allow maximum use of resources, reduce down-time, and balance the losses from services in the introductory or decline stages with profits from services in the growth or early maturity stages.

Video Program Notes

Western Cruise Lines, a service company providing cruise vacations aboard the SS *Azure Seas* to a wide range of consumer segments, is the subject of the video program for this lesson. This program shows how the service marketing manager developed a marketing mix for selected target consumers. The marketer had to decide what services to offer (for example, the kinds of entertainment, food, and accommodations; the length of each cruise; the destinations); what prices to charge; and how and where to promote each service.

As you watch the video program, consider the following questions:

1. What services does Western Cruise Lines provide?

2. What consumer need does a cruise fulfill?

3. Why didn't Western's attempt to duplicate Eastern Cruise Lines' marketing strategies work?

4. Why is the cruise considered both "intangible" and "perishable"?

5. What factors were considered in setting the price of the cruise?

6. Who serves as Western's sales force to consumers?

7. How did Western Cruise Lines solve its problem of extremely low consumer recognition?

Learning Objectives

After completing your study of this lesson, you should be able to:

1. Define the following terms as they relate to the marketing of services:

gap	service
goods-services continuum	service encounter
productivity	service quality
relationship quality	tertiary industry

2. Distinguish between goods and services.

3. Identify the primary characteristics of services.

4. Describe the determinants of service quality.

5. Outline possible outcomes of a service encounter.

6. Develop a classification system for services.

7. Explain how environmental factors affect services.

8. Discuss marketing mix and market segmentation for services.

Review Activities

Key Concepts

Identify each of the following concepts related to the marketing of services by writing the letter of the appropriate term in the blank next to the corresponding description.

a . service
b . service encounter
c . service quality
d . relationship quality
e . productivity
f . gap
g . goods-services continuum
h . tertiary industry

_____ 1. a way of visualizing the differences and similarities between goods and services

_____ 2. intangible task that satisfies the needs of consumers or business users

_____ 3. the primary determinant of consumer satisfaction or dissatisfaction

_____ 4. difference between expected service quality and perceived service quality

_____ 5. interaction point between the customer and service provider

_____ 6. industry involved in the production of services

_____ 7. a worker's output

_____ 8. buyer's trust in and satisfaction with a seller

Completion

Fill each blank in the following paragraphs with the most appropriate term from the list of completion answers below. A term may be used once, more than once, or not at all.

assurance	inseparable	responsiveness
business	intangible	services
competitive	involved	social-cultural
consumer	needs	standardize
demographic	perishable	stored
development	political-legal	tangibility
economic	provider	technological
empathy	pure	variable
goods	reliability	wants

1. According to the textbook, consumers buy goods and services for the same basic reasons. Therefore, a company's basic objective should be to offer goods and services that satisfy consumer _____ and _____.

2. The intangible tasks that satisfy the needs of consumers and business users when efficiently developed and distributed to chosen market segments are classified as _____.

3. A goods-services continuum is a diagram used to help visualize the differences and similarities between _____ and _____.

4. Some products have no service component and are called _____ goods. Similarly, pure services, at the other end of the goods-services continuum, have no _____ component.

5. Services have certain characteristics that distinguish them from goods. In contrast to goods, services are _____ and _____. In buyers' minds, services are _____ from the service provider, and buyers are often _____ in the development and distribution of services. Another characteristic of services is that it is often impossible to _____ offerings among sellers of the same service or even the service of a single provider. Finally, the quality of services is highly _____.

6. Service facilities may be idle during slack periods because services cannot be _____ until later periods. Therefore, services are considered _____.

7. The expected and perceived quality of a service offering is referred to as service quality, which is determined by five variables. One of these variables is the physical evidence of the service, or _____. Other variables include the consistency of performance and dependability, also known as _____; the willingness and readiness of employees to provide service, or _____; the confidence communicated by the service provider, or _____; and the service provider's efforts to understand the customer's needs, or _____.

8. Although _____ expenditures for services have increased rapidly, the growth in _____ expenditures for services has been even more marked.

9. Because they shape the kinds of services customers want, changes in the _____ environment have a significant impact on the offering and marketing of services.

10. Future growth in the service sector may be determined primarily by the _____ environment.

11. The most commonly used segmentation variable for service marketers is _____.

Self-Test

| Select the best answer. |

1. The method presented in the textbook for visualizing the differences and similarities between goods and services is the
   a. product profile.
   b. goods-services continuum.
   c. goods-services analysis.
   d. service index.

2. The intangible tasks that satisfy the needs of consumers and business users when efficiently developed and distributed to chosen market segments are referred to as
   a. the goods-services continuum.
   b. services.
   c. intangible products.
   d. pure goods.

3. Products that have no service component are known as
   a. tangibles.
   b. pure services.
   c. service voids.
   d. pure goods.

4. Consumer services may be defined as services
   a. made by consumers.
   b. for the ultimate consumer.
   c. performed to sell goods.
   d. that are consumed.

5. Pure services at one end of the goods-services continuum have no
   a. consumers.
   b. sellers.
   c. goods component.
   d. distribution component.

6. A service is
   a. intangible.
   b. indescribable.
   c. inert.
   d. undefinable.

7. Service facilities may sometimes be idle, because a service cannot be
   a. measured.
   b. distributed.
   c. stored.
   d. used.

8. Services are difficult to
   a. obtain.
   b. standardize.
   c. price.
   d. buy.

9. In comparison to marketers of goods, marketers of services have
   a. more interaction with customers.
   b. less interaction with customers.
   c. about the same amount of interaction with customers.

10. In comparison to the promotion of goods, the promotion of services is
   a. more difficult.
   b. less difficult.
   c. about the same in difficulty.

Applying Marketing Concepts

Sally Smith, owner of Sally Forth, Inc., is assessing the progress of her new business venture, shopping for people who don't have time to shop for themselves. Sally Smith is quite pleased; she has had to hire five additional shoppers to handle the avalanche of requests for things that people need to buy but can't find time to go out and get. The 20 percent surcharge over the cost of any merchandise purchased doesn't seem to bother many of the people who call to request the service.

Select the best answer.

1. Sally Forth provides a
   a. consumer service that's equipment based.
   b. business service that's people based.
   c. consumer service that's people based.
   d. business service that's equipment based.
   e. business service with a goods component.

2. The need for a service like Sally Forth arises from changes in the
   a. economic environment.
   b. social-cultural environment.
   c. political-legal environment.
   d. technological environment.
   e. competitive environment.

3. If intended use were the basis, Sally Forth would be classed as a
   a. consumer convenience service.
   b. consumer specialty service.
   c. diversified consumer service.
   d. general business service.
   e. specialty business service.

Additional Activities

Experiential Exercise

The purpose of this exercise is to help you understand the goods-services continuum.

- First, list five companies that demonstrate a range across the goods-services continuum and state whether each company is people-based or equipment-based. Indicate where the company belongs on the goods-services continuum by writing the number of the company where appropriate. Hairstyling, for example, is a people-based service that would be placed toward the pure service end of the continuum.

```
┌─────────────────────────────────────────────────┐
│           Goods-Services  Continuum             │
│                                                 │
│  Pure Good                          Pure Service│
│ ─────────────────────────────────────────────  │
│                                                 │
│    |      |      |      |      |      |      |   │
│                                                 │
│                                                 │
│    1.                                           │
│                                                 │
│    2.                                           │
│                                                 │
│    3.                                           │
│                                                 │
│    4.                                           │
│                                                 │
│    5.                                           │
│                                                 │
└─────────────────────────────────────────────────┘
```

- Next, name five companies that produce goods that might be considered "pure goods." Next to each company, list two or three services that the company might offer to move it toward the center of the goods-services continuum (and perhaps give the firm a competitive edge).

Questions for Exploration

Conceptual

You are an architect. When you are finished with a client, he or she walks out the door with a very tangible set of drawings that will lead to the existence of a very tangible building. What are you marketing—a good or a service? Why?

Practical

What is Western Cruise Lines really selling—and to whom? Identify a good that could meet a need currently being fulfilled by Western Cruise Lines. How would the marketing effort for the good differ from the marketing effort for the service used by Western Cruise Lines?

Answer Key

Key Concepts	1. g	4. f	7. e
	2. a	5. b	8. d
	3. c	6. h	

Completion

1. wants, needs (either order)
2. services
3. goods, services
4. pure, goods
5. intangible, perishable (either order); inseparable, involved, standardize, variable
6. stored, perishable
7. tangibility, reliability, responsiveness, assurance, empathy
8. consumer, business
9. social-cultural
10. technological
11. demographic

Self-Test	1. b	5. c	9. a
	2. b	6. a	10. a
	3. d	7. c	
	4. b	8. b	

Applying Marketing Concepts	1. c
	2. b
	3. a

*The simplest, most direct marketing channel is
not necessarily the best . . .*

—Boone and Kurtz

13

Channels

Assignments

For the most effective study of this lesson, we suggest that you complete the
assignments in the following sequence:

1. Read the study guide Overview (Lesson Notes and Video Program
    Notes) and the Learning Objectives for this lesson.

2. Read *Contemporary Marketing Wired*, 9th edition, Chapter 14,
    "Distribution," pages 462-470 and 477-492. (The balance of the chapter
    will be assigned in the next lesson.)

3. View "What Makes Amos Famous: A Case Study in Channel Strategy"
    video program.

4. Review the textbook assignment for this lesson.

5. Complete the Review Activities (Key Concepts and Completion),
    Self-Test, and Applying Marketing Concepts for this lesson.

6. Check your answers against the Answer Key at the end of the lesson,
    and review when necessary.

7. Complete any of the Additional Activities (Experiential Exercise and
    Questions for Exploration) that interest you or that are assigned by your
    instructor.

Overview

In marketing, **distribution channels** provide the means by which goods and services are moved from the producer to the consumer or business user. Marketing intermediaries (wholesalers and retailers) are the institutions that operate between the producer and consumer or business user.

Distribution channels and wholesaling intermediaries are essential to the marketing process because they create three of the four types of utility. The channels make products available when the consumers want to purchase them (time utility) and where consumers can conveniently purchase them (place utility), and they enable title to pass from the producer to the purchaser (ownership utility).

For marketers, the challenge is to select the distribution channel most appropriate for both the product and the consumer from among the hundreds of available channels. These channels range from the short, simple, and direct producer to consumer or business user to the long, more complex, and indirect producer to agent/broker to wholesaler to retailer to consumer. A marketer can also choose to use two or more different channels to reach the same target market, a practice known as **dual distribution**.

Of increasing importance to marketing are **reverse channels**, in which goods move from the user back to the producer. The channels are most often used for recycling materials and for product recalls and repairs.

For a distribution channel to perform its functions efficiently, one member of the channel makes decisions and resolves conflicts among members, who often are separate, independent, and even competitive entities. The channel member that fulfills this role is known as the **channel captain**. In the past, this role was usually played by the producer or wholesaler, but retailers, especially large chains, are increasingly taking this role.

One reason that retailers are emerging as channel captains is that they control limited retail space. In that position, they can control how many, if any, of a manufacturer's products are available in their stores. Some retailers require **slotting allowances** and various other fees in exchange for giving shelf space to manufacturers.

Selection of a specific channel or channels for distribution is an important strategy decision for marketers. Among the factors marketers consider are the market (consumer or business), nature of the product, resources of the producer, and the competition. Above all, however, the most important consideration is where, when, and how consumers buy the good or service.

The degree of distribution intensity desired for a product also influences the choice of distribution channel. Manufacturers of convenience goods, for example, usually want **intensive distribution** of their products in order to saturate the market. Other manufacturers may have a **selective distribution** policy, in which they select only a limited number of dealers to carry their products. This policy reduces total marketing costs and facilitates working relationships within the channel. A third distribution policy is **exclusive distribution**, in which a firm grants exclusive rights to a wholesaler or retailer to sell a specific product in a particular geographic area. Exclusive distribution is common in the automobile industry and is frequently found in the marketing of major appliances and clothing. Exclusive distribution can entail several different distribution practices, such as exclusive-dealing agreements, closed sales territories, and tying agreements. Because these practices may reduce competition or create a monopoly, they may present legal problems.

As a response to some of the problems of traditional distribution channels, **vertical marketing systems (VMS)** have evolved. These systems are preplanned distribution channels organized to be cost effective and improve the efficiency of distribution. The three types of VMS are the **corporate system**, in which one entity owns all stages of the distribution channel; the **administered system**, in which the dominant channel member exercises its power to achieve a high-level of coordination among channel members; and the **contractual system**, which is characterized by formal agreements among members of the distribution system.

Video Program Notes

The video program for this lesson traces the history of the Famous Amos Chocolate Chip Cookie Company and how the distribution strategy that evolved under Wally Amos, founder and owner of the original company, was changed when the company was sold in 1989. The program illustrates how a product's characteristics (in this instance, perishability) influence selection of distribution channels and describes how the specific channels work to move the product from the producer to the ultimate consumer. The program also shows how Famous Amos Chocolate Chip Cookies competed for shelf space in supermarkets with other cookies and one innovative solution the company developed. The new owners substantially redirected the distribution strategies of the original company, and in the program, a company representative clearly explains the reasons for the redirection.

As you watch the video program, consider the following questions:

1. What role did Wally Amos play in establishing the firm's brand with consumers and marketing intermediaries?

2. To what types of organizations did the original Famous Amos sell the firm's products?

3. Who were the channel members in the "hot bake" store distribution?

4. Why did the original Famous Amos prefer selective distribution to certain wholesalers rather than intensive distribution?

5. What in-store locations were used for the original Famous Amos product? Why?

6. Why did the original Famous Amos choose franchising as a method of distribution instead of establishing company-owned stores?

7. What characteristics of the distribution channels and of consumers led the original company to expand into offering ice cream in its "hot bake" stores?

8. Why was efficient distribution of product especially important for the original product? Why is it important to the new owners of Famous Amos?

9. What distribution channels are used by the new company in the United States? In the foreign market?

10. What are the reasons for the marketing strategy of the new owners?

Learning Objectives

After completing your study of this lesson, you should be able to:

1. Define the following terms as they relate to marketing channels:

administered marketing system	exclusive distribution
	franchise
channel captain	gray goods
closed sales territory	industrial distributor
contractual marketing system	intensive distribution
	marketing
corporate marketing system	intermediary
	reverse channel
direct selling	selective distribution
distribution channel	slotting
dual distribution	allowance
exclusive-dealing agreement	tying agreement
	vertical marketing system (VMS)

2. Describe the functions and major types of distribution channels.

3. Describe the concept of channel leadership and the role of channel captains in controlling the channel.

4. Identify the major considerations in developing a channel strategy.

5. Identify the categories of market-coverage intensity and the types of products using each category.

6. Identify the three major types of vertical-marketing systems.

Review Activities

Key Concepts

Identify each of the following fundamental marketing-channel concepts by writing the letter of the appropriate term in the blank next to the corresponding description.

a. distribution channel
b. marketing intermediary
c. slotting allowance
d. industrial distributor
e. intensive distribution
f. selective distribution
g. exclusive distribution
h. exclusive-dealing agreement
i. closed sales territory
j. tying agreement
k. channel captain
l. vertical marketing system
m. franchise
n. corporate marketing system
o. administered marketing system
p. contractual marketing system
q. direct selling
r. dual distribution
s. reverse channel
t. gray goods

_____ 1. policy in which a company grants exclusive rights to a wholesaler or retailer to sell in a particular geographic region

_____ 2. exists when a manufacturer restricts the geographic regions in which a distributor can sell

_____ 3. strategy of saturating the market, often practiced by manufacturers of convenience goods

_____ 4. marketing intermediary in a business channel that takes title to the goods it handles

_____ 5. arrangement between a manufacturer and marketing intermediary that requires the intermediary to carry the manufacturer's full product line in exchange for an exclusive dealership

_____ 6. contractual arrangement in which a wholesaler or retailer agrees to meet the operating requirements of a manufacturer

_____ 7. firm that operates between the producer and the consumer or business purchaser, sometimes called the *middleman*

_____ 8. planned distribution channel organized to be cost effective and to improve distribution efficiency

_____ 9. policy in which a firm chooses only a limited number of retailers to handle its product line

_____ 10. marketing institutions responsible for the physical and title flow of goods and services from producer to consumer or business user

_____ 11. arrangement between a manufacturer and marketing intermediary that prohibits the intermediary from handling competing products

_____ 12. fee paid by a manufacturer to a retailer for shelf space

_____ 13. vertical marketing system in which one firm owns every stage of the distribution channel

_____ 14. dominant and controlling member of a distribution channel

_____ 15. vertical marketing system that achieves channel coordination through the exercise of power by the dominant channel member

_____ 16. vertical marketing system characterized by formal agreements among channel members

_____ 17. when a firm uses two or more channels of distribution to reach the same target market

_____ 18. situation where the buyer and seller have personal contact

_____ 19. also called parallel goods

_____ 20. path of goods from consumers to manufacturers

Completion

> Fill each blank in the following paragraphs with the most appropriate term from the list of completion answers below. A term may be used once, more than once, or not at all.
>
> | | | |
> |---|---|---|
> | administered | general | product |
> | agents | horizontal | recalls |
> | captain | indirect | repairs |
> | Clayton | industrial | retail |
> | competitive | distributors | retailer |
> | competitors | intensity | retailers |
> | consumer | intensive | reverse |
> | contractual | leadership | selection |
> | cooperative | lieutenant | selective |
> | corporate | market | Sherman |
> | direct | operating | time |
> | dual | ownership | tying |
> | exclusive | place | vertical |
> | forward | power | wholesaler |
> | franchise | producer | wholesalers |

1. The basic purpose of distribution channels is to bridge the gap between _____ and _____.

2. In moving products to a location convenient for the consumer, channels provide the utilities of _____ , _____ , and _____.

3. In addition to providing time utility by having products available *when* the customer wants to buy, distribution channels move products to locations *where* customers can buy them. By doing so, the distribution channels create _____ utility.

4. The distribution channel that provides the customer with physical possession of the product and title to the product creates _____ utility.

5. Marketing intermediaries are firms operating between the _____ and consumer or business buyer; they include both _____ and _____.

6. Wholesalers and retailers are defined by the purpose for which purchases are made. If most of the purchases are made by persons or companies for resale to others, the seller is considered to be a _____.

7. The simplest, most direct distribution channel is that from _____ to consumer or business user.

8. Sometimes a seller (such as Avon, Tupperware, and Amway) has direct contact with the consumer; this type of distribution is known as _____ selling.

9. The traditional distribution channel for consumer goods, one that is used by many small manufacturers, is from manufacturer to _____ to retailer to consumer.

10. In the distribution channel, wholesalers that take title to the goods they handle are called _____.

11. When goods are produced by a large number of small companies, the distribution channel that is often used consists of producer to agent to wholesaler to _____ to consumer.

12. Marketing intermediaries used by service firms are usually brokers or _____.

13. Use of multiple channels is known as _____ distribution.

14. Because of the growing emphasis on recycling, _____ channels are of particular importance to marketers.

15. Reverse channels are also used for product _____ and _____.

16. If a distribution channel is to be effective, one of the channel members must exercise _____.

17. Channel leadership is a function of the member's _____ within the channel.

18. The controlling member of a distribution channel is called the channel _____.

19. The functioning of a distribution channel can be disrupted by two types of conflict: _____ and _____.

20. The channel captain may be at any channel level. In the past, the channel captain was usually a manufacturer or a wholesaler. More recently, however, the role of channel captain is being assumed by _____ , because of their growth in size and power.

21. Conflict between members at the same level is _____ conflict. Conflict between members at different levels is _____ conflict.

22. In developing a channel strategy, marketers must make several decisions. The most basic decision is _____ of a specific distribution channel. The second decision is identifying the level of distribution _____ , and the third decision concerns the issue of _____ marketing systems.

23. In selecting a specific distribution channel, marketers must consider _____ factors, _____ factors, _____ factors, and _____ factors.

24. The three general levels of distribution intensity are _____ , in which a manufacturer attempts to saturate a market; _____ , in which a firm chooses only a limited number of retailers to handle its products; and _____ , in which a firm grants sole rights to a wholesaler or retailer to sell in a specific area.

25. Contracts that prohibit a marketing intermediary from handling competitors' products are known as _____ dealing agreements. In some situations, however, such contracts may violate the _____ Act.

26. Agreements that require an exclusive dealer for a manufacturer's products to carry inventories of other products of the manufacturer are known as _____ agreements. Such agreements may be violations of the Sherman Act and Clayton Act if they keep _____ out of major markets.

27. Traditional distribution channels consisting of independent intermediaries who behave autonomously are being replaced by professionally managed and centrally planned networks called _____ marketing systems.

28. The three types of vertical marketing systems are
_____ , _____ , and _____.

29. A vertical marketing system in which a single firm owns every stage of the marketing channel is known as a _____ marketing system.

30. A vertical marketing system in which coordination is attained by a dominant channel member is known as an _____ marketing system.

31. A vertical marketing system that is characterized by formal agreements is a _____ marketing system.

32. Three types of contractual vertical marketing systems exist: _____-sponsored voluntary chains, _____ cooperatives, and _____ operations.

33. In wholesaler-sponsored voluntary chains, retailers agree to buy from one _____. Conversely, retailers set up their own wholesaling operations when they form a retail _____.

34. Under the franchise system, a wholesaler or retailer (the franchise) agrees to meet the _____ requirements of a manufacturer or other franchiser.

Self-Test

Select the best answer.

1. The traditional distribution channel for consumer goods is producer to
   a. agent to wholesaler to retailer to consumer.
   b. wholesaler to retailer to consumer.
   c. consumer.
   d. retailer to consumer.

2. When a business user places relatively small numbers of large orders, the producer is more likely to use
   a. multiple channels.
   b. channels that include wholesalers.
   c. longer channels.
   d. shorter, more direct channels.

3. When a manufacturer wishes to have a close working relationship with marketing intermediaries and to maintain an image of quality and prestige, the manufacturer is likely to follow
   a. an exclusive-dealing policy.
   b. an exclusive distribution policy.
   c. an intensive distribution policy.
   d. a selective distribution policy.

4. A contractual vertical marketing system in which dealers agree to meet the operating requirements of a manufacturer is a
   a. closed sales territory system.
   b. wholesale-sponsored chain.
   c. retail cooperative.
   d. franchise.

5. An example of a product that is sold with intensive distribution is
   a. McDonald's Big Mac hamburger.
   b. Crest toothpaste.
   c. General Electric television sets.
   d. Porsche automobiles.

6. An agreement between the manufacturer and the marketing intermediary that requires the intermediary to carry the manufacturer's full product line in exchange for an exclusive dealership is known as
   a. a closed sales territory.
   b. an exclusive-dealing agreement.
   c. a tying agreement.
   d. a vertical marketing system.

7. The three types of vertical marketing systems are
   a. corporate, administered, and contractual.
   b. independent, contractual, and exclusive.
   c. managed, contractual, and independent.
   d. administered, contractual, and integrated.

8. The three basic types of distribution intensity are
   a. selective, permissive, and exclusive.
   b. administered, intensive, and selective.
   c. intensive, selective, and exclusive.
   d. competitive, intensive, and exclusive.

9. The firm that controls the distribution channel is known as the channel
   a. master.
   b. administrator.
   c. captain.
   d. manager.

10. Distribution channels help create for the consumer each of the following utilities EXCEPT
   a. time.
   b. form.
   c. place.
   d. ownership.

Applying Marketing Concepts

Jane McGraw is the newly appointed marketing manager for SportFad, a company that manufactures recreational products such as in-line skates, skateboards, snowboards, and surfboards. Because it is relatively small, this West Coast company has marketed only to local retailers.

One of McGraw's first projects is to test the potential of selling SportFad's products by direct-mail advertisements to large retailers around the country. She discovers a great deal of interest in SportFad's attractive, high-quality products, but the company has limited financial resources for nationwide marketing and distribution. In spite of the limited funds, management decides to risk expansion and assigns McGraw the task of establishing an efficient, low-cost distribution channel.

1. To achieve her company's objectives, McGraw should probably hire a sales staff to sell her company's products directly to retailers.
   a. true
   b. false

2. If McGraw decides to sell the products to a limited number of retailers, she will be engaged in
   a. reverse channels.
   b. closed selling.
   c. intensive distribution.
   d. selective distribution.

3. If McGraw decides to use one wholesaler to distribute products to all retailers, she will be employing
   a. an industrial distributor.
   b. a buying agent.
   c. a channel captain.
   d. an exclusive distributor.

4. If McGraw sells through wholesalers to retailers, who then sell to consumers, and she also sells to consumers using direct mail and mail-order advertisements, she will be using dual distribution.
   a. true
   b. false

5. If McGraw sells SportFad products only to intermediaries who agree not to carry competitive products, she will be engaging in
   a. franchising.
   b. exclusive dealing.
   c. exclusive distribution.
   d. horizontal conflict.

Additional Activities

Experiential Exercise

The purpose of this exercise is to help you understand the process used to develop distribution channels. The exercise requires familiarity with channel options and factors affecting channel choice.

- For this exercise, select and describe a distribution channel for each of the following products: high-quality lawn mowers, fine china, medium-priced outdoor jackets, natural fruit candy, motorcycles, and high-quality precision hoses and couplings. In your description of the channel for each product, include the degree of exposure (intensive, selective, or exclusive) that you are recommending, the channel you have selected (based on Figure 13.2 in the textbook), the services you expect the different marketing intermediaries to provide, and the reasons for your choices.

Questions for Exploration

Conceptual

Distribution channels are often constrained by government antitrust regulations. What are these government efforts trying to protect or prevent? What would the business world be like without these regulations?

Practical

Evaluate the channels originally selected by Famous Amos in the video program for this lesson (franchise stores, supermarkets, convenience stores). How have the new owners of Famous Amos changed the channel strategy for the company? Do you think the new channel strategy is the correct one for the product? If it is not, how would you change it?

Answer Key

Key Concepts	1. g	6. m	11. h	16. p
	2. i	7. b	12. c	17. r
	3. e	8. l	13. n	18. q
	4. d	9. f	14. k	19. t
	5. j	10. a	15. o	20. s

Completion

1. producer, consumer
2. time, place, ownership (any order)
3. place
4. ownership
5. producer; wholesalers, retailers (either order)
6. wholesaler
7. producer
8. direct
9. wholesaler
10. industrial distributors
11. retailer
12. agents
13. dual
14. reverse
15. recalls, repairs (either order)
16. leadership
17. power
18. captain
19. horizontal, vertical (either order)
20. retailers
21. horizontal, vertical
22. selection, intensity, vertical
23. market, product, producer, competitive (any order)
24. intensive, selective, exclusive
25. exclusive, Clayton
26. tying, competitors
27. vertical
28. corporate, administered, contractual (any order)
29. corporate
30. administered
31. contractual
32. wholesaler, retail, franchise
33. wholesaler, cooperative
34. operating

Self-Test	1. b	5. b	8. c
	2. d	6. c	9. c
	3. b	7. a	10. b
	4. d		

Applying Marketing Concepts	1. b	4. a
	2. d	5. b
	3. d	

*You can do away with the wholesaler but you
can't do away with the functions he performs.*
                                    —An old wholesaler's saying

14

Wholesaling

Assignments

For the most effective study of this lesson, we suggest that you complete the
assignments in the following sequence:

1. Read the study guide Overview (Lesson Notes and Video Program
    Notes) and the Learning Objectives for this lesson.

2. Read *Contemporary Marketing Wired,* 9th edition, Chapter 14,
    "Distribution," pages 470-477, and review pages 464-470.

3. View "The Fresh Connection: A Case Study in Wholesaling"
    video program.

4. Review the textbook assignment for this lesson.

5. Complete the Review Activities (Key Concepts and Completion),
    Self-Test, and Applying Marketing Concepts for this lesson.

6. Check your answers against the Answer Key at the end of the lesson,
    and review when necessary.

7. Complete any of the Additional Activities (Experiential Exercises and
    Questions for Exploration) that interest you or that are assigned by your
    instructor.

Overview

Wholesaling encompasses the various activities of wholesaling intermediaries that sell goods or services almost exclusively to retailers, business users, or to other wholesaling intermediaries.

These **wholesaling intermediaries** provide seven basic **marketing functions**: buying, selling, storing, transporting, providing **market information**, financing, and risk taking. In providing these services, wholesaling intermediaries also provide the marketing utilities of time, place, and possession or ownership. All the services provided by wholesaling intermediaries must be performed for a marketing channel to function. The services may be shifted among various types of providers, but they cannot be eliminated.

Wholesaling intermediaries are categorized in several ways. One basic distinction is between those who take title to the goods they handle and those who do not take title to the goods.

Wholesaling intermediaries are also categorized according to ownership. Some are owned by the manufacturers of the goods they sell, others are independent establishments, and still others are owned by retailer-owned cooperatives and buying offices.

Manufacturers of goods can distribute those goods directly through **sales offices** and **sales branches**. Both operations serve as offices for sales representatives, but sales branches also carry inventory and process orders from available stock. Manufacturers can also market their goods at **trade fairs**, periodic exhibitions where retail and wholesale buyers can inspect goods, and **merchandise marts**, where goods are on permanent display.

Independent wholesaling intermediaries include both merchant wholesalers and agents and brokers. **Merchant wholesalers** take title to goods and perform a wide range of services, tailored to meet the needs of individual customers. One kind of merchant wholesaler is the **rack jobber**, who provides display stands, fills and refills stands and shelves, and prices the goods. Rack jobbers frequently provide these services to such retailers as supermarkets and discount, drug, hardware, and variety stores.

Truck wholesalers typically transport perishable items such as bread, tobacco, and candy to retailers who wish to maintain a small, fresh inventory for their customers. Truck wholesalers promote the products they carry. **Drop shippers** process orders of large, bulky, nonagricultural commodities and arrange to have producers send them directly to buyers. Drop shippers do not physically handle the goods they sell. **Cash-and-carry wholesalers** sell items to small retailers. As the name implies, these wholesalers neither perform the delivery function nor extend credit. **Mail-order wholesalers** use catalogues to contact customers and the postal service and package services to deliver goods.

In comparison to merchant wholesalers, **agents and brokers** never take title to goods, although some agents may temporarily take possession of goods. Most often, the basic function provided by agents and brokers is bringing buyers and sellers together. This type of independent wholesaling intermediary can be divided into five categories: commission merchants, auction houses, brokers, selling agents, and manufacturer's agents.

Commission merchants are frequently involved in the marketing of such agricultural products as grain, produce, and livestock, acting as the producer's agents when the product is sold.

Auction houses bring buyers and sellers together at one place, so that buyers can inspect goods before purchasing them. Auction houses are often used in the marketing of tobacco, used cars, art, livestock, furs, and fruit.

Brokers usually function on a one-time basis to represent either the buyer or the seller in a transaction. Brokers never take possession of the goods.

Selling agents, also known as **independent marketing departments,** are usually responsible for the entire output of a producer and constitute the firm's entire marketing effort. The coal, lumber, and textile industries frequently use selling agents.

Manufacturer's agents, or manufacturer's reps, usually operate in a specified geographic area and represent several different manufacturers of related but noncompeting products. Manufacturer's agents are often used by companies when entering new sales territories or introducing unrelated product lines.

In addition to wholesaling services provided by manufacturers and independent wholesaling intermediaries, some retailers are performing wholesaling functions by forming buying clubs and establishing centralized buying offices.

Today, wholesaling is a dynamic part of marketing that continues to evolve in response to changing conditions. Merchant wholesalers, for example, account for about 60 percent of all wholesale sales. Some wholesalers are growing vertically by opening retail outlets, while other have expanded to serve national and international markets.

Video Program Notes

In the video program for this lesson, a major food wholesaler, Northern Produce, performs a wide variety of functions to facilitate the flow of goods (in this case, produce) from producers to ultimate consumers. A brief visit with a farmer and a major food user (a cruise ship line) indicates that, without the wholesaler, the farmer and cruise ship line would be unable to operate their respective businesses in an efficient, cost-effective way. The program also explores each of the functions that major wholesalers perform, including buying and selling, storing, transportation, acquiring and disseminating market information, financing, and risk taking for the supplier and the consumer. One especially important lesson is taught in this program: "You can shift the functions wholesalers perform but you can't do away with them."

As you watch the video program, consider the following questions:

1. What type of wholesaler is Northern Produce?

2. Who are Northern Produce's customers?

3. Why does Northern Produce maintain alternate sources of supply?

4. What risks does Northern Produce assume when it performs the warehousing function?

5. What marketing functions and services does Northern Produce provide to Western Cruise Lines?

6. How do Northern Produce buyers arrive at the price of items such as mushrooms?

7. What advantages are there for Northern Produce in offering financing?

8. What marketing functions and services does Northern Produce provide to growers?

9. Why does Northern Produce publish a newsletter?

10. What additional services and marketing functions does Northern Produce offer that add to its operating costs?

Learning Objectives

After completing your study of this lesson, you should be able to:

1. Explain the following terms as they relate to wholesaling:

agents and brokers	merchant wholesaler
auction house	rack jobber
broker	sales branch
cash-and-carry wholesaler	sales office
commission merchant	selling agent
drop shipper	trade fair
mail-order wholesaler	truck wholesaler
manufacturer's agent	wholesaler
merchandise mart	wholesaling intermediary

2. Identify functions and services typically provided by wholesaling intermediaries.

3. Identify the criteria for classifying two basic types of wholesaling intermediaries.

4. Describe the operations and services of various types of manufacturer-owned wholesaling.

5. Describe the operations and services of various types of independent wholesaling intermediaries.

Review Activities

Key Concepts

> Identify each of the following wholesaling concepts by writing the letter of the appropriate term in the blank next to the corresponding description.
>
> | | | | |
> |---|---|---|---|
> | a. | wholesaler | j. | broker |
> | b. | agents and brokers | k. | rack jobber |
> | c. | sales branch | l. | cash-and-carry wholesaler |
> | d. | mail-order wholesaler | | |
> | e. | sales office | m. | truck wholesaler |
> | f. | trade fair | n. | drop shipper |
> | g. | merchandise mart | o. | commission merchant |
> | h. | merchant wholesaler | p. | auction house |
> | i. | manufacturer's agent | q. | selling agent |

_____ 1. provides limited service in the marketing of perishable food items by regular deliveries to retail stores

_____ 2. independent salesperson who works for a number of manufacturers of related but noncompeting products and who receives a commission based on a percentage of sales

_____ 3. establishment maintained by a manufacturer that serves as a warehouse for a particular sales territory; carries inventory and serves customers from available stock

_____ 4. full-function merchant wholesaler who markets specialized products to retail stores and provides the services of merchandising and arrangement, pricing, maintenance, and stocking of displays

_____ 5. brings buyer and seller together and may represent either on a one-time basis; does not take title to or possession of goods

_____ 6. firm or person who performs wholesaling functions and takes title to the goods sold

_____ 7. permanent facility in which manufacturers in a particular industry display their products for wholesale and retail buyers

_____ 8. sells on commission and provides a place where buyer and seller can get together in one location; allows potential buyers to inspect merchandise prior to purchasing it

_____ 9. company-owned facility designed to serve company sales personnel; does not carry product inventory

_____ 10. most often found acting as the producer's agent in the marketing of agricultural products; takes possession of goods when they are shipped to a central market

_____ 11. often referred to as *independent marketing department*

_____ 12. wholesaling intermediary that takes title to the goods handled

_____ 13. forwards orders from customers to producers (which ship directly to customers) and takes title to the goods without taking possession of them

_____ 14. limited-function merchant wholesaler that uses catalogues rather than a sales force to contact customers

_____ 15. limited-function merchant wholesaler that does not perform delivery or financing functions

_____ 16. periodic show at which manufacturers in a particular industry display their products to wholesalers and retailers

_____ 17. persons or firms that perform wholesaling functions but do not take title to the goods

Completion

Fill each blank in the following paragraphs with the most appropriate term from the list of completion answers below. A term may be used once, more than once, or not at all.

agents	functions	rack jobber
agents and brokers	independent	sales branch
	limited	sales office
auction	mail order	selling agent
brokers	manufacturer's agent	several
channels		trade fairs
consumers	merchandise	truck
customers	marts	wholesalers
deliver	merchants	wholesaling
eliminated	possession	wholesaling intermediary
finance	producers	
full-function	product	

1. Distribution _____ are made up of institutions such as wholesalers and retailers.

2. Organizations that perform buying, selling, transportation, storage, information, financing, and risk-taking functions in the distribution channel are _____.

3. By representing many manufacturers for a single customer, retailers and _____ reduce the number of transactions between the manufacturer and _____.

4. Marketing intermediaries perform a number of marketing functions; these functions can be shifted from wholesaler to manufacturer, but they cannot be _____. For example, large manufacturers and retailers may perform their own wholesaling _____.

5. Manufacturer-owned _____ operations are usually carried out through a sales branch or a sales office. The major difference between these two facilities is that the _____ carries inventory, while the _____ serves principally as a home base for salespeople.

6. In addition to sales offices and sales branches, manufacturers may market through permanent exhibitions at _____ and through periodic displays at _____.

7. Merchant wholesalers and agents and brokers make up the largest wholesaler group in both number and sales. This group is known as _____ wholesaling intermediaries.

8. Wholesalers that provide a complete range of services for the buyer are known as _____ merchant wholesalers.

9. A full-function wholesaler who provides drug stores, hardware stores, variety stores, and supermarkets with racks and merchandise and who prices and maintains the displays is known as a _____.

10. The _____-function merchant wholesaler provides specialized services designed to meet the needs of a segment of retail and business buyers.

11. One example of the limited-function merchant wholesaler is the cash-and-carry wholesaler, who provides merchandise at a low price and does not _____ or _____ it.

12. Functions such as sales, delivery, and collection for items such as bread, tobacco, and candy are often performed by _____ wholesalers.

13. A drop shipper is a limited-function merchant wholesaler who receives orders from _____ and forwards them to _____ who ship directly to buyers. The drop shipper usually sells bulky goods, often makes purchases in carload lots, but never takes _____ of the goods.

14. Catalogues are used by _____ wholesalers to contact customers.

15. Wholesalers who are instrumental in bringing buyers and sellers together but who do not take title to the goods they sell are known as _____.

16. Commission merchants, auction houses, brokers, selling agents, and manufacturer's agents are the five major types of _____.

17. Commission _____ sell agricultural products for producers. They not only take possession of the _____ but attempt to obtain the best price possible for the owner.

18. Companies that specialize in bringing buyers and sellers together to allow buyers to inspect merchandise before purchasing are called _____ houses.

19. Wholesalers whose primary function is to bring buyers and sellers together are known as _____. Unlike commission merchants, they can represent either the seller or the buyer.

20. An intermediary who is capable of representing the seller on a continuing basis, selling all of the firm's output, and even making price and promotion decisions is the _____.

21. An independent salesperson with a territory may be used by a manufacturer to develop new territories or represent the firm in areas where it is inefficient for company salespersons to operate. This _____ usually sells a line of related but noncompetitive products and represents _____ manufacturers in his or her territory.

Self-Test

Select the best answer.

1. Which of the following statements is **NOT** true of wholesaling?
   a. Wholesalers and retailers serve as important information links.
   b. Wholesalers and retailers may provide financing by providing goods on credit.
   c. The major function of wholesalers is probably bulk-breaking.
   d. Some marketing functions can be eliminated by an efficient channel system.

2. By definition, a merchant wholesaler
   a. provides the same functions as an agent.
   b. is another name for a wholesaling intermediary.
   c. applies only to wholesaling intermediaries that take title to goods.
   d. sells only to retailers.

3. The two major categories of independent wholesaling intermediaries are
   a. merchant wholesalers and agents and brokers.
   b. agents and wholesalers.
   c. brokers and agents.
   d. full-function and limited-function.

4. Of the following merchant wholesalers, the one that does NOT take possession of the product before selling it is the
   a. rack jobber.
   b. drop shipper.
   c. truck wholesaler.
   d. cash-and-carry wholesaler.

5. A major difference between a selling and a manufacturer's agent is that a
   a. selling agent sells on commission while a manufacturer's agent works for a yearly fee.
   b. manufacturer's agent sells on commission while a selling agent works for a yearly fee.
   c. manufacturer's agent sells all of the products produced by the firms it represents, while a selling agent does not.
   d. selling agent sells all of the products produced by the firms it represents, while a manufacturer's agent does not.

6. Facilities that are owned by manufacturers and carry inventory are known as
   a. sales offices.
   b. public warehouses.
   c. sales branches.
   d. private warehouses.

7. The functions of providing storage, information, and financing for manufacturers are often performed by
   a. retailers.
   b. agents and brokers.
   c. retailers and wholesalers.
   d. sellers and buyers.

8. A merchandise mart differs from a trade fair because the merchandise mart is
   a. only held from time to time.
   b. only held in open-air facilities.
   c. open all year round.
   d. closed to retailers.

9. Wholesaling intermediaries often found in the marketing of agricultural products are known as
   a. agricultural distributors.
   b. commission merchants.
   c. merchant wholesalers.
   d. farmers.

10. The wholesaling intermediaries with the largest operating expenses are usually the
    a. drop shippers.
    b. merchant wholesalers.
    c. commission merchants.
    d. selling agents.

Applying Marketing Concepts

Janet LaRue is the owner and only officer of LaRue Enterprises, a newly formed company that manufactures decorative metal wastepaper baskets. LaRue's innovative basket was shown at the regional trade show with tremendous success, and she received so many orders at the show that she decided to market nationally.

As is often the case, success introduced new problems, and LaRue has some important decisions to make. Unfortunately, her education in marketing has not given her the background necessary to make effective decisions.

The following people have asked to represent her product line to retailers, indicating that they can solve her marketing problems:

Billy Joe Sussking. A spirited individual who is offering to represent LaRue Enterprises in the Great Lakes area for a 12-percent commission. Sussking says he personally knows all the gift-shop owners in that area since he has been selling home accessory products to gift stores in the Great Lakes region for 15 years.

Dunn and Dorio Company. A large firm that boasts it has 25 salespersons. Donna Dunn, company vice president, tells LaRue that Dunn and Dorio would market the wastepaper baskets nationwide. LaRue Enterprises would not need a marketing department at all. Dunn and Dorio would not, however, carry inventory or be responsible for anything but promoting and selling the product. Like Sussking, the company would work for a commission.

Flylow, Incorporated. Flylow, Inc., a firm located in Boston and serving the New England area, is offering to buy wastebaskets and stock and inventory them. The company would then sell the baskets to retail stores located in its trade area.

Red Jackson. Jackson is an old college friend of LaRue. He had been a marketing major and is currently working as a salesman for a consumer-goods firm. Jackson has told LaRue that she should hire him to sell the wastebaskets; he would then hire additional salespersons to work from regional locations. Each location would carry a supply of wastebaskets for delivery to retail buyers. Jackson expects to be the national sales manager.

LaRue talked about these offers with a relative who worked as a marketing manager for a large carpet company. She felt her best advice came from that source: "Identify all your options and their costs. Then go ahead and make some decisions."

1. Billy Joe Sussking is a
   a. full-function wholesaler.
   b. commission merchant.
   c. broker.
   d. limited-function wholesaler.
   e. selling agent.
   f. manufacturer's agent.

2. Dunn and Dorio Company is a
   a. full-function wholesaler.
   b. commission merchant.
   c. broker.
   d. limited-function wholesaler.
   e. selling agent.
   f. manufacturer's agent.

3. Flylow, Incorporated, is a
   a. full-function wholesaler.
   b. commission merchant.
   c. broker.
   d. limited-function wholesaler.
   e. selling agent.

4. Red Jackson is offering to set up a system of
   a. sales offices.
   b. sales branches.
   c. auction houses.
   d. distribution warehouses.
   e. drop shippers.

5. An option that LaRue has not yet identified would bypass the need for either independent wholesalers or a sales force. This option is:
   a. mail order.
   b. auction houses.
   c. agents or brokers.
   d. commission merchants.

Additional Activities

Experiential Exercises

1. The purpose of this exercise is to familiarize you with wholesalers located in your area.

   - Using a map of a city in your area, plot the location of the following wholesalers: plumbing fixtures and supplies, meat wholesalers, photographic equipment and supplies, grocery wholesalers, and a wholesaler of your choice. Write a brief statement explaining the pattern (such as clustering or scattering) you find. You can use the Yellow Pages of the telephone directory to identify wholesalers in the various categories. Chambers of commerce and other trade groups may also have printed directories of wholesalers located in your area.

2. This second exercise will help you understand the functions performed by a merchant wholesaler. The exercise involves an intensive study of a selected merchant wholesaler.

   Visit a merchant wholesaler in your area and obtain answers to the following questions:

   - Type of merchant wholesaler?

   - What product lines does the firm carry?

   - Approximately how many firms does this wholesaler represent?

   - Approximately how many customers are served on a regular basis?

   - What types of businesses are they?

   - Does this wholesaler sell to other wholesalers?

   - Describe the wholesaler's trade area (either in miles from its location or by naming the cities or counties where the customers are located).

   - What functions does this wholesaler perform for its customers or for the firms it represents?

- How many salespeople does this wholesaler normally employ?

- What is the biggest challenge facing the wholesaler at this time?

- What else about marketing did you learn from your visit?

Questions for Exploration

Conceptual

Marxian criticism of capitalism has often focused on wholesaling as an example of capitalism's tendency to increase prices without adding any real value to a product. Write a letter to Karl Marx. Explain to him why he's either (a) right on the mark or (b) way off base.

Practical

Northern Produce is not exactly the prototype of a calmly routinized wholesaling operation. Given the market it serves, would it be better off if it routinized its operation, dropped exotic food lines, and moved away from the hectic process shown in the video program? Why?

Answer Key

Key Concepts				
	1. m	6. a	11. q	16. f
	2. i	7. g	12. h	17. b
	3. c	8. p	13. n	
	4. k	9. e	14. d	
	5. j	10. o	15. l	

Completion		
	1. channels	12. truck
	2. wholesalers	13. customers, producers, possession
	3. wholesalers, consumers	14. mail order
	4. eliminated, functions	15. agents
	5. wholesaling, sales branch, sales office	16. agents and brokers
	6. merchandise marts, trade fairs	17. merchants, product
	7. independent	18. auction
	8. full-function	19. brokers
	9. rack jobber	20. selling agent
	10. limited	21. manufacturer's agent, several
	11. deliver, finance (either order)	

Self-Test			
	1. d	5. d	8. c
	2. c	6. c	9. b
	3. a	7. c	10. b
	4. b		

Applying Marketing Concepts		
	1. f	4. b
	2. e	5. a
	3. a	

*Keep thy shop and thy shop will
keep thee.*

—George Chapman (1605)

15

Retailing I

Assignments

For the most effective study of this lesson, we suggest that you complete the assignments in the following sequence:

1. Read the study guide Overview (Lesson Notes and Video Program Notes) and the Learning Objectives for this lesson.

2. Read *Contemporary Marketing Wired*, 9th edition, Chapter 15, "Retailing," pages 496-511. (The balance of the chapter will be assigned in the next lesson.) Also read Chapter 10, pages 354-357 "Electronic Data Interchange," "National Account Selling," and "Vendor-Managed Inventory."

3. View "Because It's There: A Case Study in Retailing" video program.

4. Review the textbook assignment for this lesson.

5. Complete the Review Activities (Key Concepts and Completion), Self-Test, and Applying Marketing Concepts for this lesson.

6. Check your answers against the Answer Key at the end of the lesson, and review when necessary.

7. Complete any of the Additional Activities (Experiential Exercise and Questions for Exploration) that interest you or that are assigned by your instructor.

Overview

Lesson Notes

This lesson is the first of two on retailing and covers the history of retailing and retailing strategy. The next lesson will look at shopping centers, the bases on which retailers are classified, and the different types of retail outlets in each classification.

Retailing is broadly defined as "all activities involved in selling goods and services to ultimate consumers." In the United States, retailing has evolved from itinerant peddlers who carried their stores on their backs, to the general store, to downtown shopping districts, to today's hypermarkets and regional shopping centers. The **wheel of retailing** is a hypothesis that has been offered to explain how retailing changes over time. Briefly, the hypothesis states that established retailers are displaced when new retailers enter the market selling products at lower prices, which they can charge because they have reduced or eliminated services. Eventually, these retailers add services and increase prices, becoming vulnerable to being displaced by new retailers.

In the United States, retail outlets represent, in effect, the distribution channel to most consumers. Regardless of the products they sell, where they sell them, or to whom they sell them, all retailers, if they are to be successful, must first identify a target market and then develop a retailing mix to satisfy the needs of the target market.

The overall retailing strategy comprises six distinct elements: merchandise strategy, customer service, pricing, target market analysis, location-distribution, promotion, and store atmosphere. When these elements are combined, they project a desired **retail image** or consumer's perception of the store and the shopping experience it offers.

Basic to the retailing operation is **merchandise strategy**: selection of the types of merchandise that will appeal to the target market. The retailer must also make decisions on product lines, specific products, and depth and width of the selection offered to the market. In making merchandise decisions, the retailer must consider what competing retailers are offering. Also, marketing research can be quite valuable in helping retailers understand the needs and wants of the target market and tailor their merchandise strategy.

In addition, a merchandise planning method known as **assortment management** combines market research with technology. In this method, retailers attempt to offer the desired product at the desired time and place to the customer. A data warehouse is a collection of information about marketing and merchandising combined with customer intelligence. This decision support system improves the effectiveness of a retailer's merchandise mix.

A retailer's **customer service strategy** can range from "no-frills" to highly attentive personal assistance. Common customer services include gift wrapping, alterations, and delivery. Other services can be personal shopping, gift registries, wardrobe consulting, and interior design. The retailer must decide not only which, if any, services to offer but also what the charges, if any, will be for those services. Customer services can be especially valuable in attracting and keeping customers, so the retailer should carefully evaluate the kinds and level of customer service that will be offered.

Retailers determine the prices consumers pay for products. The **pricing strategy** adopted by the retailer can significantly influence how consumers perceive the retailer. In setting prices, the retailer adds a **markup** to the product's cost. Markups are usually stated as a percentage of the product's selling price or as a percentage of its cost to the retailer. Markups are based in part on the retailer's judgment on the amount consumers will be willing to pay for a product. Other factors that influence setting the original price are services performed by the retailer and the rate at which the inventory will turn over. To reduce prices for sales and similar promotions, retailers use a **markdown**, a percentage reduction on the original selling price.

The **location-distribution** component of retail strategy includes where the retail outlet is physically situated and the amount of inventory to keep on hand for consumers. Location is considered by many to be critical to the success of a retail outlet. Apart from geographic location, a retailer also has to decide whether to locate apart from other retail businesses, in a central business district, or in a planned shopping center. Where an outlet is located is usually influenced by the type of merchandise sold, the retailer's financial resources, the target market's characteristics, and availability of sites.

Promotional strategy includes advertising, special events, and sales promotions. This strategy, in combination with other strategies, establishes the store image in the minds of consumers. Promotional activities also provide consumers with essential information about the store's merchandise, prices, locations, and hours of business. Often, retailers target their promotions directly via their customer database. Others promote products over the Internet or at interactive kiosks in stores. The salespeople in the store can also be an important part of retail strategy. By encouraging a customer to buy a higher-priced item than he or she originally intended, the salesperson is practicing **selling up**. Another way that a salesperson can increase the sale is **suggestion selling**, in which the salesperson encourages the customer to add to the original purchase by buying related items (a tie to go with a shirt, a scarf to go with a dress) or items on a special promotion.

Another method of retail strategy growing in popularity is **atmospherics**, the combination of the interior and exterior physical characteristics of the store and the amenities that the retailer provides to the customers. Atmospherics can contribute significantly to the store's retail image. Especially imaginative and creative atmospherics can attract consumers to the store who might not normally shop there.

Video Program Notes

The video program for this lesson offers an in-depth look at West Ridge Mountaineering, a specialty store that offers goods and services specifically for its target market of mountain climbers and skiers. West Ridge Mountaineering has a clearly developed retail strategy, and the program examines the major components of that strategy.

West Ridge Mountaineering has built much of its success on a high level of customer service, combined with an enthusiastic, knowledgeable, and helpful sales force. The video program also includes interviews with the owner, who talks about his philosophy for building foot traffic and displaying merchandise, how the sales representatives help him to keep the store supplied with the correct amount of inventory, and how he uses print advertising, commercials on cable television, and direct mail to promote the store.

In all, the story of West Ridge Mountaineering shows how a retailer can build a bridge to the consumer by selecting the right products and store location, setting reasonable prices, creating a favorable image of the store, and developing a sales force that makes sales and wins repeat customers.

As you watch the video program, consider the following questions:

1. Generally, what goods and services does West Ridge Mountaineering sell?

2. What is the owner's philosophy about foot traffic?

3. Why does West Ridge offer low-profit services such as ski rentals, waxing, and binding adjustments?

4. What kinds of free services does the store offer? Why?

5. Is the store's location (on a busy intersection in a metropolitan area) a good one? Why was that location chosen?

6. What are some merchandise display techniques that help West Ridge increase sales?

7. How important is a knowledgeable sales force to the store's success? How well does the store owner deal with his employees?

8. What are some of the ways manufacturers help West Ridge retail its products?

9. What are some of the concerns of the store's buyer when purchasing inventory?

10. How does West Ridge target its sales promotion and advertising to potential customers?

Learning Objectives

After completing your study of this lesson, you should be able to:

1. Define the following terms as they relate to retailing:

assortment	retail image
management	retailing
atmospherics	selling up
electronic data	suggestion selling
interchange (EDI)	vendor-managed
markdown	inventory (VMI)
markup	wheel of retailing

2. Briefly describe the evolution of retailing in the United States and how the wheel of retailing explains that evolution.

3. Identify the major components of retailing strategy.

4. Describe the role of the target market, merchandise, customer service, pricing, location-distribution, promotion, and store atmosphere in retailing strategy.

5. Describe how relationship marketing incorporates electronic data interchange, national account selling, and vendor-managed inventories.

Review Activities

Key Concepts

> **Identify each of the following retailing concepts by writing the letter of the appropriate term in the blank next to the corresponding description.**
>
> a. retailing
> b. assortment management
> c. wheel of retailing
> d. retail image
> e. suggestion selling
>
> f. selling up
> g. atmospherics
> h. markup
> i. markdown
> j. electronic data interchange (EDI)

_____ 1. activities in the sale of goods and services to the ultimate consumer

_____ 2. retail selling that attempts to broaden the customer's purchase with related items or seasonal merchandise

_____ 3. planning method that combines market research and technology

_____ 4. consumer's perception of the store and the shopping experience it provides

_____ 5. hypothesis that describes the patterns of retail change by stating that new retailers enter the market with lower prices and fewer services

_____ 6. combination of a store's physical characteristics and amenities provided by the retailer

_____ 7. convincing a consumer to buy a higher-priced item than he or she originally intended

_____ 8. amount that the retailer adds to cost of merchandise to establish a selling price

_____ 9. amount that the retailer reduces the original selling price of a product

_____ 10. computer-to-computer exchange of invoices, orders, and other business documents

Completion

Fill each blank in the following paragraphs with the most
appropriate term from the list of completion answers below.
A term may be used once, more than once, or not at all.

atmospherics	merchandise	retailers
customer service	promotional	services
location	retail image	target market
markdown	prices	ultimate
markup		

1. Retailing involves the sale of goods and services to the
   _____ consumer.

2. The wheel of retailing, an image used to predict change in
   retailing, is based on the hypothesis that new types of
   retailers gain entry to the marketplace by offering lower
   _____ and reducing or eliminating _____. Over
   time, however, these retailers add services, raise prices, and
   in turn become vulnerable to new, lower-priced _____.

3. The combination of merchandise, customer service, pricing,
   target market, promotion, location-distribution, and store atmosphere projects the store's _____.

4. The first step in developing a retailing strategy is
   selecting a _____.

5. Making decisions about the type of merchandise a store will
   offer is the basis of developing a _____ strategy.

6. Gift wrapping, personal shopping, design consultation, and
   installation are examples of _____ .

7. Retailers are directly responsible for setting _____.

8. Prices are set when the retailer adds a _____ to the
   cost of an item.

9. The amount of service offered and the inventory turnover rate
   are two of the factors retailers use in determining the amount
   of _____.

10. The retailer can reduce prices with a _____.

11. The retailer's financial resources, characteristics of the target market, type of merchandise, and site availability are all factors that influence _____ strategy.

12. Advertising, special events, and sales are part of a retailer's _____ strategy.

13. The interior and exterior design of a store and amenities that the retailer offers to customers are part of the store's _____.

14. A system in which the seller determines how much product a buyer needs and ships new supplies automatically is called _____.

Self-Test

> **Select the best answer.**

1. All the activities involved with the sale of goods and services to the ultimate consumer are known as
   a. wholesaling.
   b. selling.
   c. retailing.
   d. marketing.

2. According to the wheel of retailing, as a retail store evolves, it
   a. offers fewer services.
   b. narrows its product lines.
   c. adds services and raises prices.
   d. competes with itself.

3. An exception to the wheel of retailing can be found in
   a. chain stores.
   b. supermarkets.
   c. convenience food stores.
   d. discount department stores.

4. Making decisions about the items a retailer will offer to consumers is part of
   a. merchandise strategy.
   b. retailing strategy.
   c. target market.
   d. retail image.

5. The main purpose of customer services is to
   a. enhance the store's prestige.
   b. justify increases in prices.
   c. emulate the competition.
   d. attract and retain customers.

6. According to real estate professionals, the one factor that may determine the success or failure of a retail business is the
   a. retail image.
   b. location.
   c. product line.
   d. customer service.

7. The retail image of a store is the
   a. owner's perception of the store.
   b. suppliers' perception of the store.
   c. consumers' perception of the store.
   d. competitors' perception of the store.

8. Two methods of setting and adjusting retail prices are
   a. turnover and discount.
   b. markup and markdown.
   c. the percentage method and the wheel of retailing.
   d. profit analysis and factoring.

9. Atmospherics and amenities provided to shoppers are key factors that contribute to
   a. the level of service.
   b. retail image.
   c. pricing strategy.
   d. location strategy.

Applying Marketing Concepts

Snow Unlimited is an independently owned retail store that sells skis, boots, poles, and miscellaneous equipment for both cross-country and downhill skiing. In addition, it offers a complete line of men's and women's ski clothes, a ski rental service, a ski repair service, and various instructional classes.

> **Select the best answer.**

1. This ski repair service is principally part of the retailer's
   a. atmospherics.
   b. promotional strategy.
   c. distribution strategy.
   d. customer-service strategy.

2. In selling equipment for both downhill and cross-country skiing, Snow Unlimited made a decision about its
   a. merchandise strategy.
   b. customer-service strategy.
   c. distribution strategy.
   d. atmospherics.

Additional Activities

Experiential Exercise

The purpose of this exercise is to develop your understanding of the operations of retail stores located outside shopping centers. You are asked to select a specific store and examine its overall retail image and retailing strategy.

Visit a retail store that is located in a downtown business district, near your campus or home, or any location other than in a shopping center. If the store is small and independently owned, speak with the owner. If not, speak with the manager. Ask questions to gather information about the following areas and then write a report summarizing your findings.

- Name of the store and a description of the merchandise it sells.

- What is the store's target market?

- How was the merchandise mix selected?

- How are prices determined? When are sales held?

- Why was the location selected? Does the owner think the store could be in a better location? Why?

- How is the store advertised and promoted?

- What, if any, special design and decorative features have been incorporated into the store?

- If you were the owner of the store, what changes, if any, would you want to make in the store's retailing strategy?

Questions for Exploration

Conceptual

The textbook notes several exceptions to the wheel-of-retailing hypothesis, but concludes that "the wheel pattern has held sufficiently consistent in the past to make it a useful general indicator of future retailing developments." Do you agree or disagree with the conclusion? Why?

Practical

Based on what you saw in the video program for this lesson and on your reading of textbook Chapter 15, what are the top three things that West Ridge Mountaineering has done right? What are the top three things you would suggest the store do differently?

Answer Key

Key Concepts	1. a	5. c	8. h
	2. e	6. g	9. i
	3. b	7. f	10. j
	4. d		

Completion	1. ultimate	8. markup
	2. prices, services, retailers	9. markup
	3. retail image	10. markdown
	4. target market	11. location
	5. merchandise	12. promotional
	6. customer service	13. atmospherics
	7. prices	14. vendor-managed inventory

Self-Test	1. c	4. a	7. c
	2. c	5. d	8. b
	3. c	6. b	9. b

Applying Marketing Concepts	1. d
	2. a

The chief business of the
American people is business.
                              —Calvin Coolidge

16
Retailing II

Assignments

For the most effective study of this lesson, we suggest that you complete the assignments in the following sequence:

1. Read the study guide Overview (Lesson Notes and Video Program Notes) and the Learning Objectives for this lesson.

2. Read *Contemporary Marketing Wired,* 9th edition, Chapter 15, "Retailing," pages 511-523, and review pages 506-508, "Locations in Planned Shopping Centers."

3. View "Jewels, Jeans, and Jogging Shoes: A Case Study in Retailing" video program.

4. Review the textbook assignment for this lesson.

5. Complete the Review Activities (Key Concepts and Completion), Self-Test, and Applying Marketing Concepts for this lesson.

6. Check your answers against the Answer Key at the end of the lesson, and review when necessary.

7. Complete any of the Additional Activities (Experiential Exercise and Questions for Exploration) that interest you or that are assigned by your instructor.

Overview

Lesson Notes

Perhaps one of the most significant trends in retailing in the last half of the 20th century has been the movement of retail stores from the downtowns of cities to planned shopping centers in the suburbs.

A **planned shopping center** is a group of stores planned, coordinated and marketed as a unit to shoppers in a specific geographic area. There are three basic types of planned shopping centers, distinguished mainly by their retail mix, physical size, and size of population served. The smallest, the **neighborhood shopping center,** is characterized by stores offering convenience goods and some shopping goods. Typically it has from five to fifteen stores and serves from 5,000 to 50,000 shoppers who live within a few minutes' traveling time. The next largest center is a **community shopping center**, featuring ten to thirty retail stores with more shopping goods. The community shopping center is often anchored by a large variety store or a branch of a local department store and serves a trade area from 20,000 to 100,000 people who live within a few miles. The largest center is the **regional shopping center**, encompassing at least 400,000 square feet of shopping space and as many as 200 stores, including at least one major department store, offering convenience, shopping, and specialty goods, along with professional and personal service facilities. Successful regional shopping centers are usually located in an area where at least 250,000 people live within 30 minutes' driving time.

In recent years, the growth of planned shopping centers in the United States has slowed, with customers preferring discount stores that offer convenient one-stop shopping. Many malls are now offering more services to attract customers, along with recreation and entertainment facilities. Also, specialty store shopping centers are beginning to emerge. These centers, designed to attract upscale consumers, contain specialty stores and restaurants.

At present, the United States has about 2.7 million retail outlets in shopping centers, downtown business districts, and other locations where customers' needs can be served. Because retailing constantly changes in response to consumer demand, it is not possible to apply a single classification system to retail operations. However, retail businesses can be categorized on the following five bases: shopping effort expended by customers, services provided to customers, product lines, locations of retail transactions, and forms of ownership.

In terms of the **shopping effort** that consumers are willing to expend to purchase a particular item, retail outlets can be classified as convenience retailers, shopping stores, and specialty retailers. This classification reflects the classification of consumer goods described in Lesson 10. **Convenience retailers**, such as food stores, are easily accessible and have long hours. **Shopping stores** offer goods that consumers typically "shop around" for before making a purchase decision, such as clothing, furniture, and appliances. Because of their merchandise, services, and reputation, **specialty retailers** are stores that consumers make a considerable effort to go to for shopping excursions.

In classifying retailers by services provided, the range extends from almost no services or few services (self-service and self-selection) to complete individualized attention to the customer's needs and wishes (full-service).

The three major groupings of retailers by product line are specialty stores, limited-line retailers, and general merchandise retailers. A **specialty store**, often an independent retailer such as a bakery, carries only part of a single product line, although the store stocks that product in depth, or variety. In comparison, a **limited-line** store carries a large assortment of one product line or a few closely related product lines. Home furnishings and some clothing stores are examples of limited-line retailers.

Category killers are stores that offer huge selections and low prices combined in single product lines. These stores have taken away business from general merchandise discount stores which cannot compete.

Finally, **general merchandise retailers** carry a broad variety of product lines and stock them in some depth. Traditional types of general merchandise retailers include variety stores and department stores. Within this category, **mass merchandisers** also offer a wide product line, but offer fewer services and lower prices than department stores. **Discount houses, off-price retailers, hypermarkets,** and catalogue retailers are all types of mass merchandisers. Off-price retailers, many of which are concentrated in **outlet malls,** are stores that stock only designer labels or brand-name clothing and resell it at low prices. **Supercenters** are smaller versions of hypermarkets.

One of the most basic classifications of retailers is by location of retail transaction: in the store or outside the store (nonstore). Almost all retail transactions do occur in a store, but nonstore retailing in the form of direct selling, direct-response selling, and automatic merchandising is important for some products. Direct selling, usually in the consumer's home, is often used for products that can be demonstrated: household products and encyclopedias, for example. Direct-response selling allows customers to order merchandise by telephone, mail, fax machine, or computer or by visiting a mail-order desk. **Home shopping** is a recent innovation in nonstore selling in which customers view merchandise on cable-television networks, then place their orders by telephone. In Internet retailing, customers buy products through the World Wide Web. Automatic merchandising refers to sales by vending machines, of everything from soft drinks to lottery tickets.

The last basis on which to classify retailers is by form of ownership. The two major categories are chain stores and independent retailers. **Chain stores,** which are centrally owned and managed and carry the same product lines, enjoy considerable economies of scale from their ability to purchase large volumes of products. **Independent retailers,** although not as prominent as the large national chains, account for almost 75 percent of all retail sales in the United States.

One interesting recent trend in retailing is **scrambled merchandising.** To match changing consumer shopping patterns, some retailers are now carrying dissimilar product lines in an attempt to increase sales volume. The gas station that sells groceries is an example of scrambled merchandising, as is the supermarket that carries motor oil.

The future of retailing is likely to be filled with many changes that benefit consumers, including the expansion of innovations such as the Internet and home shopping that have already proved successful. Other innovations, such as detailed receipts and faster checkout from computerized checkout stations, also benefit consumers and will be more widely used in the future. With new forms of retailing emerging at a fairly rapid pace, the field of retailing has much to offer the innovative, energetic marketer.

Video Program Notes

The video program for this lesson illustrates retailing by examining the diverse mixture of stores in South Coast Plaza, a large regional shopping center in Orange County, California. Henry Segerstrom, owner and developer of South Coast Plaza, describes how the shopping center started in the mid-1960s with a Sears, one other department store, and about 80 small stores, designed principally to serve middle-class shoppers. In the late 1970s, South Coast Plaza began to evolve from its rather conventional beginnings and expand into a major center of high-end destination stores offering distinctive goods and services to upscale consumers.

Included in the program are examples of the great variety of stores within South Coast Plaza to show how retailers offer different atmospheres, provide different levels of customer service, and use different product-line strategies. Officials of South Coast Plaza discuss their ongoing efforts to attract distinctive retailers to the center in order to maintain a retail mix that draws customers not only from southern California but from throughout the world.

As you watch the video program, consider the following questions:

1. What type of shopping center is South Coast Plaza?

2. What anchor stores are identified in the program?

3. Are anchor stores as important to South Coast Plaza today as they were when the center first opened?

4. What was the original target market for South Coast Plaza? How did that change over time?

5. Why do shopping centers feature seasonal events, such as Christmas with its elaborate decorations and strolling carolers?

6. What does the management of South Coast Plaza consider when acquiring new lessees?

7. What is the "retail image" of stores that locate in South Coast Plaza?

8. What examples of "destination stores" are shown in the program?

9. Why does South Coast Plaza have an art museum, a currency exchange outlet, and "fine dining"?

10. How does the management of South Coast Plaza support the individual retailers in the shopping center?

Learning Objectives

After completing your study of this lesson, you should be able to:

1. Define the following terms as they relate to retailing:

category killer	mass merchandiser
chain store	off-price retailer
department store	outlet mall
discount house	planned shopping center
general merchandise retailer	scrambled merchandising
home shopping	specialty store
hypermarket	supercenter
limited-line store	variety store

2. Identify the five bases used to classify retailers.

3. Describe the main types of nonstore retailing.

4. Describe and give examples of the types of retailers in each of the five classifications: shopping effort,

services provided, product line, location, and form of ownership.

5. Explain the concept of scrambled merchandising.

Review Activities

Key Concepts

Identify each of the following retailing concepts by writing the letter of the appropriate term in the blank next to the corresponding description.

a. chain store
b. planned shopping center
c. scrambled merchandising
d. automatic merchandising
e. home shopping
f. outlet mall
g. limited-line store
h. general merchandise retailer
i. neighborhood shopping center
j. variety store

k. community shopping center
l. department store
m. regional shopping center
n. mass merchandiser
o. discount house
p. off-price retailer
q. hypermarket
r. category killer
s. specialty store

_____ 1. one of a group of retail stores centrally owned and managed and carrying the same product lines

_____ 2. retailing practice of carrying dissimilar product lines in an effort to increase sales

_____ 3. a form of nonstore retailing in which products are dispensed by machines

_____ 4. group of retail stores planned, coordinated, and marketed as a unit to consumers within a geographical trade area

_____ 5. use of cable television to sell products through telephone orders

_____ 6. retailer that offers a large assortment within a single product line or closely related lines

_____ 7. shopping center consisting entirely of off-price retailers

_____ 8. store that carries a wide variety of product lines in some depth

_____ 9. a retailer that has a huge selection in a single product line and low prices

_____ 10. the smallest of the three main types of shopping center

_____ 11. giant mass merchandiser of soft goods and groceries, operating on a low-price, self-service basis

_____ 12. retail store selling products at lower-than-normal prices, but not offering typical retail services

_____ 13. retailer that sells well-known brand-name clothing at lower than usual retail prices

_____ 14. store that offers a wider line of goods than a department store, but usually not the same depth of assortment

_____ 15. large retail firm that handles a variety of merchandise, including clothing, appliances, and furniture

_____ 16. a center with a trade area that has from 20,000 to 100,000 people

_____ 17. a center with a trade area that has at least 250,000 people

_____ 18. a store offering an extensive range and assortment of low-price merchandise

_____ 19. retailer that offers only part of a single product line

Completion

Fill each blank in the following paragraphs with the most
appropriate term from the list of completion answers below.
A term may be used once, more than once, or not at all.

automatic	full	ownership
automatic	general	planned
merchandising	merchandise	shopping center
chain	home shopping	product
community	hypermarket	regional
convenience	independent	scrambled
department	limited-line	self
dependent	location	services
direct	mass	shopping
direct-response	merchandisers	shopping effort
direct-response	mixed	specialty
selling	neighborhood	specialty store
direct selling	off-price	variety
discount house	outlet malls	

1. The shift of retail trade away from downtown to the suburbs
   started in the 1950s. In the suburbs, a group of retail stores
   planned, coordinated, and marketed as a unit to shoppers in
   a specific geographical trade area is known as a _____.

2. The three main types of planned shopping centers are,
   in sequence from smallest to largest, _____ shopping
   centers, _____ shopping centers, and _____
   shopping centers.

3. In neighborhood shopping centers, the product mix is
   mainly _____ goods and some _____ goods.

4. Community shopping centers serve 20,000 to 100,000 people
   in trade areas extending a few miles. In addition to the stores
   found in neighborhood shopping centers, community shopping
   centers are likely to have more stores with _____ goods.

5. Successful regional shopping centers are usually built in areas
   in which 250,000 people live within 30 minutes' driving time.
   These centers are built around one or more major _____
   stores.

6. A recent trend in shopping centers is targeted at upscale consumers. These _____ shopping centers feature specialty shops and restaurants.

7. Because of the ongoing evolution of retailing, no single classification system has been devised. Retail operations, however, can be categorized on five bases: _____ expended by customers, _____ provided to customers, _____ lines, _____ of retail transactions, and form of _____.

8. Stores classified by shopping effort fall into three categories. Stores such as grocery stores that are easily accessible, have long store hours, and easy parking are known as _____ retailers. Furniture stores and appliance retailers are in the category known as _____ stores. Stores that provide a combination of product lines, services, or reputations in an attempt to convince consumers to expend considerable effort to shop at their stores are _____ retailers.

9. Another basis for classification of retail stores is the degree of service offered to customers. At one extreme is customer _____-service and at the other is _____-service.

10. When retailers are classified by the type of product line handled, there are three major categories: _____ stores, _____ stores, and _____ retailers.

11. General merchandise retailers carry a large number of product lines and stock them in some depth. This category of retailers includes many different variations, including _____ stores, _____ stores, and _____.

12. Although they account for less than 1 percent of all retail sales in the United States, _____ stores are very popular in other parts of the world.

13. A store that carries diverse merchandise, including personal and household items, clothing, furniture, and linens, and offers a wide variety of services such as return privileges and gift wrapping is a _____ store.

14. Stores that stock a wider line of goods than a department store, although usually with less depth, are classified as _____.

15. The type of mass merchandiser that charges lower-than-normal prices but does not offer sales assistance or home delivery is a _____.

16. A type of discount house that sells well-known brand-name clothing at less than usual retail prices is an _____ retailer. Recently, many of these retailers are concentrating in _____.

17. A store that usually has at least 200,000 square feet of retail space and sells grocery and general merchandise at discount prices is a _____.

18. Not all retail transactions take place in stores. Three common types of nonstore retailing are _____, _____, and _____.

19. The form of selling that provides maximum convenience for the consumer and allows the manufacturer to control its distribution channels is _____ selling.

20. Retailers that take consumers' orders by mail or via telephone, computer, or fax machine are practicing _____ selling.

21. Current retailing trends include _____ retailing and shopping via cable television. The latter method, called _____, enables consumers to phone in orders for merchandise that is presented on television.

22. The last type of nonstore retailing is principally through vending machines and is known as _____ merchandising.

23. Stores classified by ownership fall into two major groups: corporate _____ stores and _____ retailers.

24. The retailer's attempt to satisfy consumer demands for convenient, one-stop shopping by offering dissimilar product lines is known as _____ merchandising.

Self-Test

1. Sunnybrooke is a shopping center that has ten stores, with a retail store mix of mostly convenience-goods retailers and some shopping-goods retailers. It serves about 10,000 people living within a commuting radius of a few minutes. Sunnybrooke is a
   a. neighborhood shopping center.
   b. community shopping center.
   c. regional shopping center.
   d. downtown shopping district.

2. East Gate offers shopping at over 200 stores, including four anchor stores, plus free parking. It also has professional offices, two bank branches, and a savings and loan. It does *not* have a supermarket. East Gate is located within thirty minutes of a quarter of a million people. East Gate is a
   a. downtown shopping district.
   b. neighborhood shopping center.
   c. regional shopping center.
   d. community shopping center.

3. The type of retail store that carries the narrowest assortment of goods is the
   a. department store.
   b. hypermarket.
   c. specialty store.
   d. mass merchandiser.

4. A major difference between a discount store and a department store is that a discount store
   a. is smaller.
   b. is larger.
   c. offers fewer services.
   d. is less conveniently located.

5. Gem-Mart is a retail store occupying 220,000 square feet and selling soft goods and groceries, with few services, at extremely low prices. Gem-Mart is a
   a. hypermarket.
   b. department store.
   c. supermarket.
   d. discount store.

6. Round the Clock—a retail store that is conveniently located, charges moderately high prices, is open 24 hours, and offers rapid checkout service—can be classified as a
   a. supermarket.
   b. convenience store.
   c. limited-line store.
   d. specialty store.

7. A principal difference between a limited-line store and a specialty store is that a limited-line store
   a. carries only part of a single line of products.
   b. carries a few related lines of merchandise.
   c. offers fewer services.
   d. offers lower prices.

8. Which of the following stores are types of general merchandise retailers?
   a. variety store, department store, hypermarket
   b. department store, specialty store, supermarket
   c. discount store, department store, supermarket
   d. limited-line retailer, hypermarket, discount store

9. Any retailer that offers a wide assortment of products and lower prices and makes a profit by selling more and offering fewer services is a
   a. mass merchandiser.
   b. hypermarket.
   c. variety store.
   d. general merchandise store.

10. The major advantage of chain-store operations over independent retailers is
    a. location.
    b. prestige.
    c. customer loyalty.
    d. economies of scale.

Applying Marketing Concepts

Juel Lee owns Oriental Imports, a store specializing in fine antiques and art objects from China, Japan, and other parts of Asia. Because much of his merchandise is exclusive and unusual, his prices are quite high. For some time, he has been dissatisfied with his store's location in the downtown business district. The other stores on his block include a discount camera store, a travel agency, a mini-blind store, a hardware store, a drugstore, and an outlet store that sells sportswear. Mr. Lee thinks that a different location could help him to attract more customers, and he is willing to pay the higher rent that would probably result from the move.

In evaluating possible locations for his new store, Mr. Lee is looking at a small shopping center near his home in the suburbs, a community shopping center that has a branch of a local department store and that is very busy on the weekends, a regional shopping center that has more than 200 stores, and a new shopping center that has restaurants and jewelry stores, home furnishings stores, and high-fashion stores.

1. Mr. Lee's store is probably classified as a
   a. general merchandise store.
   b. variety store.
   c. specialty store.
   d. shopping store.

2. Customers of Mr. Lee's store probably are
   a. not willing to expend much effort to get to his store.
   b. willing to travel up to five miles to visit his store.
   c. willing to travel more than ten miles to visit his store.

3. The best location for Oriental Imports is probably either the
   a. small shopping center or community shopping center.
   b. community shopping center or regional shopping center.
   c. small shopping center or new shopping center.
   d. regional shopping center or new shopping center.

Additional Activities

Experiential Exercise

In this exercise you will study a variety of characteristics of planned shopping centers.

- Using a map of a city near your campus or home, carefully identify the locations of two different types of r' nned shopping centers. Next, measure the driving distance between the two centers. What are the logical reasons for the location of each planned shopping center? If you were to build a neighborhood shopping center in or near your community, where would you build? Why?

- Visit a planned shopping area and draw a map showing the location of each retail store in the center. (If the center you have selected is very large, draw a map of only one section or level.) Also show all parking areas and walkways. Select a group of four stores next to one another and classify each store by each of the following bases: customer shopping effort, services provided, product line, and ownership.

- If you were able to rent space in the center that you visited, what type of store would you open? Why? In what part of the center would you like to rent? Why?

Questions for Exploration

Conceptual

For many people, the act of shopping provides two kinds of satisfaction. The first is the efficient acquisition of products to satisfy a perceived need or want. The second is emotional and is derived from the experience of shopping: interacting with salespeople, the atmosphere of the store or shopping center, examining different types of merchandise.

Home shopping on cable television may very well provide the first kind of satisfaction, but can it provide the second kind? If it does, how?

If not, how could home shopping be changed to provide that satisfaction? If it cannot be changed, will home shopping ever be widely accepted?

Practical

Is South Coast Plaza a regional shopping center or is it becoming a specialty store shopping center as described in the textbook?

Compare and contrast South Coast Plaza with other regional shopping centers with which you are familiar. What kind of atmosphere does South Coast Plaza have?

Is atmosphere really that important to retailing? Why?

Answer Key

Key Concepts	1. a	6. g	11. q	16. k
	2. c	7. f	12. o	17. m
	3. d	8. h	13. p	18. j
	4. b	9. r	14. n	19. s
	5. e	10. i	15. l	

Completion

1. planned shopping center
2. neighborhood, community, regional
3. convenience, shopping
4. shopping
5. department
6. specialty store
7. shopping effort, services, product, location, ownership
8. convenience, shopping, specialty
9. self, full
10. limited-line, specialty, general merchandise
11. variety, department (either order); mass merchandisers
12. variety
13. department
14. mass merchandisers
15. discount house
16. off-price, outlet malls
17. hypermarket
18. direct selling, direct-response selling, automatic merchandising (any order)
19. direct
20. direct-response
21. Internet, home shopping
22. automatic
23. chain, independent
24. scrambled

Self-Test	1. a	5. a	8. a
	2. c	6. b	9. a
	3. c	7. b	10. d
	4. c		

Applying Marketing Concepts	1. c
	2. c
	3. d

If you got it, it came by truck.
　　　　　　　　—Trucking industry slogan

17

Physical Distribution

Assignments

For the most effective study of this lesson, we suggest that you complete the assignments in the following sequence:

1. Read the study guide Overview (Lesson Notes and Video Program Notes) and the Learning Objectives for this lesson.

2. Read *Contemporary Marketing Wired,* 9th edition, Chapter 16, "Logistics and Value Chain Management," pages 528-549.

3. View "Deliverance: A Case Study in Physical Distribution" video program.

4. Review the textbook assignment for this lesson.

5. Complete the Review Activities (Key Concepts and Completion), Self-Test, and Applying Marketing Concepts for this lesson.

6. Check your answers against the Answer Key at the end of the lesson, and review when necessary.

7. Complete any of the Additional Activities (Experiential Exercises and Questions for Exploration) that interest you or that are assigned by your instructor.

Overview

Lesson Notes

Logistics encompasses far more than just the act of transporting information, goods, and services from one place to another. Logistics is an important part of any firm's overall marketing effort. **Efficient physical distribution,** one part of logistics, is critical to providing customer service, and customer satisfaction depends heavily on giving customers what they need, when they need it.

Effective distribution requires proper management of the **supply (value) chain,** or the order in which suppliers create and deliver goods and services. **Value-added service,** a component of the chain, adds an improved or supplemental service that is not normally anticipated or received.

In order to reduce logistics costs, **third-party (contract) logistics firms** handle logistical activities for other companies.

The physical-distribution **system** includes several different components: customer service, transportation, warehousing, warehouse site selection, inventory control, order processing, and protective packaging and materials handling. The components are interrelated: a decision about one component may impact all the other components.

The basic goal of a logistics system is to achieve a specified level of customer service while minimizing the costs of moving the good from where it is produced to the ultimate purchaser. Suboptimization results when companies maximize cost but interfere with progress toward broader company goals. One example concerns the use of **maquiladoras** to cut labor and tariff costs. Reduction in logistics cost should help maintain **customer-service standards.**

Of the major elements of physical-distribution systems, transportation accounts for 40 to 60 percent of total distribution costs. Five major transportation modes are available for use in physical distribution: railroads, motor carriers, water carriers, pipelines, and air freight.

Railroads still control the largest share of the ton-miles in the United States. Railroads are especially efficient for moving bulky goods over long distances, such as lumber, iron and steel, coal, automobiles, and grain and chemicals.

Motor carriers (trucks) provide relatively fast, consistent transportation for shipments of all sizes. In comparison to railroads, motor carriers move more manufactured products such as clothing, furniture and fixtures, lumber and plastic products, food products, leather products, and machinery.

Water carriers, including inland barge lines and oceangoing ships, are relatively slow but quite inexpensive. Barges are often used for transporting bulky commodities such as grain, gravel, lumber, sand, and steel. Deepwater ships carry goods between U.S. ports on the Great Lakes and across oceans in international trade. Among products frequently transported by water carriers are fuel, oil, coal, chemicals, minerals, and petroleum products.

Pipelines are a highly specialized transport mode. Although slow, pipelines are extremely efficient transporters of natural gas, oil (both crude and refined products such as gasoline, jet fuel, diesel fuel, and kerosene), and coal in slurry form.

Air freight provides the fastest and most expensive method of moving goods. Air carriers are moving increasing amounts of freight, and forecasters expect air cargo loads to double by 2013. Because of the high cost of air freight, air carriers are used primarily for valuable or highly perishable goods such as computers, fresh flowers, and specialty foods.

In addition, small quantities of products can be shipped via bus, United Parcel Service, Federal Express, DHL International, and the U.S. Postal Service.

In selecting the best transportation mode, logistics managers must consider such factors as speed, reliability, frequency, availability, flexibility, and cost. For some products and some situations, a combination of transportation modes can be used, including piggyback (truck and railroad), fishyback (truck and water carrier), and birdyback (truck and air carrier).

There are two basic types of warehouses: **storage warehouses**, where goods are stored for a moderate to long periods of time, and **distribution warehouses**, where goods are assembled, redistributed and stored for only a short time. Many manufacturers, to reduce transportation costs, have developed distribution centers. Break-bulk centers break down large shipments into smaller ones and distribute them to individual customers. Make-bulk centers consolidate several small shipments into one large shipment and deliver the shipment to the customer. Through automation, logistics managers can cut distribution costs and improve customer service. Selecting sites for warehouses and distribution centers entails numerous considerations, including transportation accessibility, proximity to customers, cost and availability of labor, taxes, and state laws.

Inventory control is an especially important element in logistics systems. Basically, the logistics manager must determine how much inventory to hold at each location. In determining optimum inventory levels, the logistics manager may use a number of techniques, including the **just-in-time (JIT) system**, which involves minimizing inventory to reduce inventory-carrying costs.

The logistics manager is also concerned with order processing and materials handling. Efficient order processing is critical to meeting the firm's customer-service standards. Order processing usually includes several steps: a credit check, recording the sale, making accounting entries, and locating and shipping the item and adjusting inventory records. A **stockout** occurs when an order for a product is not available for shipment. **Materials handling** refers to all activities involved in moving goods from within the manufacturer's plants and warehouses through to the transportation company's terminals. Materials handling included **unitizing** (combining as many packages as possible into one load) and **containerization** (placing several unitized loads into a large container).

A properly operating physical-distribution system can be a marketing plus; an inefficient system can be a disaster. All marketing managers should make the effort to understand the organization's physical-distribution system and be constantly alert for opportunities to improve it.

Video Program Notes

A marketer must make certain decisions to ensure that a product is satisfactorily distributed from the manufacturer to the ultimate consumer. Through the marketing operations of a major water distributor, Arrowhead Water Company, the video program shows that even the simplest logistics system is filled with marketing choices that affect the smooth, profitable operation of the company and the ultimate satisfaction of the consumer. By comparing Arrowhead's direct-to-home distribution system and its retail-grocery-store distribution, the program depicts the choices a marketing manager must make, choices that facilitate the handling of products and their delivery to the ultimate consumers. The marketing manager must solve the problems of producing targeted levels of customer service and satisfaction at the lowest overall cost by balancing marketing variables related to transportation, inventory control, materials handling, order processing, and warehousing. Every single decision that the marketer makes on the logistics of products affects the *overall* efficiency and effectiveness of its distribution.

As you watch the video program, consider the following questions:

1. What methods of transportation does Arrowhead use to get the product to its plant for processing?

2. What are the products Arrowhead offers in its bottled-water product line?

3. How many days' inventory of its various products does Arrowhead try to keep?

4. Who plays the key role in achieving the standard of customer service at Arrowhead?

5. What are some of the functions performed by the route salesman?

6. How is order processing handled at Arrowhead?

7. What size products are sold to grocery chains?

8. How did Arrowhead management decide how many bottles to put in each case?

9. How does Arrowhead use the concept of unitizing?

10. Since it has no fleet for wholesale delivery, how does Arrowhead get its products to the grocers' shelves?

Learning Objectives

After completing your study of this lesson, you should be able to:

1. Define the following terms as they relate to physical distribution:

class rate	stockout
commodity rate	storage warehouse
containerization	system
customer-service standards	suboptimization
distribution warehouse	supply (value) chain
just-in-time (JIT) system	third-party
logistics	(contract)
maquiladora	logistics firm
materials handling	unitizing
physical distribution	value-added service

2. Explain the role of logistics in an effective marketing strategy.

3. Identify and compare major components of a physical-distribution system.

4. Outline the suboptimization problem in logistics.

5. Explain the impact of transportation deregulation on logistics activities.

6. Compare the major transportation alternatives on the basis of speed, dependability, cost, frequency of shipments, availability in different locations, and flexibility in handling products.

7. Discuss how transportation intermediaries and combined transportation modes can improve physical distribution.

Review Activities

Key Concepts

> **Identify each of the following physical-distribution concepts by writing the letter of the appropriate term in the blank next to the corresponding description.**
>
> a. physical distribution
> b. customer-service standards
> c. class rate
> d. commodity rate
> e. storage warehouse
> f. distribution warehouse
> g. maquiladora
> h. system
>
> i. third-party logistics firm
> j. materials handling
> k. unitizing
> l. containerization
> m. stockout
> n. just-in-time system
> o. suboptimization
> p. value-added service

_____ 1. components organized according to a plan for achieving a specific objective

_____ 2. standard transportation rate for moving specific commodities between any two points

_____ 3. activities dealing with the movement of goods from completion of production to acquisition by consumer

_____ 4. combining several unitized loads for ease and speed in shipping

_____ 5. quality of service that a firm attempts to provide to its customers

_____ 6. assembly plant set up by a U.S. firm in Mexico

_____ 7. company that specializes in handling logistics activities for other firms

_____ 8. place to assemble and then redistribute goods rapidly (rather than simply storing them)

_____ 9. combining as many packages as possible into one load, preferably on a pallet, to expedite movement and reduce damage and pilferage

_____ 10. rate given by carriers to shippers as a reward for regular use or large-quantity shipments

_____ 11. place where goods are kept for a period of time to help balance supply and demand for both buyer and seller

_____ 12. activities associated with moving goods within plants, warehouses, and transportation terminals

_____ 13. inventory-control system designed to minimize inventory at production plants

_____ 14. an item not available for shipment or sale

_____ 15. part of the physical-distribution system's focus on customer service

_____ 16. a condition that occurs when the manager of each physical-distribution function attempts to reduce costs but, because of the impact of each task on the others, produces less than optimal results

Completion

Fill each blank in the following paragraphs with the most appropriate term from the list of completion answers below. A term may be used once, more than once, or not at all.

air carriers	inexpensive	protective
automated	inland	packaging
break-bulk	inventory-carrying	and materials
class	inventory control	handling
commodity	inventory-holding	railroad
common	just-in-time (JIT)	railroads
components	make-bulk	storage
containerization	materials-handling	suboptimization
contract	motor carriers	systems
costs	oceangoing	time
customer	order-processing	transportation
customer service	physical distribution	trucking
delivery	pipelines	unitizing
distribution	place	warehousing
expensive	private	water carriers
freight forwarders		

1. Customer service, transportation, inventory control, packaging and materials handling, order processing, and warehousing comprise the key elements of _____.

2. By providing customers with the utilities of _____ and _____ , physical distribution contributes greatly to _____ satisfaction and therefore assists firms in implementing their marketing strategies.

3. The study of logistics is an example of the _____ approach to business problems.

4. A system is an organized group of _____ designed to achieve specific objectives.

5. A frequent problem in physical distribution is _____. This problem occurs when the manager of one distribution function attempts to minimize _____ but, because of the impact of one function on the others, the results are unsatisfactory.

6. Logistics managers have two goals: reduction of _____ and maintenance of the required level of _____.

7. Once an acceptable level of customer service has been established, the physical-distribution system should achieve that goal through the five elements of _____ , _____ , _____ , _____ , and _____.

8. The largest expense item in logistics is _____ cost.

9. There are two basic types of freight rates: class and commodity. Standard rates for every commodity moving between two places are _____ rates. Carriers often give _____ rates to shippers for large-quantity shipments or regular use.

10. There are three basic classifications of carriers: common, contract, and private. Carriers that serve the general public are known as _____ carriers. Carriers that do not offer their services to the general public are known as _____ carriers. Carriers that transport products only for a particular firm are known as _____ carriers.

11. The five principal transportation alternatives open to the logistics manager are _____ , _____ , _____ , _____ , and _____.

12. The transportation mode that moves the greatest amount of freight and is one of the most efficient methods for moving bulk commodities is the _____.

13. The transportation mode that has grown rapidly in recent decades and offers fast and consistent service for both large and small shipments is the _____ industry.

14. There are two basic types of water carriers: _____ and _____. Water carriers provide _____ transportation services for bulk commodities, but they are slow.

15. Third only to railroads and motor carriers in the number of ton-miles of materials transported are _____.

16. The relatively expensive transportation mode used to transport items that are valuable or highly perishable is _____.

17. Shippers may use transportation intermediaries who consolidate shipments and forward them to common carriers. These intermediaries, called _____, offer shippers lower _____ and faster delivery service.

18. Transportation modes are also combined to provide better service. Piggyback, fishyback, and birdyback are the names used to describe these modes. Piggyback, the most common, involves the combination of the _____ and railroading industries. Fishyback involves the combination of motor carriers and _____. Birdyback involves the combination of motor carriers and _____.

19. There are two types of warehouses. As the name indicates, _____ warehouses are used to store goods. Places where goods are assembled and redistributed are known as _____ warehouses.

20. Recently, manufacturers have developed central-distribution centers to cut transportation costs. The two types of central-distribution centers are _____ and _____.

21. Centers that consolidate shipments from many suppliers into one or more larger shipments are called _____ centers.

22. Centers that divide up large shipments into many smaller shipments are called _____ centers.

23. Some warehouses depend on machinery and computers for the efficient flow of materials. These _____ warehouses can reduce labor costs, worker injuries, pilferage, fires, and breakage; they also assist in inventory control.

24. The location of warehouses is a major decision for a firm. It is a complex decision involving the analysis of warehousing costs, _____ costs, and _____ costs from warehouse to customer.

25. The inventory-control system designed to minimize inventory at production plants by timing the arrival of shipments with the need for those materials is known as the _____ inventory system.

26. In order to meet its customer-service standards, a firm may have to use premium transportation services or increase the number of field warehouses if its _____ system is inefficient.

27. The practice of using pallets and special wrapping systems to combine as many packages as practical into one load that can be handled by modern equipment is known as _____. This practice requires less labor per unit, speeds movement, and reduces theft and damage.

28. To facilitate intermodal transfers, several unitized loads can be combined and placed in an 8-foot-wide box, from 10 to 40 feet long. This practice is known as _____.

Self-Test

1. Physical distribution includes each of the following activities **EXCEPT**
   a. customer service.
   b. inventory control.
   c. production control.
   d. materials handling.

2. One reason for increased attention to logistics activities is that
   a. transportation costs are up due to deregulation.
   b. most production problems have been solved.
   c. physical distribution accounts for almost 50 percent of marketing costs.
   d. technological breakthroughs are occurring in physical-distribution methods.

3. A major advantage of the just-in-time (JIT) system is that it
   a. minimizes inventory-carrying costs at production facilities.
   b. gets the product to customers just when they need it.
   c. reduces the time it takes to deliver inventory.
   d. eliminates inventory at the retailers.

4. The transportation mode that moves the largest amount of freight and is the most efficient is
   a. railroads.
   b. motor carriers.
   c. water carriers.
   d. air freight.

5. A freight forwarder is
   a. not used in international transportation.
   b. a supplemental carrier.
   c. a firm that consolidates shipments for shippers.
   d. an air-freight expediter.

6. Costs for which components of the physical-distribution system are the most expensive?
   a. warehousing
   b. transportation
   c. inventory control
   d. order processing
   e. administrative

7. The lowest ton-mile costs are achieved by
   a. water carriers.
   b. motor carriers.
   c. railroads.
   d. air carriers.

8. The principal difference between class rates and commodity rates is that class rates
   a. are special rates granted to shippers as a reward.
   b. are standard rates established for shipping various commodities.
   c. are illegal in some states.
   d. do not apply to shipping commodities.

9. Which of the following is **NOT** a form of intermodal transportation?
   a. piggyback
   b. fishyback
   c. horseyback
   d. birdyback

10. The two basic types of warehouses are
    a. storage and shipping.
    b. break-bulk and storage.
    c. make-bulk and distribution.
    d. storage and distribution.

Applying Marketing Concepts

The Tall-Low Company is a medium-sized chain of retail stores catering to very tall and very short men and women. It carries a full line of clothes and accessories for those markets. The company has had a brief but exciting history. Tall-Low began ten years ago with one store in a small southwestern city; it now has more than 200 stores nationwide. Such growth has brought not only profits to the company but also problems. The key problem facing the top management of Tall-Low is the challenge of physical distribution.

Currently, more than 300 suppliers ship directly to each Tall-Low store. Each store manager places orders directly and handles all shipping and materials-handling matters individually. This method has serious disadvantages for a firm the size of Tall-Low. First, the suppliers charge more for many small shipments than they would for one shipment to a company warehouse. Second, by purchasing in larger quantities, the company could obtain quantity discounts not received under the current method of operation. Third, shipments are sometimes lost or late in arriving at Tall-Low stores. Fourth, inspection, returned goods, and special orders place a burden on the local store manager. Fifth, the main office simply cannot control the buying activities of the local stores, much less keep a firm control of inventory. Sixth, sales are being lost because of too many stockouts in the retail stores.

One suggestion is to set up one central automated warehouse to receive all supplier shipments. From that location, goods could be shipped to the individual stores by common carrier. A second suggestion is to set up several strategically located automated warehouses, thereby cutting delivery time.

Some questions that need to be answered before a decision can be made are: Should the company buy a fleet of trucks or use common carriers? Should all buying, returned goods, and the like be coordinated with the main office?

1. The Tall-Low Company is thinking of setting up a
    a. store warehouse.
    b. distribution warehouse.
    c. public warehouse.
    d. common warehouse.

2. A key function of the warehouse the Tall-Low Company is thinking of building is
    a. unitizing.
    b. containerizing.
    c. break-bulk.
    d. make-bulk.

3. If the Tall-Low Company uses a common carrier to deliver orders to the individual stores, the type of rate it would be charged is the
    a. class rate.
    b. commodity rate.
    c. tariff rate.

4. The complaint that the Tall-Low Company is losing sales because of stockouts in stores means that
    a. customer-service standards are not being met.
    b. the stores are too far from the suppliers.
    c. the company needs to hire better store managers.

Additional Activities

Experiential Exercises

1. The purpose of this exercise is to help you understand the logistics system of a manufacturing firm. You are asked to visit a manufacturer and discuss the organization and the effectiveness of its logistics system.

Visit a medium- or large-sized manufacturing firm and discuss the logistics system with the manager. Obtain the information necessary to answer the following questions.

- What department is responsible for logistical functions in the firm? Draw an organization chart showing the departmental responsibility for the following functions: transportation, in-plant warehousing, field warehousing, inventory control, order processing, and materials handling. Be certain to include the title of each manager responsible for a logistical function.

- Is the authority to make decisions concerning logistics centralized or decentralized? Support your answer.

- What customer-service standards have been set for the logistics system? Are these standards being met?

- What steps has the company taken to avoid suboptimization?

- Does the company believe its logistical functions can be improved? If the answer is yes, where does it believe improvement can be made?

- Has deregulation of the transportation industry affected the company's logistics system? If so, how?

2. For this exercise, visit a company-owned warehouse and observe the materials-handling and order-processing systems. Obtain the information necessary to answer the following questions:

- Draw a floor plan that illustrates the various loading and storage areas and routes used to transfer materials. Use different-colored arrows to indicate the flow of traffic to and from storage

and loading areas. Why do the materials flow
that way? Could the flow be improved?

- Describe the order-receiving and order-processing
  systems. Does the warehouse use a computerized
  order-processing system? On the average, how
  much time passes between the moment an order
  is received and sent?

- Describe the materials-handling system.
  Is it automated?

Questions for Exploration

Conceptual

"Except for special cases (such as shut-ins), home delivery of
consumer nondurable products is a nonproductive use of a firm's
resources."

Agree or disagree with the preceding statement. Argue your case
and cite examples.

Practical

As described in the video program, Arrowhead Water Company
sells 25 percent of its bottled-water product to grocery outlets and
75 percent to business and residential customers. If the sales
proportions were reversed, with 75 percent to grocery outlets and
25 percent to business and residential customers, what changes
would probably occur in Arrowhead's distribution activities?
Would the company be better off or worse off? Why?

Answer Key

Key Concepts	1. h	5. b	9. k	13. n
	2. c	6. g	10. d	14. m
	3. a	7. i	11. e	15. p
	4. l	8. f	12. j	16. o

Completion

1. physical distribution
2. time, place (either order); customer
3. systems
4. components
5. suboptimization, costs
6. costs, customer service
7. transportation, warehousing, inventory control, order processing, protective packaging and materials handling (any order)
8. transportation
9. class, commodity
10. common, contract, private
11. railroads, motor carriers, water carriers, pipelines, air freight (any order)
12. railroad
13. trucking
14. inland, oceangoing (either order); inexpensive
15. pipelines
16. air freight
17. freight forwarders, costs
18. trucking, water carriers, air freight
19. storage, distribution
20. break-bulk, make-bulk (either order)
21. make-bulk
22. break-bulk
23. automated
24. materials-handling, delivery
25. just-in-time (JIT)
26. order-processing
27. unitizing
28. containerization

Self-Test	1. c	5. c	8. b
	2. c	6. b	9. c
	3. a	7. a	10. d
	4. a		

Applying Marketing Concepts	1. b	3. a
	2. c	4. a

Thou art not for the fashion of these times,
where none will sweat but for promotion.
—Shakespeare

18
Promotion

Assignments

For the most effective study of this lesson, we suggest that you complete the assignments in the following sequence:

1. Read the study guide Overview (Lesson Notes and Video Program Notes) and the Learning Objectives for this lesson.

2. Read *Contemporary Marketing Wired,* 9th edition, Chapter 17, "Integrated Marketing Communications," pages 558-596.

3. View "Polishing the Apple: A Case Study in Promotion" video program.

4. Review the textbook assignment for this lesson.

5. Complete the Review Activities (Key Concepts and Completion), Self-Test, and Applying Marketing Concepts for this lesson.

6. Check your answers against the Answer Key at the end of the lesson, and review when necessary.

7. Complete any of the Additional Activities (Experiential Exercises and Questions for Exploration) that interest you or that are assigned by your instructor.

Overview

Lesson Notes

The purpose of **promotion** is to inform, persuade, and influence the consumer's purchase decision. **Communication**—the transmission of a message from a sender to a receiver—is an essential part of a promotional strategy. The term **marketing communications** is used specifically for any messages that deal with buyer-seller relationships, including word-of-mouth advertising and other spontaneous forms of communication. A planned promotional strategy is the most important part of marketing communications.

With so many messages being sent, a consumer can easily become confused and may even tune out messages. To prevent a consumer from losing attention, marketers use **integrated marketing communications (IMC)** to coordinate all promotional activities, producing a unified, customer focused, rather than product-focused, promotional message.

An effective promotional strategy must, first, gain the receiver's attention; second, be understood by both the receiver and the sender, and, third, stimulate the receiver's needs and suggest an appropriate method of satisfying them. These characteristics are similar to those of **AIDA concept**, which stands for attention-interest-desire-action. This concept explains the steps a person goes through before deciding to purchase a product. A more detailed analysis of the communications involved in a promotional strategy begins with the *sender* (the marketing manager) who *encodes* (translates into understandable terms) the message in a form such as a sales presentation or advertisement, for delivery by a *channel* (a salesperson, public relations outlet, or advertising medium) to the receiver (consumer) who *decodes* (interprets) the message and makes a decision. The receiver's response to the message is *feedback*, which may be in the form of an attitude change, purchase, or nonpurchase. Feedback, in the form of marketing research, field sales reports, and other marketing data, goes back to the marketing manager who began the communications process.

It is generally agreed that promotion has five basic objectives. The first—and traditional—objective is to provide information about a particular good or service to potential consumers. An especially important objective of most promotion is to increase demand, especially selective demand, the demand for a specific brand. Two closely related objectives concern the product itself: differentiating the product and accentuating the value of the product. In differentiating the product, the promotion stresses the product's distinctive features; in accentuating the value, the promotion emphasizes the usefulness of the product to the potential consumer. The final objective of promotion is stabilizing sales, which is an attempt to reduce seasonal and other variations in demand for a product.

To achieve these promotional objectives, the marketer develops a **promotional mix**, a blending of nonpersonal and personal selling. **Nonpersonal selling** encompasses four distinct activities: advertising, sales promotion, direct marketing, and public relations. **Personal selling** involves a seller making a promotional presentation on a person-to-person basis with a prospective buyer. The major types of nonpersonal selling and personal selling will be covered in detail in the four lessons following this lesson.

Because the promotional mix comprises a variety of activities, one of the most challenging tasks for the marketer is designing the right combination of activities to achieve the desired objective. The composition of the promotional mix will usually be influenced by five factors: the nature of the market, the nature of the product, the stage in the life cycle of the product, the price of the product, and the funds available for promotion. For example, the promotional mix is likely to emphasize personal selling for a product when the market is limited and concentrated, when the nature of the product is complex and it is a business product, when a product is in its introductory or early growth stages, and when the price per unit is high. In contrast, advertising is usually emphasized when the market is large and widely dispersed, when a product is standardized and a consumer product, when a product is in the latter part of the growth stage or in the maturity and early decline stages, and when the price per unit is low.

The promotional mix is also affected by whether a pulling strategy or a pushing strategy is being used. In a **pulling strategy**, the marketer's goal is to stimulate demand for the product by the final user, who will then put pressure on the distribution channel to carry the good or service. The two components of the promotional mix often used in a pulling strategy are advertising and sales promotion, such as sponsoring special events and awarding prizes. In a **pushing strategy**, the marketer's goal is to sell the product to various members of the marketing channel (wholesalers and retailers), who will then "push" the product through the marketing channel to consumers. Personal selling, supplemented by cooperative advertising, trade discounts, and other dealer supports, is usually the principal means of carrying out a pushing strategy.

Promotion, regardless of the mix, requires money. Since no firm has unlimited resources, promotion expenditures must be budgeted. Four methods have traditionally been used to set promotional budgets: **percentage of sales, fixed sum per unit, meeting competition, and task objective.** The first three methods are rather arbitrary and sometimes are not sufficiently flexible to enable the marketer to respond to changing conditions and to meet promotional objectives. The **task-objective method** is considered by many to be the best for modern marketing. In this method, a firm first defines its promotional objectives in quantitative terms and then determines the amount and type of promotional activity required to achieve each objective.

Marketers must continually review and evaluate the effectiveness of the promotional effort. Although factors beyond the marketer's control make it difficult to isolate the effects of promotion, evaluation of past activities provides a solid foundation on which to build effective future promotional activities.

Video Program Notes

The video program for this lesson examines how Apple Computer, Inc., has made innovative and effective use of sales promotion and advertising in marketing its products over the years.

Apple entered the high-risk, high-technology field of computers in the early 1980s. Apple's original strategy was to offer new and distinctive products and to promote them with expensive and unconventional campaigns. The program shows a typical example of Apple's promotional strategy, with footage of the product roll-out held to introduce the Apple IIc. This "event marketing," attended by more than 4,000 Apple dealers, created enthusiasm among dealers and extensive press coverage of the Apple IIc.

Apple's advertising strategy, especially in television, is illustrated by several Apple commercials, including the classic "1984" that introduced U.S. consumers to the Macintosh, as well as later commercials that stressed the theme of "giving people the power to do their best." In addition to television commercials, the program shows Apple's extensive use of print advertising to create consumer demand, which was then reinforced by personal selling in retail stores.

The program also traces Apple's direct challenge to IBM in its efforts to position Macintosh computers as suitable for business use. Although early attempts were not completely successful, Apple gained entry to the business market because its computers and laser printers were being used for desktop publishing by creative departments and similar operations within businesses.

Another aspect of Apple's promotional strategy covered in the video program is how the company initially established itself in the educational marketplace and how Apple has responded to challenges to its position.

Although Apple's original market was principally the United States, the company now has extensive international distribution, and the program concludes with company representatives discussing the international marketing strategy and examples of television commercials that are part of that strategy.

As you watch the video program, consider the following questions:

1. What characteristics of the types of products Apple sells influence the promotional strategy?

2. Who are the targets for Apple's event marketing (sales promotion shows)?

3. Is Apple's event marketing a "push" or a "pull" strategy?

4. How does Apple attempt to blend advertising and personal selling efforts?

5. Which medium does Apple use to interest potential buyers? To interest dealers?

6. What strategy did Apple use when it first tried to enter the business market?

7. Why does Apple heavily promote its products to industry analysts?

8. Why was desktop publishing referred to as a "Trojan horse"?

9. What role does the educational market play in Apple's overall promotional strategy?

10. How do Apple's commercials reinforce the company's international marketing?

Learning Objectives

After completing your study of this lesson, you should be able to:

1. Define the following terms as they relate to promotion:

   AIDA concept
   fixed-sum-per-unit method
   integrated marketing
      communications (IMC)
   marketing communications
   meeting-competition method
   percentage-of-sales method

   personal selling
   promotion
   promotional mix
   pulling strategy
   pushing strategy
   task-objective method

2. Describe the communications process and the tasks any message must accomplish in order to be effective in the promotional strategy.

3. Identify and explain the specific objectives of promotion.

4. Describe the concept of the promotional mix and its relationship to the marketing mix.

5. Identify the elements of the promotional mix and describe the factors that influence the promotional mix.

6. Describe the two major alternative promotional strategies and the situations in which each is most appropriate.

7. Briefly explain various methods of allocating a promotional budget, including percentage of sales, fixed sum per unit, meeting competition, and task objective.

Review Activities

Key Concepts

Identify each of the following promotion concepts by writing the letter of the appropriate term in the blank next to the corresponding description.

a. promotion
b. marketing communications
c. AIDA concept
d. promotional mix
e. percentage-of-sales method
f. fixed-sum-per-unit method
g. task-objective method

h. pulling strategy
i. pushing strategy
j. meeting-competition method
k. integrated marketing communications (IMC)

_____ 1. promotional effort by a seller to stimulate demand by final users, who will then exert pressure on the distribution channel to carry the good or service

_____ 2. promotional-budget allocation method in which a firm allocates promotional efforts on the basis of the specific objectives to be accomplished

_____ 3. transmission of messages from a sender to a receiver of messages dealing with buyer-seller relationships

_____ 4. combination of personal selling and nonpersonal selling by marketers in an attempt to achieve promotional objectives

_____ 5. promotional-budget allocation method in which allocated funds are based on a specified percentage of either past or forecasted sales

_____ 6. acronym for the steps an individual takes prior to making a purchase decision

_____ 7. activity designed to inform, persuade, and influence the consumer's purchase decision

_____ 8. promotional-budget allocation method in which promotional expenditures are a predetermined dollar amount for each sales or production unit

_____ 9. promotional effort by a seller to members of the marketing channel to stimulate personal selling of a good or service

_____ 10. promotional-budget allocation method that matches the promotional expenditures of competitors

_____ 11. coordination of promotional activities to produce a customer-focused unified message

Completion

> **Fill each blank in the following paragraphs with the most appropriate term from the list of completion answers below. A term may be used once, more than once, or not at all.**
>
> | | | |
> |---|---|---|
> | advertising | market | publicity |
> | buyer | meeting-competition | public relations |
> | communications | nonpersonal | pulling |
> | decrease | percentage-of-sales | pushing |
> | demand | personal | sales promotion |
> | differentiate | personal selling | seller |
> | fixed-sum-
    per-unit | price | stabilize |
> | funds | private | task-objective |
> | increase | product | trade promotion |
> | information | promotion | value |

1. Of the four variables a marketing manager works with in developing a marketing mix, the function of informing, persuading, and influencing the consumer's purchase decision is known as _____.

2. Promotional strategy is closely related to the process of _____.

3. Marketing communications are those messages that deal with relationships between the _____ and _____.

4. In general, the objectives of promotion are considered to be to provide _____ , to increase _____ , to _____ the product, to accentuate the product's _____ , and to _____ sales.

5. If a firm is using a pulling strategy, the promotional objective is probably to _____ demand.

6. If a firm's advertising stresses the unique features of a product, the promotional objective is probably to _____ the product.

7. If a firm's advertising emphasizes the utility of a product, the promotional objective is probably to accentuate the _____ of the product.

8. If a firm develops a strategy to even out the sales volume of a seasonal product, the promotional objective is to _____ sales levels.

9. The traditional function of promotion has been to provide _____.

10. The marketer may communicate with consumers in two basic ways: through _____ selling and _____ selling.

11. A person-to-person promotional presentation to the buyer is called _____ selling.

12. Nonpersonal selling can be divided into six categories: _____ , _____ , _____ , _____ , _____ , and _____ .

13. The nonpersonal presentation of goods and services to a large audience through various media is _____ .

14. Communications efforts that stimulate consumer purchasing and dealer effectiveness is _____ .

15. A firm's communications with its various publics is _____ .

16. Favorable attention from the media, not paid for by a sponsor, is called _____ .

17. Direct communications other than personal sales contacts between buyer and seller are defined as _____ _____ .

18. The five factors that influence the promotional mix for a specific product are the nature of the _____ , the nature of the _____ , the stage in the life cycle of the _____ , the _____ of the product, and the availability of _____ for promotion.

19. To reach a market with large numbers of customers spread over a wide area, the marketer is apt to make extensive use of _____ .

20. In the marketing of shopping goods, _____ plays an important role.

21. For a product in the introductory stage of its life cycle, emphasis is usually placed on _____ to inform the marketplace of the new product.

22. For low-value consumer goods, such as chewing gum, soft drinks, and snack foods, the dominant component of the promotional mix is _____ .

23. Implementation of any promotional strategy requires the availability of _____.

24. When a seller uses a promotional effort to stimulate demand for a product by final users, the seller is using a _____ strategy.

25. When a seller uses a promotional effort to stimulate members of the marketing channel to sell a product, the seller is using a _____ strategy.

26. The four traditional methods of budgeting for promotion are the _____ method, _____ method, _____ method, and _____ method.

27. The most common way of establishing promotional budgets is the _____ method.

28. Instead of a percentage of sales, some firms allocate a _____.

29. A method that does not necessarily pertain to promotional objectives and thus is probably inappropriate for most marketing programs is the _____ method.

30. The method that is based on a sound evaluation of a firm's promotional objectives is the _____ method.

Self-Test

| Select the best answer. |

1. The most significant components of the promotional mix are
   a. personal selling, nonpersonal selling, and distribution.
   b. research, personal selling, and sales promotion.
   c. advertising, personal selling, and sales promotion.
   d. public relations, publicity, and pricing.

2. Personal selling is used
   a. for business goods.
   b. for higher-value items.
   c. during the sales transaction.
   d. for all of the above.

3. Advertising is used primarily for
   a. business goods.
   b. closing the sale.
   c. lower-value goods.

4. Pushing strategy relies heavily on
   a. personal selling.
   b. advertising.
   c. sales promotion.

5. Pulling strategy relies on
   a. sales promotion.
   b. advertising.
   c. personal selling.
   d. advertising and sales promotion.

6. A general term for the transmission of a marketing message from a seller to a buyer is
   a. personal selling.
   b. sales promotion.
   c. marketing communications.
   d. publicity.

7. A person-to-person presentation to a potential buyer is called
   a. promotion.
   b. sales promotion.
   c. marketing communications.
   d. personal selling.

8. Favorable "free" media attention for a firm or its product is known as
   a. sales promotion.
   b. public relations.
   c. advertising.
   d. publicity.

9. The marketer's communication of a favorable image about the firm to various groups (such as customers, suppliers, stockholders, employees, the government, and society) is known as
   a. sales promotion.
   b. marketing communications.
   c. public relations.
   d. publicity.

10. The overall function of influencing a purchase decision by informing or persuading the customer is called
    a. marketing.
    b. promotion.
    c. selling.
    d. advertising.

Applying Marketing Concepts

You have been hired as the product manager for ST-34, an industrial chemical used by many firms nationwide in manufacturing cleaning compounds. The chemical is relatively easy and inexpensive to manufacture, and therefore has a low unit price. Since ST-34 will be sold to other firms that manufacture cleaning compounds, it will be treated by them as a raw material.

> **Select the best answer.**

1. Marketing ST-34 will probably require a promotional strategy with heavy emphasis on
   a. personal selling.
   b. advertising.
   c. sales promotion.
   d. public relations.

2. If your firm manufactured a cleaning compound for sale to ultimate consumers, the promotional mix would probably
   a. be evenly divided between personal and nonpersonal selling.
   b. place more emphasis on personal selling.
   c. place less emphasis on personal selling.
   d. emphasize sales promotion.

The Penmate Manufacturing Company manufactures and markets a line of ballpoint pens. These pens are relatively low-priced and are sold in boxes containing a gross (12 dozen) of pens. Each box of pens is used as a marketing unit for sales and cost analyses. Promotional expenditures are also allocated on a per-box basis. Currently, Penmate allocates 10¢ per box for promotion.

3. Penmate's promotional budget is based on the
   a. percentage-of-sales method.
   b. fixed-sum-per-unit method.
   c. meeting-competition method.
   d. task-objective method.

4. If 5 percent of total sales had been used to allocate promotional expenditures, this would be an example of the
    a. percentage-of-sales method.
    b. fixed-sum-per-unit method.
    c. meeting-competition method.
    d. task-objective method.

Additional Activities

Experiential Exercises

1. The purpose of this exercise is to help you understand how marketers use a different promotional mix not only for different products but also depending on the stage of the purchasing process: before the sale, during the sale, and after the sale.

    Develop an after-the-sale promotional mix for each of the following products: personal computer, cruise to Alaska, and business accounting services.

    Example: Personal Computer. Send customers a letter congratulating them on their decision to buy the computer; remind customers that the company has great warranty service; and give a name and an address to write to and a telephone number to call if they have any questions.

    *   Using the same three products, describe your promotional mix for the before-the-sale stage.

    *   How do the objectives of promotion differ before, during , and after the sale?

2. The purpose of this exercise is to help you understand the importance of customs, holidays, and other special occasions to marketing strategies and promotional campaigns.

    Tremendous numbers of goods are sold and countless services rendered because of cultural or social customs. For example, many churchgoers feel obliged to wear dressy apparel to church on Easter. Holidays, such as Christmas, Valentine's Day, the Fourth of July, Labor Day, and Halloween, generate demand for goods and services such as gifts, apparel, special foods, fireworks, and travel services. Special occasions also generate high-volume sales. Birthdays, job promotions, cruises, and graduations motivate many people to lavish gifts and attention upon others. Consider such things as how people select gifts, whether they give what they personally would want for themselves or what they think the receiver wants or needs, and the impact of price on gift giving.

- Make a chart listing three customs, holidays, or special occasions that, in the United States, require some type of extra purchase or activity. Indicate the goods or services required—such as flower delivery—for each custom, holiday, or occasion listed.

  In addition, indicate the types of promotion you could use to promote these goods or services. You may wish to examine advertisements for a recent holiday or occasion.

Custom, Holiday, or Occasion	Goods or Services Required	Promotion

- Using the same chart, create three new special occasions, holidays, or customs that could be marked by parties, celebrations, commemorative ceremonies, special meals, or other festivities. Indicate the goods or services required and the types of promotion that could be used for each of these occasions.

Questions for Exploration

Conceptual

It has been said that if you invent a better mousetrap, the world will beat a path to your door. If that is true, why not cancel your promotional budget and transfer all those funds into your research and development budget?

Practical

The video program highlights Apple's event marketing presentation to dealers. What role does such event marketing play in Apple's overall marketing strategy? Is event marketing the best use of promotional funds? If not, how could those funds be used more effectively?

Answer Key

Key Concepts			
	1. h	5. e	9. i
	2. g	6. c	10. j
	3. b	7. a	11. k
	4. d	8. f	

Completion

1. promotion
2. communications
3. buyer, seller (either order)
4. information, demand, differentiate, value, stabilize
5. increase
6. differentiate
7. value
8. stabilize
9. information
10. personal, nonpersonal (either order)
11. personal
12. advertising, sales promotion, direct marketing, publicity, public relations, trade promotion (any order)
13. advertising
14. sales promotion
15. public relations
16. publicity
17. direct marketing
18. market, product, product, price, funds
19. advertising
20. personal selling
21. personal selling
22. advertising
23. funds
24. pulling
25. pushing
26. percentage-of-sales, fixed-sum-per-unit, meeting-competition, task-objective (any order)
27. percentage-of-sales
28. fixed-sum-per-unit
29. meeting-competition
30. task-objective

Self-Test			
	1. c	5. d	8. d
	2. d	6. c	9. c
	3. c	7. d	10. b
	4. a		

Applying Marketing Concepts	
	1. a
	2. c
	3. b
	4. a

*You can tell the ideals of a
nation by its advertisements.*
—Norman Douglas

19
Advertising

Assignments

For the most effective study of this lesson, we suggest that you complete the assignments in the following sequence:

1. Read the study guide Overview (Lesson Notes and Video Program Notes) and the Learning Objectives for this lesson.

2. Read *Contemporary Marketing Wired,* 9th edition, Chapter 18, "Advertising, Sales Promotion, and Public Relations," pages 600-624, and "Measuring Advertising Effectiveness," pages 633-635. (The remaining sections of the chapter will be assigned in the next two lessons.)

3. View "The Fastest Game in Town: A Case Study in Advertising" video program.

4. Review the textbook assignment for this lesson.

5. Complete the Review Activities (Key Concepts and Completion), Self-Test, and Applying Marketing Concepts for this lesson.

6. Check your answers against the Answer Key at the end of the lesson, and review when necessary.

7. Complete any of the Additional Activities (Experiential Exercises and Questions for Exploration) that interest you or that are assigned by your instructor.

Overview

Lesson Notes

As noted in the previous lesson, the nonpersonal selling components of promotional strategy consist of advertising, sales promotion, and public relations. **Advertising**, the nonpersonal presentation of a firm's products or services, is usually directed at large numbers of potential customers. Although much money is spent on advertising in the United States, the cost per consumer contact is usually small when compared to other methods of promotion.

Effective advertising requires setting objectives, research, and extensive planning. Advertising objectives are actually communications objectives: to inform, persuade, and remind potential consumers of a good or service. The goal of the advertising is to increase the probability that the potential consumers will become buyers of the good or service.

Advertising attempts to aim the advertiser's message at chosen segments of the market. An advertiser's message involves selecting a positioning strategy—a unique selling proposition that helps distinguish the product from its competition.

Two basic types of advertising are product and institutional. **Product advertising** deals with the nonpersonal selling of a particular good or service. **Institutional advertising** is concerned with promoting a concept, idea, philosophy, or goodwill.

Within these two types are three categories determined by the principal objective of the advertising: **informative advertising**, often used to develop initial demand during the introductory stage of the product life cycle; **persuasive advertising**, used to increase demand for a product during the growth and early maturity stages of the product life cycle; and **reminder advertising**, used during the latter part of the maturity stage and throughout the decline stage of the product.

Several advertising strategies have proved successful. For example, **celebrity testimonials** have sometimes increased reader willingness to accept advertising claims. Another strategy is **compara-**

tive advertising, in which the advertising message includes direct or indirect comparison with competing brands.

Two other types of advertising are retail and cooperative advertising. **Retail advertising** is nonpersonal advertising by stores that sell directly to the consumer. Although retail advertising is widely used, its effectiveness varies. Sometimes more effective is **cooperative advertising,** in which retailers share advertising costs with the manufacturer or wholesaler.

One of the major advertising decisions is which medium to use. The marketer must attempt to match a chosen target market with the audience characteristics of a given medium—a match that is never perfect. Among the media most commonly used by marketers are television, radio, newspapers, magazines, direct mail, outdoor advertising, and interactive media. Each medium has its own characteristics with respect to flexibility, selectivity, community prestige, life of the message, intensity of coverage, quality, and cost per contact.

Interactive media involves two-way communication used to promote products. The World Wide Web is used to supplement company messages over traditional media, such as television and newspapers.

Another important decision is the timing and sequencing of the advertisements, regardless of the media being used. Many marketers schedule their advertisements on the basis of seasonal sales patterns, repurchase activities, and the competition's plans.

Although some firms have in-house advertising departments, many firms hire **advertising agencies** to create and execute an advertising program. Usually, these agencies offer creative resources, expertise, and breadth of experience for reasonable rates. Regardless of where the advertising is produced, a successful advertisement should accomplish three goals: gain attention and interest, inform or persuade, and lead to a buying action.

Once a firm begins to advertise, it should assess whether a chosen advertising program is achieving the firm's promotional objectives. This assessment often involves pretesting and posttesting. **Pretesting** means assessing the advertisement's effectiveness before it actually appears in a medium; **posttesting** refers to the assessment made after the advertisement has appeared in the appropriate medium.

Video Program Notes

The video program for this lesson focuses on key decisions that a marketer must make in order to develop effective advertising. By learning about Chiat/Day, Inc., a successful advertising firm whose clients have included such companies as Apple Computer, Nike, and Yamaha Motorcycles, you will see how and why different companies go about developing advertising. The program identifies the objectives of advertising and how copy strategy and media selection directly affect the achievement of those objectives.

As you watch the video program, consider the following questions:

1. What is Chiat/Day's opinion on whether an advertiser can create demand?

2. What were the client concerns facing Chiat/Day when developing its ad campaign for Nike?

3. What were some of the problems Chiat/Day faced in developing an ad campaign for Porsche?

4. Why did Porsche select Chiat/Day as its advertising agency?

5. Why does Chiat/Day seem to prefer television as the best advertising medium?

6. Which media best convey the emotional reasons for buying? The logical reasons?

7. Why was Chiat/Day's introductory ad ("1984") for Apple's Macintosh computer unconventional as "introductory advertising"?

8. How did Chiat/Day subsequently use print advertising to help sell the Macintosh computer?

9. Why did Chiat/Day prepare several possible ad themes from which the Porsche executive could select?

10. Why did Porsche select the copy strategy featuring "Dr. Porsche's" commitment to continually improving the automobile?

Learning Objectives

After completing your study of this lesson, you should be able to:

1. Define the following terms related to advertising:

advertising	persuasive
advertising agency	advertising
comparative advertising	pretesting
cooperative advertising	posttesting
informative advertising	product advertising
institutional advertising	reminder advertising
interactive media	retail advertising
media scheduling	

2. Identify the two broad types and three major categories of advertising.

3. List and explain the principal communications objectives of advertising.

4. List the major advantages and disadvantages of the following advertising media: television, radio, newspapers, magazines, outdoor advertising, direct mail, and interactive media.

5. Explain the function of advertising agencies and describe how an advertisement is created.

6. Explain how advertising effectiveness is typically assessed.

Review Activities

Key Concepts

> **Identify each of the following advertising concepts by writing the letter of the appropriate term in the blank next to the corresponding description.**
>
> a. advertising
> b. retail advertising
> c. advertising agency
> d. product advertising
> e. institutional advertising
> f. comparative advertising
> g. cooperative advertising
> h. posttesting
> i. celebrity
> j. persuasive advertising
> k. reminder advertising
> l. media scheduling
> m. interactive media
> n. informative advertising
> o. pretesting

_____ 1. marketing specialist firm that plans and implements advertising programs

_____ 2. sharing of advertising costs between retailer and manufacturer of a good or service

_____ 3. promoting a concept, an idea, a philosophy, or the goodwill of an industry, company, organization, place, person, or government agency

_____ 4. nonpersonal selling of a specific good or service

_____ 5. nonpersonal selling by stores that offer goods or services directly to the public

_____ 6. assessment of the effectiveness of an advertisement after it has been used

_____ 7. nonpersonal selling technique that makes comparisons with competitive brands

_____ 8. paid, nonpersonal marketing communication by an organization seeking to inform or persuade members of a particular audience

_____ 9. assessment of an advertisement's effectiveness before it is actually used

____ 10. timing and sequence of advertisements

____ 11. advertising that announces the availability of an item and is designed to develop initial demand

____ 12. competitive, nonpersonal promotion designed to develop demand for a product in its growth or early maturity stage

____ 13. advertising that reinforces earlier promotional efforts

____ 14. communication channels that allow message recipients to participate actively in the promotional effort

____ 15. advertising associated with famous people

Completion

> Fill each blank in the following paragraphs with the most appropriate term from the list of completion answers below. A term may be used once, more than once, or not at all.
>
> | | | |
> |---|---|---|
> | advertising | informative | posttest |
> | billboards | institutional | pretest |
> | celebrity | intense | product |
> | comparative | magazines | quality |
> | cooperative | mass | radio |
> | direct mail | newspapers | reminder |
> | flexibility | outdoor | television |
> | high cost | persuasive | |

1. A paid nonpersonal communication that seeks to inform, persuade, or remind a particular audience is the definition of _____ .

2. There are two broad types of advertising: _____ and _____ .

3. Nonpersonal selling of a good or service is known as _____ advertising. Promoting a concept, an idea, a philosophy, or the goodwill of a business, organization, place, person, or government agency is known as _____ advertising.

4. Based on specific communications objectives, subdivisions within the two types of advertising are _____ advertising, _____ advertising, and _____ advertising.

5. The type of advertising most likely to be used in the early stages of a product's life cycle is _____ advertising. In the growth stage or early maturity stage of the product's life cycle, _____ advertising is often used. In the latter part of the maturity stage and throughout the decline stage of the product's life cycle, _____ advertising is used.

6. One way to create an impression on a market segment is to advertise a product in direct comparison with other brands. This advertising strategy is called _____ advertising.

7. Many marketers hire _____ spokespeople to make their messages more effective.

8. Six of the most commonly used media for advertising are _____, _____, _____, _____, _____, and _____ .

9. The most frequently used advertising media are _____ and _____.

10. A print medium that offers selectivity and long life is _____ . In comparison with newspapers, radio, and television, this medium has less _____ because of long lead times required.

11. _____ is the dominant medium for national advertising. This medium's primary advantages are its impact, _____ coverage, repetition, flexibility, and prestige. A less costly broadcast medium is _____ .

12. Other media choices include billboards and other forms of _____ advertising. This type of advertising is used primarily to promote products available for sale nearby. Direct mail is a medium that permits _____ coverage, selectivity of audience, speed, and _____ of format; its disadvantages include _____ per person and dependence on the _____ of the mailing list.

13. The effectiveness of an advertisement can be tested in two ways. Before an advertisement is used, the advertiser can conduct a _____ . After the advertisement appears, the advertiser can conduct a _____ .

14. Manufacturers sometimes share retailer advertising costs to help the retailer secure additional advertising. This practice is known as _____ advertising.

Self-Test

> **Select the best answer.**

1. The basic communication objectives of advertising are to
   a. inform, remind, and recall.
   b. inform and persuade.
   c. persuade and recall.
   d. inform, persuade, and remind.

2. Comparative advertising is one form of
   a. informative product advertising.
   b. persuasive product advertising.
   c. reminder product advertising.

3. Institutional advertising seeks to promote
   a. a specific institution.
   b. several products of a company at one time.
   c. a concept, an idea, a philosophy, or goodwill.

4. The largest percentage of total advertising expenditures is for advertising in
   a. newspapers and television.
   b. magazines.
   c. television and radio.
   d. direct mail.

5. Advertising that is purchased by two institutions, such as a manufacturer and a retailer, is known as
   a. institutional advertising.
   b. retail advertising.

    c.   manufacturer advertising.

    d.   cooperative advertising.

6.   "Nationwide, more Coca-Cola drinkers prefer the taste of Pepsi." This statement is an example of

    a.   unfair advertising.

    b.   competitive advertising.

    c.   comparative advertising.

    d.   cooperative advertising.

7.   An ad placed by The Software Store in the *Daily Herald* advertising a new line of IBM-compatible computer software is an example of

    a.   competitive advertising.

    b.   retail advertising.

    c.   cooperative advertising.

    d.   comparative advertising.

8.   The advertising medium to which some consumers are especially resistant is

    a.   direct mail.

    b.   newspapers.

    c.   magazines.

    d.   radio.

9.   Of the two leading advertising media, the one that offers strong impact, mass coverage, repetition, flexibility of message, and prestige, is

    a.   outdoor advertising.

    b.   radio.

    c.   magazines.

    d.   television.

10.   The advertising medium that is particularly effective in high-traffic areas and often used to promote products for sale nearby is

    a.   newspapers.

    b.   magazines.

    c.   radio.

    d.   outdoor advertising.

11. A type of advertising media that offers consumers active participation in marketing communications is
    a. transit advertising.
    b. directory advertising.
    c. interactive media.
    d. broadcast media.

Applying Marketing Concepts

Frank Smith is developing an advertising plan for his firm for next year. He has spent many hours analyzing last year's advertising efforts. The firm spent almost $8 million on advertising, but Smith is not sure what, if anything, the advertising accomplished. No specific promotional objectives were set, but much time and effort were expended on audience analysis reports and examining results of research aimed at identifying the characteristics of those who read his company's magazine advertisements.

> **Select the best answer.**

1. Smith will probably be unable to assess the success of last year's advertising program because
   a. media audiences were not analyzed.
   b. objectives were not set.
   c. posttesting was not done.

2. The research done to identify characteristics of actual readership of this company's advertisements is an example of
   a. setting promotional objectives.
   b. budgeting for promotional expenditures.
   c. a posttest of advertising effectiveness.

Additional Activities

Experiential Exercises

1. The purpose of this exercise is to help you understand what types of goods or services rely on each of the various media.

Some products are more effectively advertised through one medium than through another.

For each medium given below, list a product or products frequently advertised through that medium. Then explain why you think that medium is commonly used for the product you listed.

For example:

Medium	Product	Reason
Newspapers	Food products	Consumers who prepare food can compare prices from the ads and can take the newspaper with them when shopping.
Magazines		
Television		
Radio		
Direct mail		
Outdoor		
Interactive		

2. Understanding advertising communication objectives is the purpose of the following exercise.

- The textbook lists two broad types of advertising (product and institutional) and three categories of advertising depending on the objective (informative, persuasive, reminder). From newspapers and magazines, cut out examples of product and institutional advertising. For each example, identify the objective of the advertisement and explain the reasons for your identification. (*Note:* A single advertisement may have more than one objective.)

3. The next exercise will help you understand some of the complexities in creating an advertisement for print media.

- Select three different magazine or newspaper advertisements for the same good or service provided by three different companies. Cut out the ads, paste them up, and identify the name and date of the magazine in which the product was advertised. Evaluate each of the ads by considering style (including layout, color, wording, and printing), emphasis (use of humor, demonstrations, educational or informational material), and unity (consistent use of graphics, titles, wording, or other elements to focus on a single idea or theme).

- What types of people would you expect to read the advertisements that you selected? What would be their probable psychographic or demographic characteristics?
- Create an advertisement for the same product, paying special attention to the factors identified above.

Questions for Exploration

Conceptual

Advertising profoundly influences the way people perceive, understand, and react to the world in which they live. Should all advertising, therefore, be regulated? Why? If so, how?

Practical

If you ran Chiat/Day, how would you have handled the Porsche campaign? Why would your way be better than the way Chiat/Day actually handled the campaign?

Answer Key

Key Concepts			
1. c	5. b	9. o	13. k
2. g	6. h	10. l	14. m
3. e	7. f	11. n	15. i
4. d	8. a	12. j	

Completion

1. advertising
2. product, institutional (either order)
3. product, institutional
4. informative, persuasive, reminder (any order)
5. informative, persuasive, reminder
6. comparative
7. celebrity
8. television, radio, newspapers, magazines, billboards, direct mail (any order)
9. newspapers, television
10. magazines, flexibility
11. television, mass, radio
12. outdoor, intensive, flexibility, high cost, quality
13. pretest, posttest
14. cooperative

Self-Test		
1. d	5. d	9. d
2. b	6. c	10. d
3. c	7. b	11. c
4. a	8. a	

Applying Marketing Concepts

1. b
2. c

The sign brings customers!
—Jean de La Fontaine (1678)

20

Sales Promotion

Assignments

For the most effective study of this lesson, we suggest that you complete the assignments in the following sequence:

1. Read the study guide Overview (Lesson Notes and Video Program Notes) and the Learning Objectives for this lesson.

2. Read *Contemporary Marketing Wired,* 9th edition, Chapter 18, "Advertising, Sales Promotion, and Public Relations," pages 624-629, "Sales Promotion."

3. View "Off and Running: A Case Study in Promotional Strategy" video program.

4. Review the textbook assignment for this lesson.

5. Complete the Review Activities (Key Concepts and Completion), Self-Test, and Applying Marketing Concepts for this lesson.

6. Check your answers against the Answer Key at the end of the lesson, and review when necessary.

7. Complete any of the Additional Activities (Experiential Exercise and Questions for Exploration) that interest you or that are assigned by your instructor.

Overview

Sales promotion is an important element of the promotional mix. The term "sales promotion" usually refers to single-use, nonpersonal selling efforts designed to supplement and extend the other aspects of promotional strategy. Sales promotion activities encompass a wide range of promotional efforts, including virtually every promotional activity that is not advertising, personal selling, or public relations.

Some firms rely heavily on sales-promotion efforts to stimulate sales, thus supplementing and extending other components of the promotional mix, such as advertising and personal selling. Even though sales promotion may be looked upon as the catchall category of the promotional mix, it can play a vital role in stimulating consumer demand and improving dealer effectiveness.

Sales promotion can be consumer oriented or trade oriented. **Consumer-oriented promotions** include samples, bonus packs, premiums, coupons, price-off deals, rebates, contests, sweepstakes, and specialty advertising. **Trade-oriented promotions** include point-of-purchase advertising, trade shows, dealer incentives, contests, and training programs.

Distribution of **samples, bonus packs, and premiums** is basically a way of encouraging a consumer to try a product. Such attempts to change consumer behavior can be an important means of expanding the customer base. Sampling, in which a product is distributed free to consumers, is often used to promote new or unusual products. In mobile sales promotions, trucks or trailers travel, demonstrating products and giving out samples. Such promotions attract attention and present opportunities to interact with customers. Bonus packs give buyers large quantities of a product at the regular price; and premiums are items that are given free or at a reduced cost with the purchase of another product.

Contests and sweepstakes are often used to introduce new products or to attract new customers or increased usage by current customers. Contests offer cash or merchandise prizes and seek to change directly, rather than simply influence, consumer purchasing behavior. In sweepstakes, winners are chosen by chance, and there's no need to buy the product. Both contests and sweepstakes are popular techniques that attract visitors to Web sites.

Coupons, price-off deals, and refunds are three of the most popular consumer promotion techniques for marketers. Coupons, the most widely used, offer discounts on future purchases of specific products. Price-off or cents-off deals give price reductions to reward current customers and encourage them to buy items again. Refunds are cash back to customers who provide proof of purchase.

In **specialty advertising**, the firm puts its name, or the name of one of its products, before the target consumer, by imprinting it on a "useful medium"—usually relatively inexpensive articles such as mouse pads, key rings, calendars, or T-shirts.

Trade promotion is a specialized form of sales promotion directed to wholesalers, retailers, and other channel members; it accounts for about 50 percent of an average promotional budget. Trade promotions offer financial incentives, bringing quick results and improving sales. **Trade allowances** are deals offered to wholesalers or retailers to purchase or promote certain products. A buying allowance gives discounts to retailers. In a promotional allowance, the manufacturer agrees to pay the reseller a fee to cover costs of displays or extensive advertising. Vendors may be required to pay special fees, or slotting allowances, before retailers agree to put a new product on the shelf.

Point-of-purchase advertising consists mostly of in-store displays. A key advantage of these displays is that they are located where the buying decision is made. To reinforce the sales message, the display is often coordinated with the firm's advertising campaign, appearing at the ends of aisles or including a celebrity.

At **trade shows**, manufacturers, suppliers, and other vendors gather in a central location for a few days to display their wares and expand business contacts. Even though a firm may participate in only a few trade shows a year, some firms invest tens of thousands of dollars in semipermanent display booths that they transport from fair to fair.

Other sales promotions include **dealer incentives, contests, and training programs.**

Video Program Notes

The video program for this lesson considers how and why a firm uses sales promotion. In this program, the Santa Anita Race Track, a major sales-promotion user, develops a variety of sales promotions. These efforts are directed at increasing the number of customers from target market segments. The program shows how the sales-promotion effort is carefully coordinated with the copy strategy and media selection of the advertising effort.

As you watch the video program, consider the following questions:

1. What is Santa Anita's good or service and who are its direct or indirect competitors?

2. Why can't Santa Anita rely on reminder advertisements?

3. Does Santa Anita's sales promotion attract old customers or new customers?

4. How does Santa Anita tie in its sales promotion with advertising?

5. Why does Santa Anita use sales promotion rather than straight advertising?

6. What are the disadvantages (experienced by Hollywood Park) of offering inexpensive giveaways every weekend?

7. What criteria are applied by Santa Anita in selecting an item as a premium?

8. How does Santa Anita evaluate its sales-promotion events?

9. Why did the $100,000 armored-car giveaway flop?

10. How does Santa Anita use demographic studies to develop appropriate sales-promotion programs?

Learning Objectives

After completing your study of this lesson, you should be able to:

1. Define the following terms related to sales promotion:

    buying allowance

    contest

    coupon

    dealer incentive

    off-invoice allowance

    point-of-purchase
      advertising

    premium

    promotional allowance

    sales promotion

    sample

    slotting allowance

    specialty advertising

    trade allowance

    trade promotion

    trade show

2. Distinguish between sales promotion and other forms of promotion.

3. Identify and cite examples of various methods of sales promotion: point-of-purchase advertising; specialty advertising; trade shows; distribution of samples, bonus packs, and premiums; contests and sweepstakes; and trade promotion.

4. Describe factors to be considered in selecting sales-promotion methods.

Review Activities

> Identify each of the following sales-promotion concepts by writing the letter of the appropriate term in the blank next to the corresponding description.
>
> a. contest
> b. coupon
> c. point-of-purchase advertising
> d. premium
> e. sales promotion
> f. sample
> g. specialty advertising
>
> h. trade show
> i. bonus pack
> j. trade promotion
> k. buying allowance
> l. dealer incentive
> m. off-invoice allowance
> n. promotional allowance

_____ 1. displays, demonstrations, and other promotions located near the site of the actual buying decision

_____ 2. a good or service given free to consumers in an attempt to obtain future sales

_____ 3. specially packaged item that gives the purchaser a larger quantity at the regular price

_____ 4. usually offers the consumer discounts on the next purchases of goods or services

_____ 5. marketing activities other than personal selling, advertising, and publicity that stimulate consumer purchasing and enhance dealer effectiveness

_____ 6. periodic show or "convention," usually organized by an industry trade association, where vendors serving a particular industry display their wares for visiting retail and wholesale buyers

_____ 7. sales-promotion technique that seeks to attract customers by offering cash or merchandise prizes

_____ 8. sales-promotion technique that offers the consumer a bonus item that is given free or at a reduced cost with the purchase of another product

_____ 9. sales promotion to reach target consumers that uses a relatively inexpensive, useful article carrying the advertiser's name, address, and advertising message

_____ 10. trade-promotion technique designed to motivate and reward channel members

_____ 11. manufacturer's reimbursement of a reseller to cover the cost of a special consumer promotion

_____ 12. a means of rewarding resellers who buy certain quantities of products

_____ 13. type of sales promotion geared to marketing intermediaries

_____ 14. type of trade promotion that gives retailers a discount on goods

Completion

> **Fill each blank in the following paragraphs with the most appropriate term from the list of completion answers below. A term may be used once, more than once, or not at all.**
>
> | | |
> |---|---|
> | advertising | premiums |
> | bonus pack | promotional allowances |
> | buying allowance | publicity |
> | contest | public relations |
> | coupons | sales promotion |
> | customers | samples |
> | dealer incentives | specialty advertising |
> | off-invoice allowances | trade promotion |
> | point-of-purchase advertising | trade show |

1. The assorted and sometimes out-of-the-ordinary marketing activities, other than selling, advertising, and publicity, that stimulate consumer demand and enhance dealer effectiveness are called _____ .

2. One type of trade-oriented promotion involves displays and demonstrations that seek to promote a product at a time and place closely associated with the actual buying decision. In-store promotion of consumer goods is a common example of this type of trade-promotion activity known as _____ .

3. Matchbooks bearing the name and address of a local restaurant would be an example of _____ . This type of sales promotion often uses such items as calendars, pens, mouse pads, T-shirts, and caps.

4. The annual furniture show in Chicago, at which furniture manufacturers display the latest styles of furniture for retail-store buyers, is an example of a sales-promotion method known as a _____ .

5. Several different sales-promotion techniques can be used to induce consumers to buy products. Small amounts of products given away free are known an _____ . Bonus items given free with a purchase, such as a toothbrush with the purchase of toothpaste, are known as _____ . A company may also offer consumers a discount on the next purchase of a product by distributing _____ .

6. Asking customers to submit short statements on why they like a product and awarding prizes for the best statements is an example of a _____ . The purpose of this technique is to attract new _____ .

7. Some stores or manufacturers carry _____, specially packaged items in larger quantities offered at the regular price.

8. A company that gives its customers pens imprinted with its name is practicing _____ .

9. Giving a prize to the boy or girl who collects the most candy-bar wrappers is an example of a _____ .

10. A major publishing company that sets up a booth at a regional marketing meeting to show its latest textbook is participating in a _____ .

11. A consumer-goods company that has its salespeople set up displays in supermarkets is practicing _____ .

12. A specialized type of sales promotion directed toward channel members is known as a _____ .

13. Frequently used sales-promotion techniques geared toward marketing intermediaries are _____, _____, _____, and _____ .

14. Resellers are often reimbursed for the costs of such promotions as point-of-purchase displays through _____ from manufacturers.

Self-Test

1. A type of nonpersonal selling that is nonrecurrent, sometimes out-of-the-ordinary, and features an assortment of techniques is
   a. publicity.
   b. sales promotion.
   c. advertising.
   d. public relations.

2. Of the following techniques, the one that is **NOT** generally considered to be a sales-promotion technique is
   a. point-of-purchase advertising.
   b. outdoor advertising.
   c. free samples.
   d. discount coupons.

3. In-store promotional displays that seek to promote a product at a time and place closely associated with the actual buying decision are known as
   a. point-of-purchase advertising.
   b. retail advertising.
   c. free samples.
   d. in-store advertising.

4. Free flyswatters that feature the name and address of a local real-estate agent are an example of
   a. gift advertising.
   b. free samples.
   c. specialty advertising.
   d. premiums.

5. An annual meeting of New England photocopier and printing-machine manufacturers held in Boston for the benefit of local distributors, retailers, and company purchasing agents is an example of a
   a. retail mart.
   b. trade show.
   c. convention.
   d. wholesale show.

6. To introduce a new shampoo, Procter and Gamble delivered a one-ounce bottle of the shampoo to each household in Bellevue, Nebraska. This distribution is an example of
   a. premiums.
   b. specialty advertising.
   c. samples.
   d. product advertising.

7. To promote a singer's new CD, the recording company offered a free poster with the purchase of the CD. The poster is an example of
   a. a free sample.
   b. a coupon.
   c. a premium.
   d. product advertising.

8. To promote the use of its line of lawn fertilizers, Ortho placed "cutout" advertisements offering discounts on the purchase of a 20-pound bag of fertilizer. This advertisement is an example of
   a. a free sample.
   b. a coupon.
   c. a premium.
   d. product advertising.

9. Sales promotion usually
   a. supplements the advertising effort.
   b. gets the largest portion of the promotion budget.
   c. includes personal selling.
   d. is impossible to evaluate.

10. Typical trade-promotion methods include
    a. bonus packs and sweepstakes.
    b. point-of-purchase displays and free merchandise.
    c. coupons and sales contests.
    d. buying allowances and promotional allowances.

Applying Marketing Concepts

That'sa Pizza is a take-out pizza parlor in Kansas City. That'sa Pizza competes with a large number of chain pizza restaurants (such as Domino's, Straw Hat, and Shakey's), as well as with other local independents. Many of That'sa Pizza's competitors offer "deals" such as "buy one large pizza and get a smaller second one for only a penny." Some run advertisements that offer discounts to customers who bring the ad to the store (for example, $1.00 off any size pizza with the ad). To counteract the big-time promotion efforts of its competitors, That'sa Pizza gave away baseball caps last summer with the name and location of the restaurant on the visor.

Recently, when introducing a new Bar-B-Que pizza, That'sa Pizza offered free slices to customers who wanted to taste the pizza before buying it.

> **Select the best answer.**

1. The promotional strategies of That'sa Pizza's competitors appear to consist mostly of
   a. coupons and premiums.
   b. coupons and specialty advertising.
   c. specialty advertising and premiums.
   d. premiums and contests.

2. The sales-promotion technique used by That'sa Pizza when introducing Bar-B-Que pizza was
   a. specialty advertising.
   b. free samples.
   c. coupons.
   d. premiums.

3. The baseball caps given away by That'sa Pizza are an example of
   a. specialty advertising.
   b. free samples.
   c. coupons.
   d. premiums.

Additional Activities

Experiential Exercise

The purpose of this exercise is to help you understand how certain firms use various sales-promotion techniques in their promotional strategy.

- Start by reviewing your local newspaper's weekly food section. Examine the advertisements for coupons, premiums, and contests. Then, go to one or more supermarkets, preferably on the weekend, to look for other sales-promotion techniques such as point-of-purchase advertising and distribution of samples.

- Make a chart listing the major sales-promotion techniques you observed. After each technique, list the types of foods and other consumer products most often promoted with that technique.

Questions for Exploration

Conceptual

It has been said that advertising and sales promotion greatly influence U.S. culture and society, especially in terms of values and material possessions. If that is true, it means that our society is being changed by what advertisers consider the "American way." How does promotion affect U.S. culture? And how does U.S. culture affect promotion?

Practical

In the video program, Santa Anita's marketing director commented that direct-mail discount coupons to former customers have the best response of all promotion efforts. If this conclusion is correct, then why shouldn't Santa Anita cancel newspaper ads, sales-promotion premiums, and sales-promotion events and concentrate entirely on direct-mail promotion?

Answer Key

Key Concepts			
1. c	5. e	9. g	13. j
2. f	6. h	10. l	14. k
3. i	7. a	11. n	
4. b	8. d	12. m	

Completion	
1. sales promotion	9. contest
2. point-of-purchase advertising	10. trade show
3. specialty advertising	11. point-of-purchase advertising
4. trade show	12. trade promotion
5. samples, premiums, coupons	13. buying allowances, off-invoice allowances, promotional allowances, dealer incentives (any order)
6. contest, customers	
7. bonus pack	
8. specialty advertising	14. promotional allowances

Self-Test		
1. b	5. b	8. b
2. b	6. c	9. a
3. a	7. c	10. d
4. c		

Applying Marketing Concepts	
1. a	
2. b	
3. a	

21

Public Relations

Assignments

For the most effective study of this lesson, we suggest that you complete the assignments in the following sequence:

1. Read the study guide Overview (Lesson Notes and Video Program Notes) and the Learning Objectives for this lesson. (Note that several important terms appear in the Lesson Notes that do not appear in the textbook.)

2. Review *Contemporary Marketing Wired*, 9th edition, Chapter 17, "Integrated Marketing Communications," pages 573-577, "Sponsorships" and "Direct Marketing" and Chapter 18, "Advertising, Sales Promotion, and Public Relations," pages 629-639 "Public Relations," "Cross Promotion," "Measuring Promotional Effectiveness," and "Ethics in Promotion."

3. View "Just Another Oil Company? A Case Study in Public Relations" video program.

4. Review the textbook assignment for this lesson.

5. Complete the Review Activities (Key Concepts and Completion), Self-Test, and Applying Marketing Concepts for this lesson.

6. Check your answers against the Answer Key at the end of the lesson, and review when necessary.

7. Complete any of the Additional Activities (Experiential Exercise and Questions for Exploration) that interest you or that are assigned by your instructor.

Overview

Lesson Notes

The principal purpose of **public relations** is to promote a favorable image of a company and its products to the various publics or groups that affect the company. Public relations is more than just a marketing function; it is a corporate function. Public relations serves broader objectives than just promotion objectives or even marketing objectives; public relations serves the long-range objectives of the entire firm.

Public relations usually represents a relatively small part of the overall promotion budget, because it is often carried out by the corporate communications division of the firm, to which marketing may or may not report. In some firms, **corporate communications** is a division concerned with marketing, public relations, and all other aspects that affect **corporate image**—how various publics perceive a firm.

One way in which a firm may enhance its corporate image is through **sponsorship**. In sponsorship, which is continually growing in usage each year, the firm contributes cash or in-kind resources to support an event or activity in exchange for direct association with that event or activity. Among the events and activities supported by firms are sports events, concerts and ballets, art exhibitions, and entertainment.

In addition to enhancing a firm's corporate image, sponsorships can also contribute to the firm's overall sales promotion strategy by placing the firm's name and products in front of potential consumers. Recently, major sports leagues recruit firms to sponsor events on the World Wide Web.

Direct marketing is growing the most rapidly of all the promotional mix elements. The technique uses many different media: direct mail, **telemarketing**, television or radio ads, home shopping channels, **infomercials**, newspapers, and magazines.

Most firms also must target specific audiences with specific messages. The target audiences of public relations are more than just customers and potential customers. Those audiences also include stockholders, boards of directors, employees, suppliers, competitors, governments, and society as a whole. A firm must be closely attuned to each of these target groups, and it must conduct a continual campaign to develop and maintain in the minds of members of each of these groups a favorable image of the firm and its products.

A firm attempts to ensure that stockholders and boards of directors hear accurate and favorable information about it in the media. The annual report is prepared especially for these groups; it is a way of informing stockholders and potential stockholders and convincing them that it is wise to invest in the firm.

A firm also tries to ensure that employees are favorably disposed toward it. It may accomplish this goal by supporting company bowling leagues or baseball teams or by supporting a company credit union. An ongoing problem that all companies face is hiring qualified people who not only want a job but also want to work for that particular firm. By maintaining good employee relations, a firm can use endorsements by current employees (and sometimes pay cash bonuses in return) to attract new employees.

Maintaining good working relationships with suppliers is also a part of public relations. Reliable suppliers are essential to the smooth, strong operation of a firm. A firm attempts to be reasonable and flexible, giving early commitments to the supplier whenever possible. In general, the firm helps ensure that the supplier stays in business to provide good service.

For companies that are heavily regulated, maintaining a favorable image with the government (federal, state, and local) is especially important. A firm that maintains a strong public-relations campaign to promote itself as a good citizen in the community may be able to avoid major conflicts with government agencies as well as with private groups. A favorable image may, in turn, forestall passage of legal restrictions and regulations that affect the firm's operations.

An important role of the marketer in the public-relations effort is to seek **publicity** by submitting publicity releases to media editors. **Publicity releases** are usually information-oriented supplements to the overall promotional campaign, supplements that feature some aspect of the corporation or its products. If used to promote the firm's products, publicity may be seen as a form of sales promotion. However, if publicity is sought primarily to enhance the firm's corporate image, then that publicity is clearly part of public relations. Media editors working for newspapers, magazines, radio, or television regularly receive corporate publicity releases. Since these editors decide, based on their perception of audience interest, whether or not to publish or broadcast such releases, placement of publicity releases can be uncertain.

In a recent trend, marketers, such as movie studios and fast-food chains, combine efforts to promote related products by using **cross promotion**. This type of promotion also occurs on the Internet.

The question of ethics is considered in many public relations campaigns, particularly advertisements that target children, involve liquor or tobacco, or exaggerate the product's capabilities (**puffery**).

The precise role the marketer plays in the firm's public-relations campaign varies from firm to firm. In most cases, the role is significant, since the marketer participates in development of the firm's image, development of strategies for implementing that image, and in dissemination of information about the firm's public-relations effort.

Video Program Notes

The video program for this lesson explains how a firm uses public relations and publicity to build a favorable company image with a variety of targeted groups. Through the example of the Atlantic Richfield Company (ARCO), the program shows that public relations is concerned with public opinion. The marketing executives of ARCO must identify and attempt to satisfy the needs and desires of various publics, including company stockholders, the board of directors, employees, dealers, customers, the local community, governments (federal, state, county, and city), suppliers, private organizations, and even competitors. This program also shows how ARCO attempts to develop, implement, and evaluate a specific public-relations plan for each of these publics. It emphasizes that publicity and public relations are not so much "calculated" as they are planned and coordinated to enhance the corporate image.

As you watch the video program, consider the following questions:

1. Why did ARCO provide funding to build the Olympic track? How did ARCO use the Olympic track in its ads?

2. What was the public-relations benefit of getting rid of credit cards?

3. How does ARCO maintain good public relations with its dealers?

4. How does ARCO maintain good public relations with its stockholders and the financial community?

5. Why did ARCO cap the crack in the ocean floor? How did it let the public know?

6. Why does ARCO maintain strong public relations with the University of California at Santa Barbara and the Santa Barbara planning commission?

7. Why did ARCO help build the Ecology Resource Center?

8. Why aren't ARCO's publicity releases to the media always effective?

9. How does ARCO's Joint Education Program maintain good public relations with employees and the community?

10. For ARCO, is corporate giving through the ARCO Foundation a luxury or a necessity?

Learning Objectives

After completing your study of this lesson, you should be able to:

1. Explain the following terms as they relate to sponsorship and public relations:

corporate communications	publicity releases
corporate image	public relations
cross promotion	puffery
direct marketing	sponsorship
infomercial	telemarketing
publicity	

2. Describe the role of sponsorships and direct marketing in integrated marketing communications planning.

3. Identify the broad objectives of any public-relations program and identify groups that should be considered in developing a public-relations program.

4. Explain the roles of publicity, public relations, and cross promotions in an organization's promotional strategy.

5. Explain how marketers assess promotional effectiveness.

6. Discuss the importance of ethics in a firm's promotional activities.

Review Activities

Key Concepts

Identify the following public-relations concepts by writing the letter of the appropriate term in the blank next to the corresponding description.

a. public relations
b. publicity
c. media editor
d. corporate communications
e. corporate image
f. publicity release
g. cross promotion
h. sponsorship
i. telemarketing

_____ 1. person who works for a newspaper, a magazine, radio station, or television station and decides whether to run publicity releases from different firms

_____ 2. information-oriented supplement to promotion produced by a company and distributed to the media

_____ 3. stimulation of demand for a good, service, place, idea, person, or organization by placing significant news about it or obtaining a favorable presentation for it that is not paid for by the sponsor

_____ 4. the public's perception of a firm

_____ 5. marketers' combined efforts to promote related products

_____ 6. a firm's communications and relationships with its various publics, including stockholders, employees, suppliers, government, customers, and the society in which it operates

_____ 7. support of an athletic event or a cultural activity in exchange for name association

_____ 8. a division of a firm that is concerned with marketing, public relations, and all other aspects that affect corporate image

_____ 9. direct marketing conducted entirely by phone

Completion

> Fill each blank in the following paragraphs with the most
> appropriate term from the list of completion answers below.
> A term may be used once, more than once, or not at all.
>
> | | | |
> |---|---|---|
> | advertising | customers | publicity |
> | boards of directors | employees | publicity releases |
> | competitors | exposure | public relations |
> | corporate | government | sales |
> | corporate communications | image | society |
> | corporate image | infomercial | sponsorship |
> | | media editors | stockholders |
> | | promotion | suppliers |

1. In exchange for sponsorship, a firm receives _____ to an audience and association with the audience's _____ of the event or activity.

2. An increasingly important element of promotion is _____, which is concerned with communications and relationships of a firm with its various publics, including _____ , suppliers, stockholders, boards of directors, employees, government, competitors, and the society in which it operates.

3. One aspect of public relations is to stimulate demand by getting what is sometimes referred to as "free advertising." This type of public relations is known as _____.

4. Because public relations is performed by all divisions of a corporation, including marketing, it is often viewed as a _____ function.

5. Public relations is usually a relatively small part of the overall _____ budget.

6. Some firms group marketing, public relations, and all other aspects that affect corporate image into a single division called _____.

7. The various publics that are targets of a firm's public-relations efforts include customers, _____ , _____ , _____ , _____ , _____ , _____ , and _____.

8. How a firm is perceived by its publics is called the firm's _____.

9. Information-oriented supplements to the overall promotional campaign are called _____.

10. The placement of publicity releases is uncertain because the decision to present a firm's publicity releases to the public is usually under the control of _____.

11. If used to promote a firm's products, a publicity release may be considered a form of _____ promotion. However, if publicity is sought primarily to enhance the firm's corporate image, that release is clearly part of the firm's _____.

12. Exaggerated claims of a product's superiority are called _____.

13. An _____ is a television commercial that runs at least 30 minutes for a single product.

14. When an organization provides cash for a sports event in exchange for direct association with that event, it is called a _____.

Self-Test

1. The element of promotion that is concerned with communications and relationships between the firm and its various publics is known as
   a. sales promotion.
   b. public relations.
   c. sponsorship.
   d. advertising.

2. When a firm provides funds for a nationally televised tennis tournament and the firm's name will be part of the tournament's name, the firm is engaging in
   a. trade promotion.
   b. specialty advertising.
   c. celebrity testimonials.
   d. sponsorship.

3. The aspect of public relations that is most directly related to promoting a company's goods or services is
   a. corporate communications.
   b. publicity.
   c. advertising.
   d. promotion.

4. Informative public-relations articles that are presented free to the media by the firm and are designed to stimulate consumer demand are called
   a. advertisements.
   b. commercials.
   c. publicity releases.
   d. fact sheets.

5. The primary focus of a public-relations effort is to promote
   a. the firm's goods or services.
   b. a favorable image of the firm and its goods or services.
   c. the firm's marketing department.
   d. the firm's publics.

6. Public relations is usually viewed as a
   a. marketing function.
   b. promotional strategy.   .
   c. corporate function.
   d. public function.

7. A corporate communications division of a firm
   is primarily responsible for
   a. all aspects of promoting the corporate image.
   b. in-house information exchange.
   c. issuing publicity releases.
   d. marketing only.

8. The attitudes and perceptions that the firm's
   various publics have about the firm it are known as
   a. the corporate image.
   b. subliminal perception.
   c. public relations.
   d. the corporate logo.

9. The decision of whether or not to publish or
   broadcast a firm's publicity releases usually
   depends on the judgment of
   a. the board of directors.
   b. the public.
   c. the marketing manager.
   d. media editors.

10. Publicity releases are considered a part of
    a. sales promotion.
    b. public relations.
    c. advertising.
    d. all of the above.

11. When Disney joins with Burger King to promote *Hercules,* the two firms are practicing
    a. telemarketing.
    b. sales promotion.
    c. cross promotion.
    d. puffery.

Applying Marketing Concepts

The American Dye Corporation recently concluded lengthy litigation with the Environmental Protection Agency, in which American Dye was charged with illegal pollution of the Kayak River. Even though all charges against American Dye were dismissed, the board of directors felt that the firm's corporate image had been greatly marred.

To help repair the damage, the board turned to Lacy Clark, director of corporate communications. To comply with the first directive to her from the board, Lacy developed a series of "fact sheets," which helped to set the record straight and, in general, favorably promoted the firm's image. The fact sheets were mailed to selected radio and television stations, as well as to newspapers and magazines, in hopes that those media would report on American Dye's innocence and its ongoing efforts to establish special wildlife preserves at several locations in the state.

> **Select the best answer.**

1. Clark's "fact sheets" about American Dye are
   a. public relations.
   b. media.
   c. publicity releases.
   d. ad copy.

2. Clark's overall responsibilities for favorably promoting the firm's corporate image are a major part of the firm's
   a. public relations.
   b. sales promotion.
   c. advertising.
   d. publicity campaign.

3. Whether or not the "fact sheets" are published or run in the media depends on the decision of
   a. media editors.
   b. the director of corporate communications.
   c. the public.
   d. the company president.

Additional Activities

Experiential Exercise

The purpose of this exercise is to help you understand some of the decisions that a firm must make in order to develop a cohesive public-relations strategy.

- Identify a firm and suggest some appropriate methods for promoting the firm's corporate image to its various publics. Begin by identifying a medium-sized manufacturing or service firm in your city or area. Select a firm that does not have a significant public-relations effort or a prominent corporate image. After you have made your selection, describe at least two methods of promoting that firm's corporate image with each of the following publics: stockholders, board of directors, employees, suppliers, government, and society.

Questions for Exploration

Conceptual

"The publicity effort of American industry has subverted the impartiality of the news media to such an extent that information provided by the news media no longer can serve as a meaningful information base for our decision." Agree or disagree with the preceding statement and argue your case.

Practical

What if ARCO's Platform Holly suddenly collapsed, causing another massive oil spill on the Santa Barbara coastline? As a marketing consultant to ARCO, what would you recommend that ARCO do to avoid a corresponding collapse in public relations with each of its publics?

Answer Key

Key Concepts		
	1. c	6. a
	2. f	7. h
	3. b	8. d
	4. e	9. i
	5. g	

Completion		
	1. exposure, image	8. corporate image
	2. public relations, customers	9. publicity releases
	3. publicity	10. media editors
	4. corporate	11. sales, public relations
	5. promotion	12. puffery
	6. corporate communications	13. infomercial
	7. stockholders, employees, suppliers, boards of directors, government, society (any order)	14. sponsorship

Self-Test			
	1. b	5. b	9. d
	2. d	6. c	10. b
	3. b	7. a	11. c
	4. c	8. a	

Applying Marketing Concepts	
	1. c
	2. a
	3. a

*Nothing happens until
somebody sells something.*
            —Red Motley

22

Selling

Assignments

For the most effective study of this lesson, we suggest that you complete the assignments in the following sequence:

1. Read the study guide Overview (Lesson Notes and Video Program Notes) and the Learning Objectives for this lesson.

2. Read *Contemporary Marketing Wired,* 9th edition, Chapter 19, "Personal Selling and Sales Management," pages 644-677.

3. View "'Tis the Seasoning: A Case Study in Selling" video program.

4. Review the textbook assignment for this lesson.

5. Complete the Review Activities (Key Concepts and Completion), Self-Test, and Applying Marketing Concepts for this lesson.

6 Check your answers against the Answer Key at the end of the lesson, and review when necessary.

7. Complete any of the Additional Activities (Experiential Exercises and Questions for Exploration) that interest you or that are assigned by your instructor.

Overview

Lesson Notes

Everyone has had experience, either as a buyer or as a seller, with **personal selling**. Personal selling, an important element in the promotional mix, involves person-to-person presentations to potential buyers and is an essential part of virtually every business.

A firm selects one or more of three different approaches to selling. These approaches include field selling, over-the-counter selling, and telemarketing. In **field selling**, salespeople make face-to-face presentations to prospective customers at their homes or places of business. In **over-the-counter-selling**, which is common in retail stores and in some wholesale operations, customers come to the seller's place of business. **Telemarketing** is based entirely on telephone, either on an outbound basis (in which salespeople contact customers) or on an inbound basis (in which customers call a number to obtain information or order a product).

Instead of one-on-one selling, recent sales trends involve sales to teams of corporate representatives. Salespeople are expected to answer technical questions, understand technical jargon, and wait sometimes years to close a single sale. As a result, companies are practicing relationship selling, consultative selling, team selling, and sales force automation. In **relationship selling**, a salesperson builds regular contact with a customer over an extended period. **Consultative selling** involves meeting customer needs, listening and caring, and building customer loyalty. **Team selling** combines salespeople and specialists in order to complete a sale.

Today, the sales function is being greatly enhanced with various technologies, including laptop and notebook computers, pagers, cellular phones, and voice and electronic mail. Use of these and other technologies is referred to as **sales force automation**. Automation both facilitates the sales process and improves customer service. The ultimate outcome of this automation is the virtual office, a workplace that only exists in electronic space.

The sales process includes different types of selling tasks: order processing, creative selling, and missionary sales. **Order processing** is part of most selling jobs, especially when the customer need is easily identified. **Creative selling**, as the name implies, requires greater skills on the part of the salesperson. In **missionary sales**, the seller provides information and technical assistance to either the customer or another salesperson.

Steps in the personal-selling process consist of **prospecting and qualifying, approach, presentation, demonstration, handling objections, closing,** and **follow-up**. If any link in this chain of tasks is not handled well by the salesperson, then the sales process may produce a dissatisfied customer or no sale at all.

Prospecting and qualifying involve finding potential customers who have the need, the money, and the authority to buy. To convince the customer that the product fits actual needs, the salesperson approaches the customer, makes a presentation, and, in many cases, performs a demonstration. The salesperson must be prepared with sufficient information to overcome customer objections, so that the sale can be closed successfully. Some basic techniques for closing a sale include the alternative-decision technique, the SRO (standing room only) technique, silence, and extra-inducement closes. The final stage of the selling process is the follow-up: contacting customers after closing to determine their satisfaction with purchases, and maintaining customers as prospects for repeat business and for referrals to new business.

The job of **sales management** includes all the activities related to recruiting, selecting, training, organizing, supervising, motivating, compensating, controlling, and evaluating the sales force. Because the total cost of a sales force is usually a major expense item for a firm, a sales manager must exercise great care in managing the sales force.

One of the sales manager's tasks is to design an effective sales compensation plan. The choice among straight **commissions**, straight **salary**, or a combination plan crucially and directly affects other areas of sales-force management. Each of these plans has distinct advantages and disadvantages. A commission plan offers the greatest incentive to salespeople and ensures that pay is related directly to performance. Salaries are advantageous, however, if management wants to guarantee salespeople a regular income and ensure that they perform nonselling activities. Bonuses are another popular type of compensation.

Video Program Notes

Through the sales and marketing divisions of Lawry's, this video program explores two key issues of selling: what the professional salesperson is and does, and how the professional sales force is managed. By following the daily routine of a professional salesperson, the program illustrates prospecting and qualifying, approach, presentation, overcoming objections, closing the sale, and follow-up. The program also describes attitudes needed to succeed in sales (ability to plan, tenacity, knowledge of the company, knowledge of the product, knowledge of the consumer's needs or problems, and interpersonal skills).

The program also shows how the marketer, as sales manager, must manage the specific functions of recruitment and selection, training, organization, motivation, compensation, evaluation, and control of the sales force. The fact that sales is the only department to bring in money in a given firm helps underscore the importance of selling in the promotional mix.

As you watch the video program, consider the following questions:

1. How does Lawry's marketing department use information from its field sales force?

2. How do the sales department and marketing department set sales quotas at Lawry's?

3. What roles do advertising and sales promotion play in the field-selling process?

4. What is the purpose of having salespeople take part in taste tests?

5. Why and how does Lawry's use video for training salespeople?

6. For what reasons does Lawry's hold a sales meeting?

7. What are the purposes of bonuses and sales awards?

8. What tasks and functions does the Lawry's sales representative perform?

9. Why is follow-up critical in professional selling?

10. How do the selling strategies for the headquarters account, the retail account, and the ultimate consumer differ?

Learning Objectives

After completing your study of this lesson, you should be able to:

1. Define the following terms as they relate to selling:

approach	over-the-counter selling
boundary-spanning role	personal selling
canned presentation	precall planning
closing	presentation
commission	prospecting
consultative selling	qualifying
creative selling	relationship selling
expectancy theory	salary
field selling	sales force automation
follow-up	(SFA)
missionary sales	sales management
national accounts	sales quota
organization	team selling
order processing	telemarketing

2. Describe the types of selling environments.

3. Describe major trends in personal selling.

4. Identify and explain the basic sales tasks.

5. Identify and explain the steps involved in the selling process.

6. Explain the role and functions of a sales manager.

7. Discuss the functions of sales management.

8. Describe how ethics play a role in personal selling and sales management.

Review Activities

Key Concepts

Identify each of the following terms related to personal selling by writing the letter of the appropriate term in the blank next to the corresponding description.

a. field selling
b. over-the-counter selling
c. prospecting
d. sales management
e. closing
f. sales quota
g. order processing
h. creative selling
i. qualifying
j. approach
k. presentation
l. canned presentation

m. commissions
n. telemarketing
o. precall planning
p. relationship selling
q. team selling
r. sales force automation (SFA)
s. boundary-spanning role
t. national accounts organization
u. expectancy theory

_____ 1. face-to-face sales presentations made at the prospective customer's home or business

_____ 2. level of expected sales for a territory, product, customer, or salesperson against which actual results are compared

_____ 3. locating and identifying potential customers

_____ 4. asking the customer for an order

_____ 5. securing, training, organizing, supervising, motivating, compensating, evaluating, and controlling a sales force to ensure effectiveness

_____ 6. face-to-face selling conducted in retail and some wholesale locations, in which customers come to the seller's place of business on their own initiative

_____ 7. selling at the retail and wholesale levels where the salesperson identifies a need, points it out to the customer, and writes up the order

_____ 8. personal-selling situation in which considerable analytical decision making by the consumer requires skillful, proposed solutions by the seller

_____ 9. incentive payments directly related to the sales or profits generated by a salesperson

_____ 10. determining whether a prospect has the need, the income, and the authority to buy

_____ 11. salesperson's initial contact with a prospective customer

_____ 12. memorized sales talk used to ensure uniform coverage of the points deemed important by sales management

_____ 13. describing the product's main features and relating them to the customer's problems or needs

_____ 14. personal selling involving the use of the telephone by salespeople who call out or by prospective customers who call in

_____ 15. use of specialists from other functional areas along with a salesperson to promote a product

_____ 16. use of information gathered during prospecting and qualifying to tailor approach and presentation to customer's needs

_____ 17. mutually beneficial relationship between salespeople and customers over an extended period

_____ 18. assignment of sales teams to a firm's largest accounts

_____ 19. a theory that motivation depends on the salesperson's expectations of his or her ability to perform a job

_____ 20. use of technology to make selling more efficient and competitive

_____ 21. function performed by the sales manager in linking the sales force to internal and external environments

Completion

Fill each blank in the following paragraphs with the most appropriate term from the list of completion answers below. A term may be used once, more than once, or not at all.

alternative decision	follow-up	prospecting
approach	"if I can show	qualifying
canned	you"	recruiting
close	missionary	salary
commission	missionary	sales force
compensation	selling	automation
control	motivation	selecting
creative	objections	silence
creative selling	order processing	standing
demonstration	organization	room only
emotional	over-the-counter	telemarketing
evaluation	personal selling	training
extra inducement	presentation	
field	processing	

1. Presentation of a firm's promotional efforts through face-to-face relationships of salespeople with potential buyers is referred to as _____.

2. Personal selling usually takes place in one of three locations. Selling conducted away from the seller's place of business is called _____ selling, face-to-face selling at the seller's place of business is called _____ selling, and selling over the telephone is called _____.

3. In some ways, sales personnel are consultants to buyers and are concerned with performing three basic sales tasks: order _____, _____ selling, and _____ selling.

4. While most sales jobs require the performance of all three tasks, these tasks can be used for classifying a sales job on the basis of the primary selling task performed. A Lawry's salesperson who replenishes a grocer's stock of packaged seasonings would be primarily concerned with performing the task of _____.

5. Some purchases involve considerable analytical decision making on the part of the purchaser. For example, a manufacturer's salesperson who is trying to convince a retailer to carry his or her company's line of appliances would be involved in _____.

6. Indirect selling, which involves selling the goodwill of a company and offering information and technical assistance to buyers, is called _____. A drug manufacturer who encourages physicians to prescribe the manufacturer's brand of products would be involved in this type of selling.

7. Selling is a challenging job, and a salesperson must take several steps to complete a successful sale. The first step involves seeking out potential customers, which is known as _____. The second step involves determining whether the customer has the need, the money, and the authority to buy, which is known as _____.

8. Once a sales representative has identified a likely prospect, the second step in the sales process involves meeting and establishing rapport with the prospective customer. This initial contact with the customer is called the _____.

9. When a salesperson informs a potential customer of the goods and services offered by the company and relates their features to a customer's needs or problems, the customer is getting a sales _____.

10. Sales presentations are usually tailored to the customer. In some cases, such as door-to-door canvassing, sales management may prefer the sales force to use a memorized, or _____ , sales talk in order to ensure uniform coverage of all sales points.

11. An automobile salesperson usually takes a prospective buyer for a ride in the automobile being considered. This ride is an example of a product _____.

12. When a sales representative attempts to answer questions and charges made by a prospect, the sales function is called handling _____.

13. A salesperson who has successfully handled the objections raised by a prospect is ready to _____ the sale, which means asking the customer for the order.

A salesperson can use a number of techniques to close a sale. For each of the five closing situations below, identify the type of closing technique being used.

14. "Somebody else is coming to look at this car this afternoon." *Type of technique: _____.*

15. The salesperson presents data to the customer to prove that a new furnace, when installed, will reduce the customer's heating bill by 25 percent. *Type of technique: _____.*

16. "If you buy the tires now, we'll throw in a free tank of gas." *Type of technique: _____.*

17. "Would you like the blue sofa or the green sofa?" *Type of technique: _____.*

18. The salesperson says nothing, waiting for the customer to talk. *Type of technique: _____.*

19. In many sales transactions, the selling process does not end with the completed sale. Postsale activities often determine whether a person will be a repeat customer. A salesperson who contacts a buyer to determine his or her satisfaction with the purchase is completing the step referred to as the sales _____.

20. Sales managers provide overall direction and control of the personal selling effort. One of the most basic functions sales managers perform is _____ and _____ persons who will be successful salespeople.

21. Once hired, management must shape the sales recruits into an effective sales organization. Among the methods used in sales _____ are on-the-job instruction, individual instruction, in-house classes, and external seminars.

22. Another responsibility of sales managers is the _____ of the field sales force, which may be based on geography, types of products, types of customers, or a combination of these factors.

23. Sales managers also must communicate with salespersons and provide the encouragement necessary for them to achieve sales goals. These activities are part of _____.

24. An important aspect of motivation is _____.

25. Two of the most difficult tasks for sales managers are _____ and _____. To accomplish these tasks, sales managers must set standards and select instruments with which to measure sales performance.

26. Salespeople are usually compensated by a straight salary, a commission plan, or a combination of the two means. Each means has its advantages and disadvantages. The means that gives salespersons the greatest incentive is _____. The means that ensures that the salespeople will perform nonselling activities is _____.

27. The use of pagers, cell phones, and laptop computers in personal selling is known as _____.

Self-Test

Select the best answer.

1. Personal selling can be defined as
   a. a promotional presentation conducted on a person-to-person basis.
   b. selling to an individual as opposed to selling to a firm.
   c. sending promotional material directly to the prospective buyer.
   d. any retail sales situation.

2. The three basic tasks to be accomplished in selling are
   a. order processing, creative selling, and missionary sales.
   b. order processing, order checking, and creative selling.
   c. creative selling, order taking, and demonstrating.
   d. missionary sales, presenting, and creative selling.

3. Two steps in the sales process are
   a. prospecting and order taking.
   b. approaching and creative selling.
   c. presenting and demonstrating.
   d. order checking and closing.

4. "Standing room only," "alternative decision," and "extra inducements" are examples of different types of
   a. follow-up methods.
   b. closings.
   c. presentations.
   d. approaches.
   e. demonstrations.

5. Training, motivation, recruitment and selection, supervision, and compensation are some of the key tasks of the
   a. salesperson.
   b. senior sales representative.
   c. sales manager.
   d. marketing manager.

6. A sales compensation plan that features only a fixed payment per period of time is called a
   a. commission plan.
   b. salary plan.
   c. sales plan.
   d. combination plan.

7. Payments directly related to the sales or profits achieved by a salesperson are called
   a. quotas.
   b. commissions.
   c. salaries.
   d. bonuses.

8. Personal selling that occurs away from the seller's place of business is known as
   a. over-the-counter selling.
   b. field selling.
   c. missionary selling.
   d. telemarketing.

9. Face-to-face selling in which the buyer comes to the seller's place of business is known as
   a. over-the-counter selling.
   b. field selling.
   c. missionary selling.
   d. telemarketing.

10. To ensure coverage of important sales points, a sales manager may require the sales force to use
    a. telemarketing.
    b. creative selling.
    c. a canned presentation.
    d. automation.

11. Recent trends in personal selling include
    a. commissions.
    b. over-the-counter selling.
    c. demonstrations.
    d. relationship selling.

12. Sales managers can reduce unethical behavior by
    a. not reporting it.
    b. eliminating consultative selling techniques.
    c. ignoring it.
    d. monitoring ethical conduct.

Applying Marketing Concepts

Sparrow Furniture, Inc., manufactures and sells modern office furniture to businesses. Sparrow's customers typically do a good deal of research before making major purchases.

Bill Jansen, sales manager for Sparrow, has implemented a new compensation plan for his sales force. The new plan is designed to increase the incentive of all salespeople in order to raise their level of sales. According to the plan, each salesperson must sell $10,000 worth of furniture every month. After the sales goal is reached, salespeople receive compensation equal to 10 percent of their gross sales.

Select the best answer.

---

1. Sparrow's sales force is primarily involved in
   a. order processing.
   b. creative selling.
   c. missionary selling.
   d. over-the-counter selling.

2. Jansen's sales force is most likely involved in
   a. field selling.
   b. telemarketing.
   c. over-the-counter selling.
   d. order processing.

3. Jansen's new compensation plan is an example of a
   a. commission plan.
   b. salary plan.
   c. combination plan.

4. The $10,000 sales goal for each salesperson is an example of a
   a. marketing objective.
   b. sales commission.
   c. sales quota.
   d. combination plan.

Additional Activities

Experiential Exercises

1. The purpose of this exercise is to help you understand how a prospect's objections can actually be an aid in selling the product. Choose a consumer product, list two objections a consumer might have to purchasing it, give possible replies to the objections, and state how this process may have helped in selling the product.

For example:

> *Objection:* "I don't like the bucket seats in this model."
> *Reply:* "We offer a variety of interiors, including bench seats and split bench seats."
> *How objection helped:* It led to a discussion of the available interiors, one of which might interest the buyer.

2. The textbook identified three basic sales tasks: order processing, creative selling, and missionary sales. Below are four situations requiring at least one of these tasks. For each situation, identify the primary task to be performed, along with any other tasks, and explain the reasons for your choice.

   • A bread salesperson calls on one of the grocery stores on his or her route and finds it is short of hamburger buns.

   • An art-supplies salesperson calls on a college bookstore to inform the manager of a highly innovative type of drawing pen.

   • A sales representative for a computer data-processing company calls on the purchasing committee of a chain of department stores to discuss the type of information system the company needs.

   • The salesperson for the computer data-processing company calls again on the people who decided to buy the equipment to determine if they are satisfied.

Questions for Exploration

Conceptual

From the standpoint of the firm, which talent is more important for the sales representative to have: the ability to overcome customer objections or the ability to help the firm alter the good or service so that customer objections disappear? Why?

Practical

Each Lawry's salesperson services about forty customers. If Lawry's dropped its field-order strategy and switched to telephone sales, it could triple the number of customers contacted weekly. Explain why such a move would not be in Lawry's best interest.

Answer Key

Key Concepts			
1. a	7. g	13. k	18. t
2. f	8. h	14. n	19. u
3. c	9. m	15. q	20. r
4. e	10. i	16. o	21. s
5. d	11. j	17. p	
6. b	12. l		

Completion

1. personal selling
2. field, over-the-counter, telemarketing
3. processing, creative, missionary
4. order processing
5. creative selling
6. missionary selling
7. prospecting, qualifying
8. approach
9. presentation
10. canned
11. demonstration
12. objections
13. close
14. standing room only
15. "If I can show you"
16. extra inducement
17. alternative decision
18. silence
19. follow-up
20. recruiting, selecting
21. training
22. organization
23. motivation
24. compensation
25. evaluation, control
26. commission, salary
27. sales force automation

Self-Test			
1. a	5. c	9. a	
2. a	6. b	10. c	
3. c	7. b	11. d	
4. b	8. b	12. d	

Applying Marketing Concepts		
1. b	3. a	
2. a	4. c	

We must look at the price system as a mechanism for communicating information if we want to understand its real function.

—Frederick August von Hayek

23
Pricing

Assignments

For the most effective study of this lesson, we suggest that you complete the assignments in the following sequence:

1. Read the study guide Overview (Lesson Notes and Video Program Notes) and the Learning Objectives for this lesson.

2. Read *Contemporary Marketing Wired,* 9th edition, Chapter 20, "Price Determination," pages 686-712.

3. View "Leader of the Pack: A Case Study in Pricing" video program.

4. Review the textbook assignment for this lesson.

5. Complete the Review Activities (Key Concepts and Completion), Self-Test, and Applying Marketing Concepts for this lesson.

6. Check your answers against the Answer Key at the end of the lesson, and review when necessary.

7. Complete any of the Additional Activities (Experiential Exercises and Questions for Exploration) that interest you or that are assigned by your instructor.

Overview

Price can be defined as the exchange value of a good or service or, in other words, what someone is willing to pay for something at a particular time and place.

Unlike other marketing elements, pricing is regulated, primarily because of antitrust legislation, which was covered in an earlier lesson. Other regulation of pricing comes from the **Robinson-Patman Act**, an amendment to the Clayton Act, which prohibits price discrimination in sales to wholesalers, retailers, and other producers that is not based on a cost differential. In the past, individual states regulated pricing through **unfair-trade laws** and **fair-trade laws.** Most fair-trade laws are no longer in effect.

In setting prices, a firm must first set pricing objectives. Those objectives should be compatible with the firm's overall objectives and specific marketing goals. The four major groups of pricing objectives are profitability, volume, meeting competition, and prestige.

Profitability objectives include **profit maximization** and **target return** on sales or investment. Volume objectives include sales maximization and market share. Research conducted by the **Profit Impact of Market Strategies (PIMS)** project identified market share as one of two important determinants of profitability. The third group of pricing objectives, meeting competition, results in increased emphasis on nonprice elements of the marketing mix, product strategies, promotional decisions, and distribution. Recently, **value pricing,** or emphasizing a product's benefits in comparison to price and quality levels of competitors, has emerged. Prestige objectives are unrelated to either profitability or sales and are intended to convey an image of quality and exclusiveness. Many firms use a combination of pricing objectives, since any one objective may not guide decision makers sufficiently in this difficult task.

How prices are determined can be analyzed through a theoretical economics approach or a cost-oriented approach. Another theory is based on **customary prices,** prices that buyers traditionally expect to pay for a product.

Microeconomic price theory assumes that all firms seek to maximize profits and considers both **supply** and **demand** factors. Supply and demand are different in four types of market structures: **pure competition, monopolistic competition, oligopoly,** and **monopoly.** Price theory also includes the concept of **elasticity,** which is the measure of responsiveness of purchasers and suppliers to a change in price. Price theory is seldom used in setting actual prices because demand cannot always be precisely determined and it is often difficult to apply theory to real-world situations.

Most often, prices are determined on the basis of a cost-plus approach, which sets a price for the product that will be sufficient to cover the cost of producing and distributing it and provide a certain amount of profit.

Two basic methods of **cost-plus pricing** are the full-cost method and the incremental-cost method. Full-cost pricing includes all fixed and all relevant variable costs in setting a price for a specific product. Incremental-cost pricing includes only those costs directly attributable to a specific output in setting prices.

The cost-plus approach to pricing also has limitations. It does not directly consider demand, and, if the marketer includes all costs plus a reasonable profit margin, the product may be overpriced to the consumer. Also, cost-plus pricing usually assumes a uniform cost and price relationship; yet cost is neither the sole nor the major determinant of the selling price. Usually, production cost can be considered a minimum figure when setting price.

Pricing decisions may also be influenced by the results of **breakeven analysis,** which is used to determine the number of products that must be sold at a specific price to generate enough revenue to cover total costs. The basic breakeven model, however, has several shortcomings, the most important of which is that it does not directly consider demand. To compensate for these shortcomings, **modified breakeven analysis**, which combines the basic model with an estimate of consumer demand, can be used to set prices.

A marketing manager must be fully knowledgeable in the theory and application of pricing. To help the firm achieve its long-term profit objectives, the marketing manager must understand the relationship between price and what the market will pay for a product, whether it serves domestic or global customers.

Video Program Notes

The video program for this lesson traces the development of a new motorcycle and shows how Yamaha Motorcycles determines prices for its goods and services. The program illustrates that many variables affect pricing decisions. Price is defined as what somebody is willing to pay for something at a particular time and place, not just the result of adding up cost, expenses, and desired profit. This fast-paced program shows how real-world problems and market conditions affect the pricing formula.

As you watch the video program, consider the following questions:

1. What roles do the product-planning meetings and focus groups play in determining price-quality relationships?

2. What pricing strategy does Yamaha employ to attract low-end, first-time buyers?

3. Why is Yamaha more anxious to determine styling requirements than product features that affect performance?

4. How does Yamaha deal with the fact that most customers expect to pay about 25 percent less than the dealer is asking?

5. What cost elements contribute to the price of the V-MAX motorcycle?

6. How did the import tariffs on motorcycles over 700 cc affect Yamaha?

7. How does national advertising affect pricing and sales volume?

8. Why does Yamaha supply dealers with P.O.P. (point-of-purchase) materials?

9. What role does price play in the customer's decision to purchase a motorcycle?

10. What pricing strategy has Yamaha used in the development of the Kenny Roberts replica bikes?

Learning Objectives

After completing your study of this lesson, you should be able to:

1. Define the following terms as they relate to pricing:

breakeven analysis	price
cost-plus pricing	Profit Impact of Market Strategies (PIMS) project
customary price	
demand	
elasticity	profit maximization
fair-trade law	pure competition
modified breakeven analysis	Robinson-Patman Act
	supply
monopolistic competition	target-return objective
monopoly	unfair-trade law
oligopoly	value pricing

2. List legal constraints on pricing.

3. Describe the major categories of pricing objectives.

4. Explain the concept of price elasticity and its determinants.

5. List the practical problems in applying price theory concepts to actual pricing decisions.

6. Explain the major cost-plus approaches to price setting.

7. List the major advantages and disadvantages of using breakeven analysis in pricing decisions.

8. Explain why modified breakeven analysis is superior to basic breakeven analysis in determining prices.

9. Identify major issues related to price determination in in international marketing.

Review Activities

Key Concepts

Identify the following pricing concepts by writing the letter of the appropriate term in the blank next to the corresponding description.

a. price
b. profit maximization
c. target-return objective
d. Robinson-Patman Act
e. modified breakeven analysis
f. value pricing
g. customary price
h. pure competition
i. monopolistic competition
j. oligopoly
k. monopoly
l. cost-plus pricing
m. demand
n. elasticity
o. breakeven analysis
p. supply
q. unfair-trade law
r. Profit Impact of Market Strategies (PIMS) project
s. fair-trade law

_____ 1. pricing strategy that emphasizes the benefits of a product in comparison to those of competing offerings

_____ 2. pricing objective designed to achieve a specified return on sales or investments

_____ 3. federal legislation that prohibits price discrimination not based on a cost differential

_____ 4. traditional price that consumers expect to pay for a certain good or service

_____ 5. exchange value of a good or service

_____ 6. pricing technique used to evaluate consumer demand and expected sales volume at various prices

_____ 7. point at which the additional revenue gained by increasing the price of a product equals the increase in total costs

_____ 8. practical approach to price setting in which the decision maker adds a markup to cover unassigned costs and provide a profit

_____ 9. market structure with many buyers and sellers in which, due to product differences, the marketer has some control over prices

_____ 10. pricing technique used to determine the sales volume required at a specified price in order to generate sufficient revenue to cover total costs

_____ 11. market structure with only one seller of a good or service for which no close substitutes exist

_____ 12. amount consumers will buy of a firm's good or service at different prices during a given time period

_____ 13. amount of a good or service a firm will offer for sale at different prices during a specified time period

_____ 14. market structure with relatively few sellers and barriers to new competitors, usually due to high start-up costs

_____ 15. market structure with so many buyers and sellers that none can influence price

_____ 16. measure of responsiveness of purchasers and suppliers to a change in the price of a good or service

_____ 17. state law requiring sellers to maintain minimum prices for comparable merchandise

_____ 18. state statute that allows manufacturers to set a minimum retail price

_____ 19. research that discovered a positive relationship between a firm's market share and its return on investment

Completion

> **Fill each blank in the following paragraphs with the most appropriate term from the list of completion answers below. A term may be used once, more than once, or not at all.**
>
> | | | |
> |---|---|---|
> | breakeven | maximization | oligopoly |
> | analysis | maximize profits | prestige |
> | consumers | meeting | price |
> | cost-plus | competition | profit |
> | costs | modified | profitability |
> | customary | monopolistic | pure competition |
> | demand | competition | sales-maximization |
> | elasticity | monopoly | target |
> | investment | objectives | volume |
> | market-share | | |

1. The exchange value of a good or service is its _____.
    Another way of saying this is: _____ is what someone
    is willing to pay for a good or service at a particular time and
    place.

2. A firm's pricing _____ are very important to the
    effectiveness of its pricing operations and should be in line
    with the firm's marketing and overall objectives.

3. The four major groups of pricing objectives are _____ ,
    _____ , _____ , and _____.

4. Profitability pricing objectives include profit _____
    and return on _____.

5. A type of profitability objective that concerns achieving
    a specified return on investments is known as a
    _____ -return objective.

6. Sales maximization and market-share objectives are types
    of _____ objectives. When the firm sets a minimum
    acceptable profit level and then seeks to maximize sales,
    the firm is using a _____ approach.

7. When using _____ pricing objectives, which are expressed as a percentage of total industry sales, the firm sets a price to achieve a specific share of the total sales of a product.

8. Some companies simplify the pricing decision by matching the prices of the industry leader. This practice falls into the pricing objective of _____.

9. When a firm seeks to give a product an image of quality and exclusivity by pricing the product high, the firm is using _____ objectives to set price.

10. Prices based on tradition and consumer expectation are known as _____ prices.

11. The theoretical approach to setting price is extremely difficult to apply in practice, mainly because it is difficult to determine _____. In addition, the theoretical approach is based on many assumptions that may not be true in a given pricing situation. According to price theory, all firms attempt to _____.

12. The theoretical approach assumes that prices are being set in one of four types of market structures: _____ , _____ , _____ , and _____.

13. When there are large numbers of buyers and sellers and prices are not significantly influenced by any one of them, a price condition of _____ exists.

14. When one seller has a product so favorably differentiated from that of the competition that the seller has some degree of control over price, the situation of _____ exists.

15. The situation in which there are few sellers and many barriers to entry into a market is known as _____.

16. A market condition with only one seller of a product and no close substitutes for the product is called a _____.

17. Because it is difficult to apply the theoretical approach, actual price determination tends to be based on some form of the _____ approach. Basically, this approach is applied by adding a markup to the base cost to cover unassigned _____ and to provide a _____.

18. Cost is not always the sole determinant of prices. Price is also set by the action of _____ in the market. Cost does, however, provide a tool for analyzing the profitability of various pricing alternatives.

19. Cost-oriented pricing has certain limitations. One limitation is that cost-oriented pricing does not adequately account for product _____.

20. Demand for a product is affected by its price. In some cases, a minor price change will almost completely eliminate _____ for a product. In other cases, price increases will have a negligible effect on demand. This variation in demand based on the relative price of a product or service is known as _____.

21. The decision maker can compare the profit consequences of different prices using a technique known as _____.

22. Breakeven analysis is useful for determining which of several prices to charge, but it does not take into consideration variations in consumer _____ at different prices. An approach that does consider different demand at different prices is known as _____ breakeven analysis.

Self-Test

Select the best answer.

1. A type of volume pricing objective is
   a. overpricing.
   b. prestige pricing.
   c. market-share pricing.
   d. target-return pricing.

2. The Profit Impact of Market Strategies (PIMS) project found
   a. no relationship between a firm's market share and its return on investment.
   b. a negative relationship between a firm's market share and its return on investment.
   c. a weak relationship between a firm's market share and its return on investment.
   d. a strong positive relationship between a firm's market share and its return on investment.

3. Modified breakeven analysis differs from basic breakeven analysis in that modified breakeven analysis takes into consideration the
   a. effects of fixed costs at different volumes.
   b. effects of variable costs at different volumes.
   c. differences in supply at different prices.
   d. differences in demand at different prices.

4. A measurement of the responsiveness of either purchasers or suppliers to a change in price is called
   a. elasticity.
   b. PIMS.
   c. the demand curve.
   d. the supply curve.

5. The most popular method of setting prices today is
   a. meeting competition.
   b. cost-plus pricing.
   c. prestige pricing.
   d. customary pricing.

6. The amount someone is willing to pay for a good or service
    at a particular time or place is one definition of
    a. costs.
    b. variable costs.
    c. price.
    d. asking price.

7. If a firm wishes to establish a high-quality image
    for a product, it will probably use
    a. profit maximization.
    b. full-cost pricing.
    c. prestige pricing.
    d. sales maximization.

8. If a firm wishes to earn a specific annual rate of return
    on sales, its pricing objective can be described as
    a. target-return.
    b. market-share.
    c. prestige.
    d. volume.

9. If a firm attempts to increase sales by accepting lower
    profits, it is using
    a. target-return objectives.
    b. market-share objectives.
    c. sales maximization.
    d. incremental-cost pricing.

10. In order to determine the number of products that
    must be sold at a given price to cover total costs,
    a marketing manager would use
    a. product analysis.
    b. price analysis.
    c. cost analysis.
    d. breakeven analysis.

Applying Marketing Concepts

Duelmont Corporation processes and sells canned spiced peaches, pears, apples, and cherries under the Duelmont Pride label. The firm does not aggressively use price to get more business. As one of the three firms marketing canned spiced fruit in a five-state area, Duelmont is satisfied with about a third of the market. Prices are set at the beginning of the year, as the harvest is finished. Those prices are maintained until the next year, except for seasonal promotional activities when necessary.

The general procedure for setting price at Duelmont consists of first estimating supply and demand for the products; next, the costs of buying and canning the fruit are determined. Costs that cannot be assigned to a particular canned fruit item are not included in those cost figures. Once costs are determined, an amount sufficient to cover selling expenses and provide about an 8-percent rate of return on sales is then added to determine list price.

> **Select the best answer.**

1. The pricing objective of Duelmont Corporation is
   a. profit maximization.
   b. target return.
   c. maximizing sales.
   d. market share.

2. The pricing approach Duelmont is using is
   a. cost-plus.
   b. economic.
   c. supply-demand.
   d. breakeven.

3. The specific method of determining cost Duelmont is using is
   a. full-cost pricing.
   b. breakeven.
   c. markup.
   d. incremental-cost pricing.

4. The market situation for Duelmont is called
   a. pure competition.
   b. monopolistic competition.
   c. oligopoly.
   d. monopoly.

Additional Activities

Experiential Exercises

1. The purpose of this exercise is to help you understand how individual business owners set price.

   From the businesses in your community, select one independently owned restaurant, coffee shop, grocery store, stationery store, gift shop, or similar retail establishment.

   Schedule an appointment with the owner/manager of the establishment and ask how he or she sets the prices for the products sold.

   - Are prices set on a cost-plus basis?
   - What are the pricing objectives? Does the owner/manager have to meet the competition on any of the products sold? Is volume a consideration? Prestige? The owner/manager may describe a pricing method known as "keystoning." In this method, a retailer multiplies the cost of a product by some "factor" to set a retail price for that item. A common keystone factor is "2," resulting in a retail price twice the cost of the product to the business. Keystoning is a pure cost-based pricing method. If the owner/manager uses keystoning, ask whether it is applied to all the products sold or only to selected items.

2. The purpose of the next exercise is to give you a greater understanding of the importance of price to a marketing manager.

- Select a firm in your area and interview the marketing manager. He or she may be a product or division manager or the general marketing manager of the firm. After learning about the marketing operation, hand the manager four cards, each containing a name of a variable of the marketing mix—price, product, distribution, or promotion.
- Ask the marketing manager to rank the variables in order of importance to the product line you have been discussing.
- Ask the manager to explain the rankings: Why, for example, is the variable chosen as most important considered to be more important than the other three variables?

Questions for Exploration

Conceptual

The video program asserted that the U.S. government had imposed import tariffs on motorcycles over 700 cc to "save Harley-Davidson." How could the marketing departments at Yamaha and other foreign motorcycle manufacturers minimize the adverse impact of these tariffs?

Practical

How would other elements of the marketing mix be affected if price were the least important factor considered when purchasing a motorcycle? If price were the most important factor?

Answer Key

Key Concepts			
1. f	6. e	11. k	16. n
2. c	7. b	12. m	17. q
3. d	8. l	13. p	18. s
4. g	9. i	14. j	19. r
5. a	10. o	15. h	

Completion

1. price, price
2. objectives
3. profitability, volume, meeting competition, prestige (any order)
4. maximization, investment
5. target
6. volume, maximization
7. market-share
8. meeting competition
9. prestige
10. customary
11. demand, maximize profits
12. pure competition, monopolistic competition, oligopoly, monopoly (any order)
13. pure competition
14. monopolistic competition
15. oligopoly
16. monopoly
17. cost-plus, costs, profit
18. consumers
19. demand
20. demand, elasticity
21. breakeven analysis
22. demand, modified

Self-Test		
1. c	5. b	8. a
2. d	6. c	9. c
3. d	7. c	10. d
4. a		

Applying Marketing Concepts

1. b
2. a
3. d
4. c

*Everything is worth what its
purchaser will pay for it.*
—Publilius Syrus (1 b.c.)

24

Pricing Strategy

Assignments

For the most effective study of this lesson, we suggest that you complete the
assignments in the following sequence:

1. Read the study guide Overview (Lesson Notes and Video Program
   Notes) and the Learning Objectives for this lesson.

2. Read *Contemporary Marketing Wired*, 9th edition, Chapter 21,
   "Managing the Pricing Function," pages 716-738.

3. View "What the Market Will Bear: Great Moments in Pricing"
   video program.

4. Review the textbook assignment for this lesson.

5. Complete the Review Activities (Key Concepts and Completion),
   Self-Test, and Applying Marketing Concepts for this lesson.

6. Check your answers against the Answer Key at the end of the lesson,
   and review when necessary.

7. Complete any of the Additional Activities (Experiential Exercises and
   Questions for Exploration) that interest you or that are assigned by your
   instructor.

Overview

Lesson Notes

A firm develops a pricing strategy in order to facilitate setting prices in recurrent situations. A strategy, however, only provides general guidance, and a firm can approach pricing in many different ways. Specific pricing strategies may be based on such factors as the market share a firm desires for a product, the price of competitive products, prevailing price levels, and the prices of the firm's other products. Regardless of the factors influencing pricing strategy, the strategy should reflect the firm's overall marketing strategies and contribute to achievement of the firm's objectives.

Basic pricing strategies for goods and services include skimming, penetration, and competitive strategies. In a **skimming strategy**, or market-plus pricing, the price is high in comparison to competitive products. A firm may use a skimming strategy when its product is substantially different from existing products or completely new. A skimming strategy also enables a firm to recover its research, development, and promotion costs quickly. In contrast, a **penetration strategy,** or market-minus pricing, involves a relatively low entry price, which is designed to capture a large market share and establish brand loyalty among consumers. The penetration pricing strategy often discourages competition. Similarly, **everyday low pricing (EDLP)** maintains low prices instead of short-term price-cutting tactics. The third pricing strategy, **competitive pricing**, establishes the price of a good or service at about the same level as that of competitive offerings. A competitive pricing strategy has the effect of nullifying the price variable in marketing strategies, thus shifting the marketing emphasis to the product, its distribution, and its promotion.

Regardless of the strategy used to set prices, the result of the pricing process is a pricing structure built on **list price**, the price that is normally quoted to potential buyers. When quoting prices, however, a firm can employ any of several methods to reduce the list price. Such reductions may be necessary because of cost structures, consumer expectations, traditional practices, or the firm's policies.

The reduced price—the price the customer actually pays—is the **market price**. Price reductions can be achieved through cash, trade, and quantity discounts; allowances; and rebates.

Cash discounts are price reductions offered in return for prompt payment. **Trade discounts**, also known as *functional discounts*, are payments to a channel member for performing marketing functions. **Quantity discounts** are reductions in price given for large-volume purchases.

The two principal types of allowances are **trade-ins**, which allow credit for a used object, and **promotional allowances**, which are advertising and sales-support allowances given by the manufacturers to other channel members.

Rebates are refunds to consumers, usually given by manufacturers, that reduce the cost of the product to consumers.

When setting and quoting prices, manufacturers also must consider the transportation components of a product's price. This consideration is particularly important in the pricing of heavy, bulky, low-unit-cost goods. These costs can be borne by either the buyer or seller or shared by both. Responsibility for transportation costs is often designated by such terms as **FOB plant,** FOB origin-freight allowed or **freight absorption, uniform delivered price, zone pricing,** and **basing point system.**

Transportation costs are an especially critical element in setting prices when a firm is seeking to expand into more geographically distant markets, where there are local competitors who can supply the product without incurring substantial shipping costs.

In making specific pricing decisions, a firm is usually guided by a **pricing policy**, which is a general guideline based on marketing objectives. Pricing policies are particularly important with regard to competitive considerations. Among the most common pricing policies are psychological pricing, price flexibility, product line pricing, and promotional pricing.

Psychological pricing assumes that some prices are more appealing to buyers than others. In addition to prestige pricing (discussed in the previous lesson), two other types of psychological pricing are odd pricing and unit pricing. **Odd pricing** is a price ending in an odd number, such as $9.99. **Unit pricing** states all prices in a recognized unit of measure or standard numerical count.

Price flexibility refers to a pricing policy that allows prices for a firm's products to vary. Price flexibility is most often found in situations where individual bargaining is common. In mass-selling situations, one-price policies are most common.

Product line pricing is the practice of marketing different lines of merchandise at a limited number of prices. The various prices for specific lines help to differentiate each of the product lines and help customers in moving up or down in their purchases of products. Product line pricing requires identifying specific market segments and then setting prices that will appeal to each segment. Product line pricing is frequently used in retail marketing.

Another pricing policy often used at the retail level is **promotional pricing**, in which a lower-than-normal price is temporarily used as part of a firm's overall marketing strategy. Stores may offer **loss leaders** priced below cost to attract customers.

One interesting element of pricing is the relationship between price and the consumer's perception of quality. The concept of price limits refers to the limits within which consumers' perceptions of a product's quality vary with the product's price.

In specialized situations, prices may be determined on the basis of competitive bidding or through contract negotiation. These approaches are often used in the business sector, the government, and institutional markets. In competitive bidding, potential suppliers are asked to quote prices on the same good or service. Negotiated prices, which are set by agreement between the buyer and seller, are often found in situations where there is only one supplier or extensive research and development will be necessary.

In large companies, a pricing problem occurs when deciding on an internal **transfer price** for moving goods between **profit centers.** How this problem is resolved depends on company philosophy. In global markets, numerous conditions, both internal and external, affect pricing strategies, as well.

Video Program Notes

Through a variety of examples, the video program for this lesson demonstrates that the market, not costs, ultimately determines price. Factors such as product cost, expenses, and desired profit help to set only the asking price. The program looks at how prices are set and on what basis they are adjusted. Companies featured include Mitsubishi, Famous Amos Chocolate Chip Cookie Company, Robert Mondavi Winery, Skyfox, Pizza Hop, Looking Good, Western Cruise Lines, Disney Productions, and several others. Pricing policies illustrated include psychological, unit, new product, flexible, penetration, product line, and promotional.

As you watch the video program, consider the following questions:

1. How is price defined in the program?

2. What pricing strategy was used to introduce the Garfield phone?

3. Which uncontrollable variable seems to affect price most?

4. Why is maintaining quality essential to price?

5. Why do Looking Good and Western Cruise Lines use a low-price strategy?

6. Why do Mitsubishi, West Ridge Mountaineering, and Disney Productions maintain a variety of products, each priced differently?

7. What role does brand recognition play in pricing?

8. Why are rebates and coupons favored by all channel members over simply lowering price?

9. What kind of pricing strategy did Arm and Hammer and Looking Good assume? Why?

10. How do Skyfox and Garrett Turbine determine prices?

11. Why are different units of meat priced differently even though the retailer buys beef at a single price?

12. What determines price?

Learning Objectives

After completing your study of this lesson, you should be able to:

1. Define the following terms as they relate to pricing strategy:

basing point system	odd pricing	rebate
cash discount	penetration	skimming
competitive	pricing strategy	pricing strategy
pricing strategy	price flexibility	trade discount
everyday low	pricing policy	trade-in
pricing (EDLP)	product line pricing	transfer price
FOB plant	profit center	uniform
freight absorption	promotional allowance	delivered price
list price	promotional pricing	unit pricing
loss leader	psychological pricing	zone pricing
market price	quantity discount	

2. Describe the alternative pricing strategies and explain when each strategy is most appropriate.

3. Describe how prices are quoted.

4. Explain the features of the various pricing policy decisions that marketers make.

5. Briefly describe the relationship between price and the consumer's perception of quality.

6. Contrast competitive bidding and negotiated prices.

7. Explain the importance of transfer pricing.

8. Compare the three alternative strategies for pricing exports.

Review Activities

Key Concepts

> Identify each of the following terms related to quoting prices by writing the letter of the appropriate term in the blank next to the corresponding description.
>
> a. list price
> b. market price
> c. cash discount
> d. trade discount
>
> e. quantity discount
> f. trade-in
> g. promotional allowance
> h. rebate

_____ 1. rate that is normally quoted to a potential buyer

_____ 2. price reduction given to a buyer for prompt payment of a bill

_____ 3. payment to a channel member—the buyer—for performing a marketing function normally performed by the seller; also called a *functional discount*

_____ 4. price reduction given for large orders because of cost savings the seller obtains from filling fewer orders

_____ 5. reduction in the price of a new item granted in return for a used item the buyer gives the seller

_____ 6. refund of a portion of the purchase price

_____ 7. actual amount that a buyer pays for a good or service

_____ 8. advertising or sales-support allowances given to a channel member in an attempt to integrate promotional strategy within the channel

> Identify each of the following terms related to transportation costs by writing the letter of the appropriate term in the blank next to the corresponding description.
>
> a. FOB plant
> b. freight absorption
> c. uniform delivered price
>
> d. zone pricing
> e. basing point system

_____ 9. pricing method in which a standard price is set by geographical areas

_____ 10. price of the product at the point where the product is shipped; does not include shipping charges

_____ 11. price quotation that permits the buyer to subtract transportation expenses from a bill

_____ 12. geographic pricing in which all buyers are given the same price for the product, including transportation costs

_____ 13. price quotation that includes price at the factory plus freight charges from a city closest to the buyer

---

Identify each of the following terms related to pricing strategy and pricing policy by writing the letter of the appropriate term in the blank next to the corresponding description.

a. psychological pricing	g. product line pricing
b. odd pricing	h. promotional pricing
c. loss leader	
d. skimming pricing strategy	i. competitive pricing strategy
e. penetration pricing strategy	j. transfer price
	k. profit center
f. price flexibility	l. everyday low pricing

_____ 14. new-product pricing strategy that uses an entry price lower than that of similar products in an attempt to secure market acceptance

_____ 15. pricing strategy involving the use of a high entry price relative to competitive offerings

_____ 16. form of psychological pricing that uses prices with uneven endings (such as $16.49 and $14.99)

_____ 17. pricing policy permitting variable prices for goods and services

_____ 18. pricing approach based on the appeal of certain prices or price ranges to buyers

_____ 19. practice of pricing products at a limited number of pricing points

_____ 20. retail price set below cost to attract consumers in the hope they will buy other items at regular prices

_____ 21. temporary use of lower-than-normal price

_____ 22. strategy that de-emphasizes price as a competitive variable

_____ 23. any part of an organization to which revenue and controllable costs can be assigned

_____ 24. pricing strategy in which prices are always lower than those of competitors

_____ 25. cost assessed when a product is moved from one profit center within a firm to another

Completion

Fill each blank in the following paragraphs with the most appropriate term from the list of completion answers below. A term may be used once, more than once, or not at all.

absorption	market	sales support
advertising	odd	seller
allowances	penetration	shared
buyer	prestige	shipping charges
cash	price flexibility	skimming
competitive	pricing	strategy
discounts	product line	trade
even	promotional	trade-in
flexibility	psychological	transportation
high	quality	uniform delivered
list	quantity	unit
loss leaders	rebates	zone
low		

1. In order to facilitate setting prices in recurrent situations, a firm must develop a pricing _____.

2. The three major types of pricing strategies are _____, _____, and _____.

3. When a firm has a product that is considerably different from existing products or entirely new, it is likely to use a _____ strategy.

4. A price that is relatively low and designed to capture a large market share and establish brand loyalty is the result of a _____ strategy.

5. The pricing strategy that has the effect of shifting the marketing emphasis to nonprice variables is a _____ strategy.

6. The price that is normally quoted to potential buyers is the _____ price. The price the buyer actually pays is the _____ price.

7. Three common methods of reducing the list price are
_____ , _____ , and _____.

8. Price reductions offered in return for prompt payment are
_____ discounts. Payments to channel members for
performing marketing functions are _____ discounts.
Reductions in price given for large-volume purchases are
_____ discounts.

9. There are two types of allowances. In one type, credit is given
for a used object; this type is known as a _____. In the
second type, the manufacturer gives a promotional
allowance to other channel members in return for _____
and _____.

10. Refunds to consumers, known as _____, are usually
given by manufacturers.

11. An important consideration in setting and quoting prices
is _____ costs. These costs can be borne by either the
_____ or _____ or they can be _____ by both.

12. A price quoted FOB (free on board) plant does not include
any additional _____. The seller simply loads the
merchandise on board the carrier and from then on the
_____ pays all costs. Through this policy, the seller's
trading area is limited, especially if _____ costs are a
major part of the cost of the delivered merchandise.

13. A seller may follow a policy of paying all transportation
expenses. When using this method, which is called freight
_____ , the seller quotes the same price regardless of
the buyer's location.

14. In some cases, transportation costs paid by the buyer as part
of the quoted price include a standard transportation charge.
When the seller quotes the same price to all buyers, regardless of their distance from the shipping point, the seller is
using a _____ price.

15. When the seller, in effect, overcharges some buyers for
transportation and undercharges others by charging all
buyers an average transportation cost, the seller is using the
_____ pricing method.

16. A system of uniform delivered pricing within geographic areas, often used by mail-order firms, is called _____ pricing.

17. To provide guidelines for decision makers, to assure consistency in pricing decisions, and to control pricing, firms usually establish _____ policies. Common pricing policies include _____ pricing, _____ pricing, _____ pricing, _____ pricing, and price _____.

18. A pricing policy that assumes that some prices are more appealing than others is known as _____ pricing.

19. A price set at $49.99 is an example of _____ pricing, one common form of psychological pricing. Another form of psychological pricing is _____ pricing.

20. Selling gasoline at a set amount per gallon is an example of _____ pricing.

21. In most retail, mass-selling situations, one-price policies are used. In contrast, situations in which individual bargaining is common are usually characterized by a policy of _____.

22. Some companies (usually retailers) price products within a limited number of price ranges (such as $79, $99, and $129). This practice, which is called _____ pricing, serves as a product quality guide for consumers. It also focuses the consumer's attention on product features rather than on price alone.

23. Decision makers must decide to what extent price will be used to increase sales volume. A pricing approach designed to increase sales volume is known as _____ pricing.

24. There are many different promotional pricing practices. When retailers price products at less than cost in order to attract customers who will probably buy other, regularly priced products, they are using _____.

25. Some consumers have price limits within which their perceptions of product _____ vary directly with price. A price below this limit is considered too _____ and a price above the limit too _____.

Self-Test

Select the best answer.

1. When the price is reduced for giving the seller a used item, the seller is providing the customer a
   a. trade discount.
   b. trade-in allowance.
   c. promotional allowance.
   d. brokerage allowance.

2. The pricing strategy that shifts the marketing emphasis to the product and its distribution and promotion is known as a
   a. skimming strategy.
   b. penetration strategy.
   c. psychological strategy.
   d. competitive strategy.

3. Of the following pricing policies, the one that is often used with new products is
   a. penetration pricing.
   b. zone pricing.
   c. psychological pricing.
   d. odd pricing.

4. If Zenith offers consumers $25.00 back on the purchase of a new television set, Zenith is using a
   a. rebate.
   b. trade discount.
   c. promotional allowance.
   d. cash discount.

5. If Somerset Pipe offers King Hardware a lower price if the store purchases over 5,000 feet of $\frac{1}{2}$-inch pipe during June, Somerset is offering a
   a. rebate.
   b. trade discount.
   c. quantity discount.
   d. cash discount.

6. Toys Galore received an invoice from Funco International marked "FOB Plant," which means that
   a. Funco pays for shipping.
   b. Toys Galore pays for shipping.
   c. the shipper pays for shipping.
   d. the plant pays for shipping.

7. Marketing Concepts, a mail-order firm in Phoenix, Arizona, charges customers in Oklahoma less for shipping than it charges customers in New York. The method of setting transportation charges that Marketing Concepts uses is
   a. zone pricing.
   b. freight absorption.
   c. uniform delivered price.
   d. FOB plant.

8. Communico, Inc., has just developed a unique line of add-on microchips that enhance the graphics of IBM computers. The company decided to price above the market until competitors develop similar microchips. The pricing policy that Communico is using can be described as
   a. flexible.
   b. penetration.
   c. psychological.
   d. skimming.

9. The Shoe Emporium offers a wide variety of different shoes at the following standard prices: $9.95, $14.95, $19.95, and $24.95. The Shoe Emporium is using
   a. price flexibility.
   b. penetration pricing.
   c. product line pricing.
   d. promotional pricing.

10. Plumb Aplomb, a manufacturer of elegant brass and wood plumbing fixtures, offers retailers discounts if they advertise Plumb Aplomb's products. Plumb Aplomb is using
    a. trade discounts.
    b. promotional allowances.
    c. promotional pricing.
    d. skimming pricing.

Applying Marketing Concepts

The Caballero Corporation is located in a midwestern city and has yearly sales of approximately $24 million. The firm manufactures a limited line of quality stereo equipment, which is sold to department and specialty stores within the United States.

Caballero has successfully sold stereo equipment nationwide and has seen both sales volume and profits double in the last five years. The firm sells through its own sales force, but also uses wholesalers in territories where sales volume is insufficient to maintain company salespeople. Of course, wholesalers buy for less than retailers.

The company has a very good name in the industry, and retailers often mention Caballero in local advertising. The firm encourages this type of activity and gives retailers a reduction in price to help pay some of the advertising costs.

Caballero is able to compete with competitors located in other parts of the country by including transportation costs in its price quotes to buyers. Thus, it quotes transportation prices to buyers based on the section of the United States in which a given buyer is located.

The firm offers stereo sets of low, medium, and high quality—and prices them accordingly. For example, the low-quality sets are priced to sell from $125 to $150, medium-quality sets sell in the $200-to-$250 range, and high-quality sets sell at $500 and up. Caballero encourages retailers to use prices ending in $7.95 (such as $127.95) instead of an even amount. The firm's marketing research indicates this pricing technique has helped sales.

Select the best answer.

---

1. The discount that Caballero Corporation gives to wholesalers who sell to retailers is called a
   a. cash discount.
   b. trade discount.
   c. cash and trade discount.
   d. trade and quantity discount.

2. The type of allowance described in this situation is a
   a. trade-in.
   b. promotional.
   c. rebate and trade-in.
   d. trade-in and promotional.

3. The geographic pricing policy used by Caballero is
   a. FOB plant.
   b. freight absorption.
   c. zone pricing.
   d. uniform delivered pricing.

4. Caballero engages in
   a. product line pricing.
   b. skimming pricing.
   c. penetration pricing.
   d. price fixing.

5. Caballero encourages retailers to engage in
   a. skimming pricing.
   b. penetration pricing.
   c. odd pricing.
   d. break-even pricing.

Additional Activities

Experiential Exercises

1. The purpose of this exercise is to improve your understanding of price limits. You are asked to visit stores and investigate the range of prices for selected products.
   - For each product listed below, determine the range of prices charged in two different stores that carry similar product lines.

     | flowering plants | boys' sport shirts |
     | electric typewriters | paperback books (best-sellers) |
     | sleeping bags | personal computers |

- Ask the manager of one of these stores about the price ranges and price limits for these products. Explain the nature of any difference you find in the price limits.

2. The following exercise was developed to help you understand the role of consumer perceptions of price in pricing decisions.
   - Select an item you have recently purchased. (*Suggestion:* Select a CD player, camera, or small appliance; do not use staple goods, such as grocery or drug items, that have widely known prices.) Show the item to ten people and ask them to estimate the price. If they give you a price range, select the midpoint within the range and write it down.
   - Ask each person why he or she chose that price, listing the reasons given most often for estimated price. Briefly summarize the price perceptions of these ten people. What are the implications of these findings for firms marketing this product?

Questions for Exploration

Conceptual

"Price is a measure of how well the marketer has handled the other elements of the marketing mix— a high price means he or she has handled them well; a low price means that he or she hasn't."

Agree or disagree with the preceding statement. Support your argument.

Practical

The video program noted that limited-edition bottlings of certain Mondavi wines sold out in less than a month even though they were priced at $50 to $60 a bottle. Should Mondavi double the price on the next limited edition of these wines? Why?

Answer Key

Key Concepts	1. a	8. g	15. d	21. h
	2. c	9. d	16. b	22. i
	3. d	10. a	17. f	23. k
	4. e	11. b	18. a	24. l
	5. f	12. c	19. g	25. j
	6. h	13. e	20. c	
	7. b	14. e		

Completion

1. strategy
2. skimming, penetration, competitive (any order)
3. skimming
4. penetration
5. competitive
6. list, market
7. discounts, allowances, rebates (any order)
8. cash, trade, quantity
9. trade-in; advertising, sales support (either order)
10. rebates
11. transportation; buyer, seller (either order); shared
12. shipping charges, buyer, transportation
13. absorption
14. uniform delivered
15. uniform delivered
16. zone
17. pricing; psychological, unit, product line, promotional (any order); flexibility
18. psychological
19. odd, prestige
20. unit
21. price flexibility
22. product line
23. promotional
24. loss leaders
25. quality, low, high

Self-Test	1. b	5. c	8. d
	2. d	6. b	9. c
	3. a	7. a	10. b
	4. a		

Applying Marketing Concepts	1. b	4. a
	2. b	5. c
	3. c	

25

Nonprofit Marketing

Assignments

For the most effective study of this lesson, we suggest that you complete the assignments in the following sequence:

1. Read the study guide Overview (Lesson Notes and Video Program Notes) and the Learning Objectives for this lesson.

2. Review *Contemporary Marketing Wired*, 9th edition, Chapter 1, pages 16-23, "Extending the Traditional Boundaries of Marketing" and Chapter 3, pages 100-110, "Marketing's Role in Society," "Current Issues in Marketing," and "Controlling the Marketing System."

3. View "The Green Machine: A Case Study in Nonprofit Marketing" video program.

4. Review the textbook assignment for this lesson.

5. Complete the Review Activities (Key Concepts and Completion), Self-Test, and Applying Marketing Concepts for this lesson.

6. Check your answers against the Answer Key at the end of the lesson, and review when necessary.

7. Complete any of the Additional Activities (Experiential Exercises and Questions for Exploration) that interest you or that are assigned by your instructor.

Overview

Lesson Notes

This lesson explores two significant aspects of contemporary marketing. The first is the growing role of marketing in not-for-profit organizations. The second is the role of marketing in society at large and the major social issues that confront marketing today.

The not-for-profit sector of the U.S. economy is large and diverse. About 1.2 million organizations employ almost 11 million people and generate $300 billion in annual revenues. Not-for-profit organizations exist in both the private and public sectors, and they may market goods, services, or both in achieving their organizational objectives. Examples of private-sector not-for-profit organizations include art museums, private colleges and universities, research institutes, labor unions, and fund-raising organizations. Public-sector not-for-profits include agencies and organizations of federal, state, and local governments, such as school districts, public-health agencies, public colleges and universities, and the U.S. military.

The chief distinguishing feature of not-for-profit organizations is that their activities, although they may produce revenue, do not produce a profit that is distributed to individuals or to shareholders. Instead, the revenue accrues to the organization to use in achieving its objectives. In order to maximize their revenues and to facilitate achievement of their objectives, increasing numbers of not-for-profit organizations are adopting traditional marketing concepts and strategies.

Although not-for-profit organizations may employ many of the same marketing techniques as for-profit organizations, not-for-profit marketing has certain distinctive characteristics. One of the most important differences is that not-for-profits direct their efforts toward two or more publics, such as clients and sponsors. In contrast, for-profits usually focus on a single target market for each product. Also, as noted earlier, not-for-profits do not generate profits, so they lack a bottom line against which to measure achievement of marketing objectives. Another major difference is that most not-for-profits, in comparison to for-profits, do not have a well-defined organizational structure but may have several overlapping organizational systems.

The types of marketing engaged in by not-for-profits can be divided into five categories: person marketing, place marketing, cause marketing, event marketing, and organization marketing. **Person marketing** is concerned with developing the interest of a target market toward a particular person, such as a political candidate or an entertainer. **Place marketing** is designed to stimulate tourism, improve a location's image, or attract new business. **Cause marketing** promotes a social issue, cause, or idea to selected target markets. **Event marketing** promotes attendance at cultural activities, athletic events, and fund-raising activities. **Organization marketing** is practiced by mutual-benefit organizations, service organizations, and government organizations to encourage people to accept their goals, receive their services, or make a contribution.

Whether an organization is not-for-profit or for-profit, marketers today are particularly aware of the role of marketing in society as a whole and of the major social issues confronting all organizations. Marketing, because it is usually the primary link between the organization and the society in which it operates, is most often responsible for dealing with any social issues affecting the organization. At present, the two major social issues facing marketing are the ethics of the profession itself and the social responsibility of organizations.

Marketing ethics concern standards of conduct and moral values: what is right and what is wrong. All areas of marketing—research, product strategy, distribution, promotion, and pricing—have the potential for creating ethical dilemmas for marketers. Often these dilemmas arise from conflict between the individual's and the organization's ethics. One way of resolving ethical conflicts is adherence to a professional ethic developed by an outside party. For marketers, the American Marketing Association has developed a detailed code of ethics for its members.

Social responsibility refers to marketing philosophies, policies, procedures, and actions that have the enhancement of society's welfare as a primary objective, along with profit and consumer satisfaction. Social responsibility is concerned with qualitative benefits to consumers and society, now and in the future, as opposed to the purely quantitative measures of sales, revenues, and profits.

One area of major concern to marketers today is the environment, particularly the issues of planned obsolescence, pollution, recycling, and resource conservation. Many government and business leaders identify the environment as the most difficult challenge facing business today. In response to growing concern about ecological issues, many companies practice **green marketing**—production, promotion, and reclamation of environmentally sensitive products.

Video Program Notes

This video program illustrates how one not-for-profit organization—the U.S. Army—has adapted the marketing-mix strategies of product, pricing, distribution, and promotion to meet the organization's objectives. The program explores the strategies and tactics employed by the Army to achieve its marketing objective: to recruit high-school graduates who have the right attitude and aptitude to contribute to today's high-tech Army. The program shows how ads and ad themes are researched and developed to create awareness and enthusiasm for the Army's product, and how promotional events, such as parachute drops at high schools and sophisticated recruitment officers, help to "close the sale." The program examines consumer motivation for enlistment and customer satisfaction and how, throughout the marketing process, the Army attempts never to lose sight of its ultimate goal: an effective fighting force, ready to die if necessary to protect our country's freedoms.

As you watch the video program, consider the following questions:

1. How does the Army's All-American Parachute Team serve as advertising, sales promotion, and field selling?

2. What social-cultural problems exist for the Army in marketing to new recruits?

3. Why is a parachute demonstration superior to old-style recruitment films?

4. What "product" does the Army "sell" to potential recruits?

5. How is a recruitment officer like/unlike a civilian salesperson?

6. What are the advertising objectives of the ads created by N. W. Ayer?

7. Why do some ads feature parental support of enlistment?

8. What seems to appeal most to young people who are considering enlisting?

9. What are some of the "prices" that a recruit may be asked to pay?

10. Who or what is the Army's competition?

Learning Objectives

After completing your study of this lesson, you should be able to:

1. Define the following terms as they relate to nontraditional marketing and social issues in marketing:

cause marketing	organization marketing
event marketing	person marketing
green marketing	place marketing
marketing ethics	social responsibility
not-for-profit organization	

2. Identify the basic characteristics of nontraditional marketing.

3. Describe five major types of not-for-profit marketing.

4. Describe the role of marketing in society.

5. Identify two major social issues in marketing.

Review Activities

Key Concepts

> **Identify each of the following concepts related to social issues and nonprofit marketing by writing the letter of the appropriate term in the blank next to the corresponding description.**
>
> a. cause marketing
> b. marketing ethics
> c. event marketing
> d. social responsibility
> e. not-for-profit organization
> f. organization marketing
> g. place marketing
> h. person marketing
> i. green marketing

_____ 1. identification and marketing of an issue or idea to chosen consumer segments

_____ 2. moral premises upon which marketing decisions are made

_____ 3. marketing of a sporting, cultural, or charitable activity

_____ 4. those marketing philosophies, policies, procedures, and actions that have the advancement of society's welfare as their primary objectives

_____ 5. organization or institution that does not have a bottom line

_____ 6. marketing that seeks to influence others to accept the goals of, receive the services of, or contribute to the organization

_____ 7. marketing that seeks to promote a favorable attitude toward an individual

_____ 8. marketing efforts to attract people and organizations to a particular geographic area

_____ 9. producing, marketing, and reclaiming environmentally sensitive products

Completion

Fill each blank in the following paragraphs with the most appropriate term from the list of completion answers below. A term may be used once, more than once, or not at all.

advertising	marketing ethics	privacy
bottom line	more	private
cause	organization	public
ethical	organizational	quality
ethics	structure	recycling
event	person	responsibility
green marketing	place	social
high	planned	responsibility
less	obsolescence	unethical
marketing	pollution	

1. Financial pressures due to increased competition for donations and reduced government funding have led many not-for-profit organizations to adopt the _____ concept.

2. Not-for-profit organizations are found in both the _____ and _____ sectors.

3. The March of Dimes is an example of a not-for-profit organization in the _____ sector. The U.S. Army is an example of a not-for-profit organization in the _____ sector.

4. The five major types of not-for-profit marketing are _____ , _____ , _____ , _____ , and _____ .

5. A political campaign manager who is promoting a candidate for governor to the residents of the state is practicing _____ marketing.

6. A convention and visitor's bureau that launches a campaign to attract tourists to a particular area is practicing _____ marketing.

7. An environmental awareness group that is encouraging residents to recycle their newspapers and aluminum cans is practicing _____ marketing.

8. A public-health clinic that is encouraging parents to bring in their children to be inoculated is practicing _____ marketing.

9. In contrast to for-profit organizations, not-for-profit organizations lack a _____.

10. In comparison to the amount of control a customer has over a for-profit organization, the individual customer or user of a not-for-profit organization has _____ control.

11. Many not-for-profit organizations lack a clear _____.

12. Traditionally, society encouraged _____ to aid in providing physical possessions to people. Now, marketing is being criticized by some people for stressing the quantities of life and neglecting the _____ of life.

13. Marketers today are concerned with a variety of social issues. Two major categories of social issues are _____ and _____.

14. Critics of the competitive marketing system identify several arguments against the system. One criticism of marketing is that marketing costs are too _____ .

15. Individuals and organizations have standards of behavior. Often there is a conflict between the individual's and the organization's _____.

16. When attempting to obtain information from and about individuals, the ethical marketer must be careful **NOT** to invade a person's _____.

17. Product quality, packaging, and other marketing strategy decisions present potential _____ problems for marketers. Regulatory mandates are narrowing choices in many of these decision areas.

18. Pricing, because of its obvious importance to the consumer and society, has long been subject to governmental regulation. Some pricing activities are not only considered _____ but have also been declared illegal.

19. One area of ethical concern in marketing is _____ aimed at children. The focus of this concern is that it may exert an undue influence on children.

20. One of the broadest issues in marketing today is _____.

21. Traditionally, management has been responsible to customers, employees, and stockholders. Now the concept of _____ has been expanded to include the entire social framework.

22. Major issues pertaining to social responsibility for the environment include _____ , _____ , and _____. One way in which some companies respond to the public's environmental concerns is through _____ .

Self-Test

> **Select the best answer.**

1. The approximate number of not-for-profit organizations in the United States is
   a. over one million.
   b. slightly less than one million.
   c. about 500,000.
   d. about 100,000.

2. A marketing effort aimed at encouraging businesses and organizations to hold their conventions in a particular city is an example of
   a. organization marketing.
   b. business marketing.
   c. place marketing.
   d. idea marketing.

3. Identification and marketing of an idea or issue to chosen consumer segments is known as
   a. event marketing.
   b. consumer marketing.
   c. cause marketing.
   d. organization marketing.

4. "Clients and sponsors" are the two publics that are usually of primary concern to the
   a. organizational marketer.
   b. person marketer.
   c. not-for-profit marketer.
   d. government marketer.

5. Marketing efforts designed to cultivate the attention, interest, and preference of a target market toward an individual are known as
   a. image marketing.
   b. person marketing.
   c. idea marketing.
   d. not-for-profit marketing.

6. Two major categories of current issues in marketing are
   a. ecology and social responsibility.
   b. ecology and morality.
   c. ethics and morality.
   d. ethics and social responsibility.

7. Marketing ethics concern
   a. product decisions.
   b. pricing.
   c. distribution decisions.
   d. promotion.
   e. the whole marketing mix.

8. Widgeco, a manufacturer of outdoor furniture, purposely uses inferior plastic that deteriorates in sunlight. Widgeco is engaged in
   a. social responsibility.
   b. planned obsolescence.
   c. consumerism.
   d. the marketing concept.

9. Marketing philosophies, policies, procedures, and actions that advance public welfare are the subject of
   a. social responsibility.
   b. consumerism.
   c. consumer rights.
   d. professional ethics.

Applying Marketing Concepts

Late Friday afternoon, Harold Mickle, marketing manager for Typack Corporation, sat down at his desk and gazed out the window of his office. "It has been quite a week," he thought. "Business sure isn't what it was back when I began selling for Typack in 1968. In those days, you could just sell your product; now, so much more has to be done."

For example, on his desk was a memorandum regarding the company's response to a local newspaper's accusation of planned obsolescence by Typack. It seems the paper received numerous complaints from individuals about Typack's products. "Those people writing to the paper probably were not even customers of Typack," thought Mickle.

Almost everywhere he had been in the last week, someone reminded him of consumers' rights. Even his son, a business major at the university, wanted to talk with him about ethics and social responsibility.

On this very Friday, someone in research had asked Mickle if a particular research study would be an invasion of personal privacy. "How would I know?" Mickle thought. "Isn't that a matter for the company's lawyers?"

> **Select the best answer.**

1. The charge of planned obsolescence made in the local newspaper refers to a product
   a. of limited durability.
   b. that does not do what it is advertised to do.
   c. that never worked.
   d. that becomes an antique.

2. The issues of social responsibility that Mickle is facing are related to
   a. the profit motive and making socially responsible decisions.
   b. being responsible to everybody all the time.
   c. making less money.
   d. whom one works for and why.

3. The invasion of privacy problem presented to Mickle is
   a. a product management problem.
   b. an ethical problem.
   c. a consumerism issue.
   d. a legal issue.

Additional Activities

Experiential Exercises

1. The purpose of this exercise is to give you a better understanding of the relationship between marketing and society in general. In this exercise you are asked to examine the social impact of advertisements.

   - Identify and describe two advertisements that are likely to cause critical reaction from groups within society. Name the companies and products. Describe the advertisements and where you saw them. State why you feel the advertisements might be considered offensive and what groups might be offended.

   - Identify and describe two advertisements that are designed to tell the public about socially beneficial programs or activities conducted by a business organization. Are the ads in good taste? Should business firms advertise in this manner? Are the projects or activities truly beneficial? Who would appreciate these advertisements?

2. The next exercise will help you understand the marketing efforts of a not-for-profit organization.

- Select a not-for-profit organization, such as a social-service agency, hospital, art museum, or college or university. Collect information about its marketing mix, marketing objectives, and environmental variables from the organization's marketing director or equivalent position. Your questions should cover such topics as the goods or services offered by the organization, the channels of distribution it uses, the prices it charges, its advertising and "sales" strategy, and its competitors.

  Example: The U.S. Army is a not-for-profit organization. Its primary marketing objective is to obtain quality recruits. The services it offers are job training, adventure, fulfillment of patriotic ambitions, and so on. Its "sales force" is located in recruitment centers around the country. The price is two years' commitment.

- Write a report on the organization's marketing program and your suggestions for strengthening its marketing program.

Questions for Exploration

Conceptual

In Chapter 3 of the textbook is a list of seven common criticisms of the competitive marketing system. What specific evidence and arguments can be presented for or against each of the seven criticisms?

Practical

In 1979, a federal ban prohibiting the U.S. Army from advertising on television for new recruits was lifted. If Congress suddenly decided to reimpose the ban on recruitment advertising on television, how could the Army redirect its promotional strategy?

Answer Key

Key Concepts	1. a	4. d	7. h
	2. b	5. e	8. g
	3. c	6. f	9. i

Completion	
1. marketing	13. marketing ethics,
2. public, private	social responsibility
(either order)	(either order)
3. private, public	14. high
4. person, place, cause,	15. ethics
event, organization	16. privacy
(any order)	17. ethical
5. person	18. unethical
6. place	19. advertising
7. cause	20. social responsibility
8. organization	21. responsibility
9. bottom line	22. planned obsolescence,
10. less	pollution, recycling,
11. organizational structure	(any order); green
12. marketing, quality	marketing

Self-Test	1. a	4. c	7. e
	2. c	5. b	8. b
	3. c	6. d	9. a

Applying Marketing Concepts	1. a
	2. a
	3. b

Nothing endures but change.
—Heraclitus

26

Marketing: Today and Tomorrow

Assignments

For the most effective study of this lesson, we suggest that you complete the assignments in the following sequence:

1. Read the study guide Overview (Lesson Notes and Video Program Notes) and the Learning Objectives for this lesson.

2. Review *Contemporary Marketing Wired*, 9th edition, Chapter 1, "Developing Relationships through Customer Focus, Quality, Technology, and Ethical Behavior," pages 2-40. Read the Appendix, "Careers in Marketing."

3. View "Movers and Shakers: The Art and Science of Marketing" video program.

4. Review the textbook assignment for this lesson.

5. Complete the Review Activities (Key Concepts and Completion), Self-Test, and Applying Marketing Concepts for this lesson.

6. Check your answers against the Answer Key at the end of the lesson, and review when necessary.

7. Complete any of the Additional Activities (Experiential Exercise and Questions for Exploration) that interest you or that are assigned by your instructor.

Overview

Lesson Notes

Marketing is a process that encompasses the planning and implementation of the conception, pricing, promotion, and distribution of goods, services, and ideas. The fundamental purpose of marketing is to create exchanges that will satisfy individual and organizational objectives. The process of exchange, in which two or more parties give something of value to each other to satisfy felt needs, is a critical part of the definition of marketing.

The want-satisfying power of a good or service has been referred to as utility. Of the four utilities, marketing creates three: time, place, and ownership. The fourth utility, form, is supplied by production. In creating these utilities, marketing performs exchange functions, physical distribution functions, and facilitating functions.

Since the end of World War II, the **marketing concept** has emerged as the predominant marketing orientation. This concept has been defined as a companywide objective of satisfying consumer wants and needs and achieving long-run success. The marketing concept focuses on the consumer, rather than on the firm's goods or services, and implies that the satisfaction of consumer wants and needs is in the best interest of the firm and its achievement of long-run success.

Because marketing is consumer oriented, development of a marketing plan begins by identifying a target market—a group of consumers to whom marketing efforts will be directed. One of the basic purposes of those efforts is to convert consumers' needs for certain goods and services into wants for specific products. Marketing achieves this conversion by focusing on the benefits of a product.

Once the target market has been identified, marketers develop a **marketing mix**, a combination of four different strategies: product, distribution, promotion, and pricing. **Product strategy** includes making decisions about what products to offer and the brand names, guarantees, packaging, and labeling of those products. **Distribution strategy** involves decisions about how to move the goods or services from producer to final consumer. **Promotional strategy** concerns the various methods a firm uses to communicate with consumers about its goods and services. **Pricing strategy** deals with establishing price levels that consumers are willing to pay and that will meet the firm's profit and distribution goals.

Marketing decisions are influenced by and made within the context of five external environments: competitive, political-legal, economic, technological, and social-cultural. In some cases, the marketer has little control over these environments, and they may be considered uncontrollable variables. In other cases, however, marketers can attempt to exercise some degree of control.

As the new century approaches, a new technological era is revolutionizing marketing. Two key developments of this era are interactive marketing and the Internet.

Marketing is a dynamic, growing field, and the need for skilled marketing professionals continues to grow. Not only must marketers be aware of change, they must be ready and willing to take actions to respond to and help effect those changes.

Today's marketers must focus on relationship marketing to maintain effective relationships with customers, employees, suppliers, and other partners.

As marketing evolves, it will continue to provide many jobs both in the field of marketing and in related fields. In fact, increased adoption of the marketing concept by not-for-profit organizations will create even more marketing jobs in the future than have been available in the past. Further, marketing changes will continue to afford people in marketing careers the chance to make relevant contributions, not only to individual firms and organizations, but to society as a whole.

Video Program Notes

The final video program for this course takes a broad view of marketing, emphasizing that marketing is an ongoing effort essential to the success of every organization.

Through examples taken from the case studies of companies featured in earlier programs, this program explores the diversity of approaches to market research, advertising, marketing strategy, sales promotion, distribution, and other important areas of marketing. The program stresses the fundamental importance of identifying consumer needs, converting them to wants, and then satisfying those wants in order to achieve the objective of long-run success.

As you watch the video program, consider the following questions:

1. Why and how do the companies featured in the program test market their products?

2. Why do some companies choose not to test market?

3. Why does Famous Amos make "all kinds" of cookies?

4. How does the Disney success show that marketing can be more than just applying market research facts?

5. What problems do high-tech products (such as computers) present to the test marketer?

6. What are the central product strategies of Western Cruise Lines, Robert Mondavi Winery, Northern Produce, West Ridge Mountaineering, and Arrowhead?

7. Do the professional advertisers presented in the program feel that they can sell anything?

8. How do the various companies presented in the program attempt to break through the clutter?

9. What role does advertising play in not-for-profit marketing?

10. How does the program define "price"?

Learning Objectives

After completing your study of this lesson, you should be able to:

1. Define the following terms as they relate to marketing:

distribution strategy
marketing concept
marketing mix
pricing strategy

product strategy
promotional strategy
utility

2. Identify the utilities that marketing provides.

3. Explain the marketing concept.

4. Describe the five factors that influence
   the marketing environment.

5. Identify the four major strategies
   of the marketing mix.

6. Briefly describe major categories of marketing
   careers.

Review Activities

Key Concepts

> **Identify each of the following marketing concepts by writing
> the letter of the appropriate term in the blank next to the
> corresponding description.**
>
> a. **utility**   e. **distribution strategy**
> b. **marketing concept** f. **promotional strategy**
> c. **marketing mix**   g. **pricing strategy**
> d. **product strategy**

_____ 1. blending of the four strategy elements of marketing decision
          making to satisfy chosen consumer segments

_____ 2. element of marketing that consists of personal selling,
          advertising, and sales promotion

_____ 3. want-satisfying power of a good or service

_____ 4. element of marketing that involves decisions about package
          design, branding, trademarks, warranties, and labeling

_____ 5. companywide consumer orientation designed to achieve long-run success

_____ 6. element of marketing that deals with the movement of goods and the selection of marketing channels

_____ 7. element of marketing that deals with balancing what consumers are willing to pay, costs, and desired profit

Completion

> **Fill each blank in the following paragraphs with the most appropriate term from the list of completion answers below. A term may be used once, more than once, or not at all.**
>
> | | | |
> |---|---|---|
> | competitive | mix | promotion |
> | consumer | ownership | social-cultural |
> | distribution | place | success |
> | economic | political-legal | technological |
> | environment | price | time |
> | form | product | **utility** |
> | marketing | production | |

1. The purpose of _____ is to satisfy the wants of chosen _____ segments by efficiently distributing goods and services.

2. In order to satisfy chosen consumer segments, the marketing manager must formulate a marketing _____.

3. The marketing manager must also be aware of how the marketing _____ affects marketing plans.

4. The power of a good or service to satisfy the wants of chosen consumer segments is called _____.

5. Utilities that marketing provides include _____, _____, and _____. Form, the fourth utility, is provided by production.

6. The marketing concept can be viewed as a companywide orientation with the objective of achieving long-run

_____. Also, the marketing concept focuses on the
_____ , not on _____.

7. The marketing mix comprises four different strategies
   related to _____ , _____ , _____ ,
   and _____.

8. The five factors that constitute the marketing environment
   are _____ , _____ , _____ , _____ ,
   and _____.

Self-Test

| Select the best answer. |

1. The development and efficient distribution of goods and
   services for chosen consumer segments is one definition of
   a. production.
   b. marketing.
   c. product strategy.
   d. the marketing concept.

2. The companywide, consumer orientation designed
   to achieve long-run success is
   a. production.
   b. marketing utilities.
   c. the marketing concept.
   d. product strategy.

3. Which one of the following questions is NOT one
   asked by marketing?
   a. Should we lower our price?
   b. How should we advertise—newspapers or magazines?
   c. How should we package the new product?
   d. How should we produce the new product?
   e. How should we move the product to the ultimate con-
      sumer?

4. The blending of product, distribution, promotional, and pricing strategies is known as the marketing
   a. mix.
   b. concept.
   c. environments.
   d. utilities.

5. Selection of methods for moving goods from production to customers is part of the
   a. product strategy.
   b. consumer strategy.
   c. planning strategy.
   d. distribution strategy.

6. Package design, branding, and trademark are part of
   a. advertising strategy.
   b. product strategy.
   c. consumer strategy.
   d. sales-promotion strategy.
   e. promotional strategy.

7. The person in an organization who is responsible for directing all the activities that project and maintain a favorable image for the organization, including arranging press conferences and exhibitions and preparing news releases, is the
   a. product manager.
   b. procurement manager.
   c. public-relations officer.
   d. brand manager.

8. The marketing function that is responsible for decisions about transportation, warehousing, inventory control, order processing, and materials handling is
   a. sales.
   b. procurement.
   c. purchasing.
   d. distribution.

9. The person in charge of purchasing merchandise from various sources, such as manufacturers, wholesalers, and importers, for resale to the ultimate consumer is the
   a. physical-distribution manager.
   b. product manager.
   c. retail buyer.
   d. wholesale buyer.

10. The person who arranges for the promotion of a company's goods or services probably works in
    a. advertising.
    b. public relations.
    c. purchasing.
    d. production.

Applying Marketing Concepts

Until recent years, Kapa Brothers, Inc., marketed two major brands of candy bar, the Fudge Bar and the Fudge Bar with Nuts. When Tom Kapa, president of the corporation, observed a decline in the market share by all makers of pure chocolate and fudge-type candy bars, he felt that what consumers were looking for was a product that was "good for them" as well as good tasting.

In an effort to capitalize on this trend, Kapa Brothers polled consumers about a chocolate-chip granola bar and a chocolate-fudge granola bar. The response to a chocolate-fudge granola bar was favorable, but some people had reservations about anything with fudge in it really being a "health-food" snack. The best response to the chocolate-chip granola bar was received from affluent, well-educated people in their twenties and thirties. Further research revealed that consumers felt the chocolate-chip granola bar was less fattening, and therefore more desirable, than the chocolate-fudge granola bar. Later this information was used to decide that the bars would be priced to sell above the market, in order to appeal especially to the targeted group that reacted most favorably to the chocolate-chip granola bar.

After consumer acceptance of the concept of a chocolate-chip granola bar had been established by market research, Kapa

Brothers ran production test samples on a small scale. The favorable reaction of consumers convinced Kapa Brothers management that it had a winner. Moving ahead, Kapa Brothers decided on an overall product image of "healthful and delicious." The silver-foil wrapping for the individual bars and the eight-pack boxes they were sold in showed a handsome, healthy-looking couple smiling at one another and enjoying the product. This strategy also included creating an attractive cardboard display stand that folded out from the shipping container to show the same young couple above a rack of the granola bars. Supermarkets could then attractively display the items in the aisle or near the checkout stands. Concurrently with the product introduction, Kapa Brothers used half-page color ads in several national, top-selling health and fitness magazines.

The final product was the result of two years of effort and the use of four outside marketing research firms. The total costs incurred for the research and the first year of production were about $1.9 million. Based on these expenditures, Tom Kapa anticipated first-year sales of 100,000 cases, and 150,000 cases and 200,000 cases for the second and third years, respectively. Annual break-even volume was figured to be 200,000.

> **Select the best answer.**

1. In developing its new product, Kapa Brothers used the
   a. production-orientation concept.
   b. marketing concept.
   c. managerial approach.
   d. product-concept approach.

2. By packaging and distributing granola bars, marketing provided each of the following utilities EXCEPT
   a. time.
   b. form.
   c. ownership.
   d. place.

3. In order to assess the wants and needs of chosen consumer segments, Kapa Brothers used
   a. break-even analysis.
   b. sampling.

    c. test marketing.

    d. market research.

4. The decision to run advertising in health and fitness magazines was a part of the Kapa Brothers'

    a. promotional strategy.

    b. pricing strategy.

    c. product strategy.

    d. distribution strategy.

5. The decision to wrap the granola bar in silver foil was part of the firm's

    a. promotional strategy.

    b. pricing strategy.

    c. product strategy.

    d. distribution strategy.

6. Kapa Brothers' decision to skim the market was part of their

    a. promotional strategy.

    b. pricing strategy.

    c. product strategy.

    d. distribution strategy.

Additional Activities

Experiential Exercise

The purpose of this exercise is to enhance your understanding of the marketing concept and the extent to which an individual organization has adopted the concept.

- Select an organization to study. You may choose any type of organization that appeals to you. However, try to select one that is accessible, cooperative, and a marketer of a consumer good or service.

- Develop a list of five-to-seven questions that could be used to determine if the organization has adopted the marketing concept. Be sure to include questions about consumer orientation versus production, marketing objectives, and the firm's marketing mix and the factors in the marketing environment that affect the mix. Use the questions you have developed to interview several people in the organization.

- Based on the results of your interviews, write a brief summary of the status of the marketing concept in the organization. Be sure to discuss the extent to which the marketing concept has been adopted, cite evidence to support your conclusions, and make suggestions about how the organization could use the marketing concept in the future.

Questions for Exploration

Conceptual

Many people have misconceptions about what marketing is. List what you feel are the three most common misconceptions about marketing, and discuss why each is a misconception.

Practical

Of all the jobs in marketing that have been shown in this and the preceding twenty-five video programs, which would be to you the most exciting and the most personally rewarding? Which marketing career seems least interesting?

Answer Key

Key Concepts	1. c	5. b
	2. f	6. e
	3. a	7. g
	4. d	

Completion	1. marketing, consumer
	2. mix
	3. environment
	4. utility
	5. time, place, ownership
	  (any order)
	6. success, consumer,
	  production
		7. product, price,
		  promotion,
		  distribution
		  (any order)
		8. competitive,
		  political-legal,
		  economic, technological,
		  social-cultural
		  (any order)

Self-Test	1. b	5. d	8. d
	2. c	6. b	9. c
	3. d	7. c	10. a
	4. a		

Applying Marketing Concepts	1. b	4. a
	2. b	5. c
	3. d	6. b